ROYAL HISTORICAL SOCIETY

STUDIES IN HISTORY

New Series

ANGLO-AUSTRALIAN RELATIONS AND THE 'TURN TO EUROPE', 1961–1972

ANGLO-AUSTRALIAN RELATIONS
AND THE 'TURN TO EUROPE',
1961–1972

Andrea Benvenuti

THE ROYAL HISTORICAL SOCIETY
THE BOYDELL PRESS

First published 2008

A Royal Historical Society publication
Published by The Boydell Press
an imprint of Boydell & Brewer Ltd
PO Box 9, Woodbridge, Suffolk IP12 3DF, UK
and of Boydell & Brewer Inc.
668 Mt Hope Avenue, Rochester, NY 14620, USA
website: www.boydellandbrewer.com

ISBN 978-0-86193-295-5

ISSN 0269-2244

A CIP catalogue record for this book is available
from the British Library

This publication is printed on acid-free paper

Printed in Great Britain by
CPI Antony Rowe, Chippenham, Wiltshire

Contents

List of Figures

List of Tables

Acknowledgements

I would like to thank the Economic and Social Research Council for funding this research project. I am also indebted to Merton College, the Department of Politics and International Relations (Oxford University), the Beit Foundation and the Royal Historical Society for funding my fieldwork both in Britain and Australia. I am also grateful to the Menzies Centre for Australian Studies (King's College London) and the University of Queensland for providing extra financial support to cover my fieldwork expenses in both Britain and Australia.

Many people generously gave up their time to discuss my research. I would like to make special mention of Douglas Anthony, Peter Bailey, Sir Bernard Burrows, Lord Carrington, Tom Critchley, Sir Allen Fairhall, Malcolm Fraser, Anthony Golds, the late Sir John Gorton, Sir Nicholas Henderson, Peter Howson, Gordon Jockel, Sir Peter Lawler, Sir Patrick Nairne, Sir Michael Palliser, Alf Parsons, Sir Edward Peck, William Pritchett, the late Sir Arthur Tange and Sir Oliver Wright. I am equally indebted to Moreen Dee, Annette Nilsson and Dugald McLellan for their help in editing the manuscript. Anne Deighton, the supervisor of my doctoral thesis at Oxford, also deserves my warmest thanks for her comments and criticism.

Finally, I would like to thank my parents for their invaluable support over the years. The book is dedicated to them.

Andrea Benvenuti
August 2008

Abbreviations

AMDA	Anglo-Malayan (later Malaysian) Defence Agreement
ANZAM	Australian, New Zealand and Malayan Area
ANZUK	Australia, New Zealand, United Kingdom
ANZUS	Australia, New Zealand, United States
BAOR	British Army on the Rhine
BDLS	British Defence Liaison Staff (Canberra)
BT	Board of Trade (Britain)
CAB	Cabinet Office (Britain)
CAP	Common Agricultural Policy
CAS	Chief of Air Staff (Australia)
CET	Common External Tariff
CGS	Chief of General Staff (Australia)
Cmnd.	Command Papers (Britain)
CNS	Chief of Naval Staff (Australia)
CO	Commonwealth Office (Britain)
COS	Chiefs of Staff (Australia)
CRO	Commonwealth Relations Office (Britain)
CSA	Commonwealth Sugar Agreement
CSR	Commonwealth Strategic Reserve
DC	Defence Committee (Australia)
DEA	Department of External Affairs (Australia)
DFA	Department of Foreign Affairs (Australia)
DO	Dominion Office (Britain)
DOD	Department of Defence (Australia)
DRWP	Defence Review Working Party (Britain)
DT	Department of Trade (Australia)
DTI	Department of Trade and Industry (Australia)
EEC	European Economic Community
EFTA	European Free Trade Area
FAD	Foreign Affairs and Defence Committee (Australia)
FCO	Foreign and Commonwealth Office (Britain)
FO	Foreign Office (Britain)
FTA	Free Trade Area
HC	House of Commons (Britain)
HR	House of Representatives (Australia)
JIC	Joint Intelligence Committee (Australia)
JPC	Joint Planning Committee (Australia)
memcon	Memorandum of conversation
MOD	Ministry of Defence (Britain)

NAA	National Archives of Australia (Canberra)
NATO	North Atlantic Treaty Organisation
NLA	National Library of Australia (Canberra)
OPD	Defence and Overseas Policy Committee (Britain)
OPD(O)	Defence and Overseas Policy Committee (Official) (Britain)
PD	Parliamentary Debates
PMC	Department of the Prime Minister and Cabinet (Australia)
PMD	Prime Minister's Department (Australia)
PREM	Prime Minister's Office (Britain)
RAAF	Royal Australian Air Force
RAF	Royal Air Force (Britain)
RAN	Royal Australian Navy
RN	Royal Navy (Britain)
SEATO	South East Asia Treaty Organisation
T	Treasury (Britain)
TNA	The National Archives
WEU	Western European Union
AEHR	*Australian Economic History Review*
AHS	*Australian Historical Studies*
AJIA	*Australian Journal of International Affairs*
AJPH	*Australian Journal of Politics and History*
FRUS	*Foreign Relations of the United States*, Washington 1994–
IA	*International Affairs*
JICH	*Journal of Imperial and Commonwealth History*
TCBH	*Twentieth Century British History*

Note on the Text

This book makes continuous reference to Britain's role and military presence in areas outside Europe. In the contemporary literature, these areas are often referred to as 'east of Suez', 'the Far East' or 'south-east Asia'. Generally, the phrase 'east of Suez' refers to a vast area stretching from the Persian Gulf to Hong Kong. The 'Far East' denotes a strategic subregion of the larger 'east of Suez' area including the British bases of Hong Kong, Singapore and Malaya/Malaysia. South-east Asia is treated as a subsection within the Far Eastern theatre, where Australia's main strategic interests lay and where the Wilson government's policy of withdrawal most affected Australian security. Reference to 'east of Suez' or the 'Far East' is therefore made either when such terminology is explicitly used in primary or secondary documents or when it purports to indicate the larger strategic context in which 'south-east Asian' issues were included.

Frequent mention is also made of terms such as 'European Economic Community (EEC)', 'Common Market' and 'Europe'. The term 'EEC' refers to the association of six European countries (Belgium, France, West Germany, Italy, Luxembourg and the Netherlands) created in 1957 by the Treaty of Rome with the aim of integrating the economies of its member states into a single common market through the removal of trade barriers and the establishment of a common external trade policy. Given these aims, it is not surprising that during the 1960s the EEC began generally to be referred to as the 'Common Market'. This book occasionally uses the expression 'Common Market'; when it does so the term is synonymous with the 'EEC'. In the contemporary literature as well as in the primary sources constant use is also made of 'EEC' as a synonym for the more accurate 'European Communities'. Britain applied not only to the EEC but also to the European Coal and Steel Community (ECSC) and the European Atomic Energy Community (Euratom). After 1967 the Communities were merged in the European Communities (EC).

An explanatory note is needed in relation to the term 'Europe' and its usage in this book. Here the term is often found in connection with expressions such as Britain's 'turn to Europe', Britain's 'shift to Europe' or its 'reorientation towards Europe'. In this context, 'Europe' loosely denotes Britain's primary sphere of action and interest within the international system as the country gradually moved away from a global and imperial role, and transformed itself into an essentially regional actor.

Politicians and Officials

AUSTRALIA

Anthony, Douglas	Minister for Trade and Industry (1971–2)
Bailey, Peter	First Assistant Secretary, PMD (1965–7)
Barnard, Lance	Deputy Prime Minister (1972–5); Minister for Defence (1972–5)
Barwick, Garfield	Minister for External Affairs (1961–4)
Bunting, John	Secretary, PMD (1959–68); Secretary, Cabinet Office (1968–71)
Campbell, Alexander	Deputy Secretary, DTI (1964–7)
Casey, Richard	Governor-General (1965–9)
Critchley, Tom	High Commissioner, Kuala Lumpur (1957–65); Senior External Affairs Representative, London (1966–9)
Cumes, James	First Assistant Secretary, DEA (1968–74)
Downer, Alexander	High Commissioner, London (1964–72)
Eastman, Allan	Senior External Affairs Representative, London (1962–5); High Commissioner, Kuala Lumpur (1965–9)
Fairhall, Allen	Minister for Supply (1961–6); Minister for Defence (1966–9)
Fleming, Allan	Special Commercial Adviser, London (1967)
Flood, Philip	Assistant Secretary, DFA (1971–3)
Fraser, Malcolm	Minister for the Army (1966–8); Minister for Defence (1969–71)
Gorton, John	Minister for the Interior (1963–4); Minister for Works (1963–6); Minister for Education and Science (1966–8); Prime Minister (1968–71); Minister of Defence (1971)
Griffith, Allan	Assistant Secretary, PMD (1964–9)
Harry, Ralph	First Assistant Secretary, DEA (1960–5); Ambassador, Brussels (1965–8)
Hartnell, G.C.	Head of Australian Joint Service Staff, London (1964–6)
Hasluck, Paul	Minister for External Affairs (1964–9); Governor-General (1969–74)
Hicks, Edwin	Secretary, DOD (1956–68)
Holt, Harold	Treasurer (1958–66); Prime Minister (1966–7)
Howson, Peter	Minister for Air (1964–8)
Jockel, Gordon	First Assistant Secretary, DEA (1964–9)
Lawler, Peter	Deputy Secretary, PMD (1964–8)
McEwen, John	Deputy Prime Minister (1958–71); Minister for

	Trade (1956–63); Minister for Trade and Industry (1963–71); Acting Prime Minister (1967–8)
McIntyre, Laurence	Deputy Secretary, DEA (1965–70)
McMahon, William	Minister for Labour and National Service (1958–66); Treasurer (1966–9); Minister for Foreign Affairs (1969–71); Prime Minister (1971–2)
Menzies, Robert	Prime Minister (1939–41, 1949–66); Minister for External Affairs (1960–1)
Plimsoll, James	Secretary, DEA (1965–70)
Renouf, Alan	First Assistant Secretary, DEA (1965–6)
Tange, Arthur	Secretary, DEA (1954–64)
Thomson, Lloyd	Assistant Secretary, DEA (1966–8)
Walker, Ronald	Ambassador, Paris (1959–68)
Waller, Keith	Ambassador, Washington (1964–70)
Westerman, Alan	Secretary, DT (1960–3); Secretary, DTI (1963–71)
Whitlam, Edward Gough	Prime Minister (1972–5)

BRITAIN

Armstrong, William	Joint Permanent Secretary, Treasury (1962–8)
Audland, Christopher	CO and Common Market Department, CO (1967)
Barber, Anthony	Chancellor of Duchy of Lancaster (June–July 1970); Chancellor of Exchequer (1970–4)
Bottomley, Arthur	Secretary of State for Commonwealth Relations (1964–6); Minister of Overseas Development (1966–7)
Bowden, Herbert	Secretary of State for Commonwealth Affairs (1966–7)
Brown, George	Department of Economic Affairs (1964–6); Secretary of State for Foreign Affairs (1966–8)
Callaghan, James	Chancellor of Exchequer (1964–7); Home Secretary (1967–70)
Carrington, Lord	Secretary of State for Defence (1970–4)
Castle, Barbara	Minister of Overseas Development (1964–5); Transport Secretary (1965–8)
Crossman, Richard	Housing and Local Government Secretary (1964–6); Lord President of Council (1966–8)
Dean, Patrick	Ambassador, Washington (1965–9)
Douglas-Home, Alec	Prime Minister (1963–4); Leader of Opposition (1964–5); Secretary of State for Foreign and Commonwealth Affairs (1970–4)
Gallagher, F. G. K.	Head of Western Economic Department, CRO (1965–6) and CO (1966–7); Head of Common Market Department, CO (1967–8)
Garner, Saville	Permanent Under-Secretary of State, CRO (1962–6) and CO (1966–8)
Gore-Booth, Paul	Permanent Under-Secretary of State, FO (1965–9)
Healey, Denis	Secretary of State for Defence (1964–70)
Heath, Edward	Lord Privy Seal with FO responsibilities (1960–3);

	Leader of Opposition (1965–70); Prime Minister (1970–4)
Jay, Douglas	President of Board of Trade (1964–7)
Jenkins, Roy	Home Secretary (1965–7); Chancellor of Exchequer (1967–70)
Johnston, Charles	High Commissioner, Canberra (1965–71)
MacLehose, Crawford	Head of Far Eastern Department, FO (1963–5); Principal Private Secretary to Secretary of State for Foreign Affairs (1965–7)
Macmillan, Harold	Prime Minister (1957–63)
Marsh, Richard	Minister of Power (1966–8); Minister of Transport (1968–9)
Mountbatten, Lord	Chief of British Defence Staff and Chairman of Chiefs of Staff Committee (1959–65)
Nairne, Patrick	Deputy Under-Secretary, MOD (1970–3)
Oliver, William	High Commissioner, Canberra (1959–65)
Palliser, Michael	Head of Planning Staff, FO (1965–6); Private Secretary to Prime Minister (1966–7)
Peart, Frederick	Minister of Agriculture, Fisheries and Food (1964–8)
Powell, Richard	Permanent Secretary, Board of Trade (1960–8)
Pritchard, Neil	Deputy Under-Secretary of State, CRO (1963–6) and CO (1966–7)
Rippon, Geoffrey	Chancellor of Duchy of Lancaster (1970–2)
Sandys, Duncan	Secretary of State for Commonwealth Relations (1960–4)
Shannon, Godfrey	Assistant Under-Secretary, CRO (1956–6) and CO (1966–8)
Snelling, Arthur	Deputy Under-Secretary of State, CRO (1961–6), CO (1966–8) and FCO (1968–9)
Stewart, Michael	Secretary of State for Foreign Affairs (1965–6); First Secretary of State (1966–8); Secretary of State for Economic Affairs (1966–7); Secretary of State for Foreign and Commonwealth Affairs (1968–70)
Thomson, George	Chancellor of Duchy of Lancaster (1966–7); Secretary of State for Commonwealth Affairs (1967–8)
Trend, Burke	Cabinet Secretary (1963–73)
Wilson, Harold	Prime Minister (1964–70)
Wright, Oliver	Private Secretary to successive prime ministers (1964–6)

FRANCE

Couve de Murville, Maurice	Minister of Foreign Affairs (1958–68)
de Gaulle, Charles	President (1958–69)
Pompidou, Georges	President (1969–74)

INDONESIA

Subandrio, Raden — Foreign Minister (1957–66)

MALAYSIA

Abdul Rahman Putra, Tunku — Prime Minister (1957–70)

NEW ZEALAND

Eyre, Dean — Minister of Defence (1960–6)

Holyoake, Keith — Prime Minister and Minister of External Affairs (later Foreign Affairs) (1960–72)

Marshall, John — Deputy Prime Minister (1960–72); Prime Minister (1972)

Nash, Walter — Prime Minister (1957–60)

SINGAPORE

Lee Kuan Yew — Prime Minister (1959–90)

UNITED STATES

Ball, George — Under-Secretary of State, Department of State (1961–6)

Berger, Samuel — Deputy Assistant Secretary of State for East Asian Affairs, Department of State (1965–8)

Bundy, McGeorge — Special Assistant to President for National Security Affairs (1964–63)

Johnson, Lyndon — Vice-President (1961–3); President (1963–9)

Kennedy, John — President (1961–3)

Kissinger, Henry — Assistant to President for National Security Affairs (1969–75); Secretary of State (1973–7)

McNamara, Robert — Secretary of Defense (1961–8)

Nixon, Richard — President (1969–74)

Rostow, Walt — Counselor of Department of State and Chairman of the Policy Planning Staff (1961–6); Special Assistant to President (1966–8)

Rusk, Dean — Secretary of State, Department of State (1961–9)

Introduction

On 7 January 1969 a frank exchange of views took place at No. 10 Downing Street between the Australian prime minister, John Gorton, his British counterpart, Harold Wilson, and the British Foreign and Commonwealth Secretary, Michael Stewart. In reviewing the state of Anglo-Australian relations, Gorton told Wilson that 'Australia would come increasingly to treat her relations with Britain in the same way as those she had with any foreign country, such as France or the United States. This was the logical consequence of the growing difference in their interests and activities.' Wilson disagreed with Gorton and suggested that 'these differences were more apparent than real, the result of the geographical separation of the two countries'. 'When the chips were down', Wilson argued, Australia and Britain 'were bound to find themselves at one'. Gorton asked what this all meant and added that 'in terms of foreign policy it was rational for Australia to regard Britain as a foreign country'. At this point Stewart commented that, as he understood it, 'Mr. Gorton was saying that there was no longer "any special relationship" between Britain and Australia … but that we should continue to work together in the closest consultation and association'. Gorton did not dissent.[1]

In the context of traditional Australia–Britain relations, Gorton's words were, at the very least, startling. No previous Australian prime minister would have thought to put the Anglo-Australian relationship in the same category as Australia's relations with other friendly but foreign governments. Despite having developed into a separate and sovereign state, Australia in the 1950s still thought of itself as a British nation and retained extremely strong ties with the 'mother country'. Australia's relations with Britain were still defined in terms of 'British race patriotism', that is, 'the idea that all British peoples, despite their particular regional problems and perspectives, ultimately comprised a single indissoluble community through the ties of blood, language, history and culture'.[2] There still existed 'a powerful sentimental assumption that the interests of Australia and the British world ought ultimately to coincide'.[3] Consequently, any attempt to liken Australia's relationship with Britain to its relations with other, particularly non-Commonwealth countries, would have seemed almost sacrilegious. Yet Gorton's comments

---

[1] John Gorton, Harold Wilson and Michael Stewart, memcon, 7 Jan. 1969, TNA, London, FCO 24/408.
[2] Stuart Ward, *Australia and the British embrace: the demise of the imperial ideal*, Melbourne 2001, 2.
[3] Ibid. 9.

were not unwarranted. Australia and Britain were indeed experiencing 'a growing difference in their interests and activities'. Although Gorton did not clarify how far apart these interests had grown, he clearly believed that they had gone far enough. The use of the term 'foreign' in describing the nature of future links between Australia and Britain appeared to sound the death-knell of the once close relationship. As, indeed, it did.

This book aims to explore the reason why Anglo-Australian relations underwent such a drastic change during the 1960s. In so doing, it analyses how the once intimate ties of empire, which had bound Australia and Britain, became, for all practical purposes, inconsequential by the early 1970s. Examining Australian post-World War II history, it is impossible to overlook the rapid and radical erosion of Anglo-Australian relations in the 1960s, even when allowing for the strains the relationship had suffered during the war and up until 1949. It is the principal contention of this book that the erosion of close relations can be attributed broadly to what has been called 'Britain's turn to Europe'. In the 1960s Britain's foreign, defence and trade policies underwent a profound revision as the government attempted to redefine Britain's post-imperial role. London gradually turned away from imperial and global commitments and its orientation became more European. David Sanders has called this process of reorientation the 'Europeanisation' of Britain's external policy.[4] It can be seen principally in the series of policies implemented by successive British governments during the 1960s and early 1970s, namely in the applications for entry into the European Economic Community (EEC) between 1961 and 1972, as well as in the decision in 1968 to withdraw from east of Suez by 1971.

This book does not imply that Anglo-Australian ties had not experienced difficult challenges prior to the 1960s. David Day has highlighted the serious rift that occurred between the Australian prime minister, John Curtin, and his British counterpart, Winston Churchill, following the fall of Singapore in 1942.[5] Chris Waters, meanwhile, has emphasised the strong disagreements over a number of issues between London and Canberra in the late 1940s.[6] During the 1950s, however, dissension became more frequent. Significant disagreements were recorded over issues such as defence, trade, management of the sterling area and decolonisation. With regard to defence, the Australian Department of External Affairs was by 1961 observing that

> United Kingdom power no longer provides an answer to our security problems. There is no longer a concept of imperial defence ... The United King-

[4] David Sanders, *Losing an empire, finding a role: British foreign policy since 1945*, London 1990, 3.

[5] David Day, *The great betrayal: Britain, Australia, and the onset of the Pacific war, 1939–42*, Melbourne 1992, and *Reluctant nation: Australia and the allied defeat of Japan, 1942–45*, Melbourne 1992.

[6] Chris Waters, *The empire fractures: Anglo-Australian conflict in the 1940s*, Melbourne 1995.

dom's contribution to the defence of South East Asia and Australia is no longer the key to our security for which we looked primarily to the US by negotiating the ANZUS Treaty and, subsequently, to SEATO.[7]

David Lee, in his examination of the political economy of Australia's post-war foreign and defence policies, has argued that in the mid-1950s the Menzies government 'reached the view that reliance on membership of the sterling area and its traditional economic relations with Great Britain was not sufficient to secure Australia's vital economic needs'.[8] According to Lee, this fact compelled Menzies 'to loosen the bonds which tied Australia's economy so closely with Britain's', and 'to diversify Australia's international economic relations'.[9] None the less, 'the underlying fissures in the relationship were invariably papered over by loud, ostentatious affirmations of the British blood ties' and 'generally confined to the realm of confidential inter-governmental discussions'.[10] For the Australian government the differences did not seem grave enough to warrant a painful rift in Anglo-Australian relations.

Britain's turn to Europe posed a challenge of a different kind altogether and was to produce an outcome, the effect of which could not have been envisaged, for both the EEC applications and the withdrawal from east of Suez involved an irreconcilable conflict of interest between the two countries. It was a conflict of great and unprecedented new magnitude. From a political viewpoint, Australia perceived British membership of the EEC as liable to draw Britain progressively into a tight bloc, which would restrict its freedom of action as a world power and as the leader of the Commonwealth. Economically, Australians believed that their traditional trade relationship with Britain would be damaged irreparably should London adopt the Community's common external tariff, and the protectionist farm regime that was gradually coming into force during the 1960s. As most of Australia's exports to Britain were agricultural, Australian export earnings could only suffer severe losses. There was also another dimension to the Common Market problem that seriously concerned the Australian government. Although EEC membership entailed no specific commitment in the field of defence, the authorities in Canberra believed that Britain was likely to reduce its 'interest in maintaining, and the ability to maintain, an effective strategic role in the world beyond Suez, where Australia's defence interests [lay]'.[11] In the event, Wilson's decision to withdraw from east of Suez resulted

---

[7] Cabinet submission 1183, 26 June 1961, NAA, Canberra, A1838/269, TS899/1/4 pt 2.
[8] David Lee, *Search for security: the political economy of Australia's postwar foreign and defence policy*, Sydney 1995, 160.
[9] Ibid. 167.
[10] Stuart Ward, 'Discordant communities: Australia, Britain and the EEC, 1956–1963', unpubl. PhD diss. Sydney 1998, 24.
[11] Cabinet submission 1183, 26 June 1961, NAA, A1838/269, TS899/1/4 pt 2.

rather from a reassessment of Britain's foreign policy options in addition to, and to conform with, domestic and financial considerations. None the less, the important factor here is that the Australian government viewed Britain's membership of the EEC as having important defence implications for Australia and indeed this book shows there was, to an extent, a 'European dimension' to Wilson's decision to pull out of the Far East.

There is no doubt that, in the Australian view, the EEC question, together with the withdrawal, created a serious conflict of interest between Britain and Australia. Not only did both these issues undermine Australia's defence strategy, then based on forward deployments into the south-east Asian region, but they did so at a time when Canberra was increasing its commitment to the war in Vietnam. It is in consideration of these factors that the degree of conflict of interest is realised and the depth of the impact on Anglo-Australian relations is revealed.

This study argues that Britain's turn to Europe was a primary cause, albeit not the only one, for the parting of the ways between Australia and Britain. The relationship which had existed until the beginning of the 1960s could not withstand the strains imposed by Britain's reassessment of its imperial role. This is not to deny the importance of the other factors that compounded the strains on the relationship. David Goldsworthy has identified the changing character of the Commonwealth and London's moves towards restrictive immigration as additional issues that fuelled the Australians' sense of grievance towards Britain during this period.[12] This book does not dismiss the relevance of such factors in reinforcing the Australian sense of estrangement. However, it contends that they should be considered no more than irritants. The crucial issue here – or rather, the fundamental cause of change in Anglo-Australian relations – was the radical redefinition of Britain's post-imperial role and Britain's concomitant reorientation towards Europe. Neither outcome accorded, nor could ever accord, with Australian political, economic and strategic interests. Elements of dissonance were introduced into communication between Canberra and London, resulting in disagreements which, in contrast to previous decades, proved impossible to reconcile. This study shows clearly that the period under consideration marks a watershed in Anglo-Australian relations. After Britain's entry into the EEC in 1973 relations between the two countries never regained the depth and range that they had enjoyed in the period preceding the Second World War. As Britain became more closely involved in the affairs of Europe, Australia increasingly looked to the Asia-Pacific region. Despite the amicable relationship that would exist between London and Canberra thereafter, bilateral ties would no longer be of great significance to either country.

---

12 David Goldsworthy, 'Point of departure: the British military withdrawal from Southeast Asia as a problem in Anglo-Australian relations', unpubl. conference paper, Australian Historical Association, Hobart, October 1999.

In addition to highlighting the widening gap between Australian and British interests as Britain sought to re-evaluate its international position, this book closely examines the reaction of the Australian government to British policies. It argues that Australia was not entirely blind to the positive aspects of British membership of the EEC, but that it failed to see beyond the perceived damaging effect it would have on Australian trade and defence interests. The inherent feeling of Australian vulnerability arising from its geographical isolation on the periphery of Asia surfaced, as concerns increased that Britain's departure from south-east Asia would create significant strategic and political problems for Australia. Australian policy sought to minimise the impact of these unwelcome changes. One option taken was to play the 'sentiment card'. During the 1961–3 EEC negotiations, the Menzies government sought to pressure Britain's prime minister, Harold Macmillan, by resorting to sentimental and emotional arguments of 'kith and kin'. Not surprisingly, these tactics proved unsuccessful. With Britain's renewed efforts to gain admission into the EEC under Wilson's new Labour government, the 'sentiment card' became even less relevant. Another option was to seek the help of the United States. However, the Menzies government discovered in 1961–2 that the Kennedy administration strongly supported British entry into the EEC, and no diplomatic support could be expected from Washington. On the other hand, Australian calls in 1966–7 for the United States, now fully committed to a war in Vietnam, to urge Britain to remain in south-east Asia met with some success. None the less, even with the Johnson administration on its side, the Australian government under its new prime minister, Harold Holt, could not prevent a British withdrawal. This book shows that there was in fact little Australia could do to achieve its objective of maintaining its trading arrangements with Britain and British strategic interests in south-east Asia. Australia's ability to influence Britain was negligible. In the end, as the modalities of change and their tempo were set by London – and they were far too rapid and far too radical for Australia's liking – Australia resorted to protests. Yet, the paradox was that, anxious not to antagonise Britain for fear that it would drift even further away, the Australian government avoided too confrontational a stance. Australian policy-makers gradually accepted the realities of the situation and looked to diversify Australia's trading options away from its traditional markets in Britain and towards the Asia-Pacific region and cautiously redefined its strategic priorities in Asia.

This study draws heavily on the work of other scholars. In the past few years there has been increased interest in the study of Australia's relations with Britain during the 1960s.[13] The recent opening of Australian and

---

[13] Until recently, the only major study in the field was H. G. Gelber's *Australia, Britain and the EEC, 1961 to 1963*, Melbourne 1966.

British archives on this period has injected new life into the topic.[14] This book acknowledges the contribution made by a number of scholars who have availed themselves of the released material to revisit and re-evaluate the importance of this particular period in Anglo-Australian relations. Stuart Ward's *Australia and the British embrace: the demise of the imperial ideal* is particularly significant as the first thorough analysis based on archival sources of Britain's first application to join the EEC. In this study, Ward not only emphasises the importance of the application to Anglo-Australian relations, but also demonstrates its effect on Australian political culture. Ward's central argument is that 'the demise of the British race patriot outlook in Australian politics can be identified, with a surprising degree of precision, in the United Kingdom's first application to join the European Economic Community'. In his view, 'the advent of the Common Market crisis in 1961 brazenly and abruptly confronted the core myth of "community in diversity" that had for so long sustained the Anglo-Australian relationship through countless imperial crises'.[15] In chapters or article-length studies, David Goldsworthy, John O'Brien, Paul Robertson and John Singleton, and Catherine Schenk have all focused on different aspects of Australia's diplomacy towards the British 1961–3 application.[16] Goldsworthy has concentrated upon the role of Prime Minister Robert Menzies as the key Australian player in the area of Anglo-Australian relations on the EEC issue. O'Brien, and Robertson and Singleton, have looked at Australian reactions to Britain's bid as a part of a more general Commonwealth response. Schenk has devoted significant attention to Australian policies although her primary focus is on the financial and monetary implications for the sterling area of an eventual British entry.

Jeppe Kristensen, in his MA thesis, 'Community of interest: Australia and Britain's "east of Suez", 1966–68', explains the role of British withdrawal from east of Suez in further undermining Australia's attachment to the ideal of Britishness in Australian political culture. While accepting Ward's assertion that the 1961–3 application radically transformed Anglo-Australian rela-

---

[14] Anglo-Australian diplomatic relations in the 1960s has been the subject of considerable work in recent years although much of it has failed to develop distinctive perspectives on key aspects of the relationship. See Annmarie Elijah, 'Better the devil you know? Australia and the British bids for European Community membership', unpubl. PhD diss. Melbourne 2003, and Daniel House, 'Rethinking the region: Australia and Britain's withdrawal from southeast Asia, 1965–71', unpubl. PhD diss. Deakin (Geelong) 2004.

[15] Ward, *British embrace*, 260–1.

[16] David Goldsworthy, *Losing the blanket: Australia and the end of Britain's empire*, Melbourne 2002, 120–38; John O'Brien, 'The British Commonwealth and the European Economic Community, 1960–63: the Australian and Canadian experiences', *Round Table* lxxxv (1996), 479–91; John Singleton and Paul Robertson, *Economic relations between Britain and Australasia, 1945–1970*, Basingstoke 2002, 166–89; Catherine Schenk, 'The UK, the sterling area, and the EEC, 1957–63', in Anne Deighton and Alan Milward (eds), *Widening, deepening and acceleration: the European Economic Community, 1957–1963*, Baden-Baden 1999, 123–37.

tions, Kristensen contends that British race patriotism did not in fact disappear overnight.[17] Although his focus is upon the diplomatic implications of British withdrawal rather than on cultural history, David Goldsworthy makes a similar point in a chapter of his *Losing the blanket: Australia and the end of Britain's empire*.[18] Both studies are valuable contributions.[19] They are the first attempts to revisit Australia's reactions to the withdrawal by relying on recently-released archival material. Yet, their brevity is a problem. Kristensen deals exclusively with the crucial phase of the British withdrawal (1966–8). This has three evident shortcomings. First, it takes British withdrawal as a given and, in so doing, fails to examine Britain's defence role east of Suez in the early 1960s. In particular, no mention is made of the growing political, economic and strategic constraints under which successive British governments found themselves operating east of Suez between the end of the 1950s and into the early 1960s. Second, it overlooks the gradual reassessment of British defence policy options undertaken by Wilson during 1965 and the Menzies government's responses to it. Third, it also fails to address Anglo-Australian defence relations in the post-1968 period, and to take into account Australia's reaction to the British decision in 1971 to maintain a token military presence in Malaysia and Singapore. Goldsworthy does put the withdrawal into a broader historical context and manages to convey the sense of growing scepticism with which, by the early 1960s, the Menzies government came to see Britain's ability to maintain a meaningful role east of Suez. He also considers Australian responses to Wilson's defence policy reassessment in 1965. Yet the brevity of his chapter is a real constraint. British policy is sketchily outlined and Goldsworthy's analysis, like Kristensen's, does not go beyond 1968.

The importance and originality of this study is that it is the first comprehensive attempt to explore the full importance of Britain's turn to Europe for Anglo-Australian relations. It is not restricted to one specific aspect or crisis in the relationship in the 1960s. Instead, it considers the political, strategic and economic consequences for the Australian government in its policy-making as it struggled to accept the inevitability of Britain's decision. To this end, the book analyses Australian policy-making in four phases of reaction and response: Britain's first application (1961–3); the British with-

---

[17] Jeppe Kristensen, 'Community of interest: Australia and Britain's "east of Suez", 1966–68', unpubl. MA diss. Southern Denmark (Odense) 2000, 5. In his article, '"In essence still a British country": Britain's withdrawal from east of Suez', *AJPH* li (2005), 40–52, Kristensen further explores the impact of the British withdrawal on Australian political culture by showing how Britain's imperial retreat pushed Australians to think harder about forging a distinctive Australian civic identity.

[18] Goldsworthy, *Losing the blanket*, ch. viii.

[19] Mention should be made of Derek McDougall, 'Australia and the British military withdrawal from east of Suez', *AJIA* li (1997), 183–94. Albeit based exclusively on secondary sources, it remains a worthy contribution to the understanding of Australian policy towards withdrawal.

drawal (1967–8); Britain's second application (1967); and, finally, Britain's reinstated application (1971–2). It should be stressed that this is not an examination of Australian foreign policy in all its dimensions, but only of Australian reactions to British initiatives. Although events are seen through the prism of Australian foreign policy, it is not an analysis of Australia's foreign policy as such, but rather of the impact of British policies upon its relationship with one of Britain's main imperial partners.

The book asserts that the Anglo-Australian relationship during this period did not deteriorate as a result of one specific crisis. Rather, it declined rapidly as a result of the cumulative effect of the four perceived crises. Their impact on the Australian mindset of vulnerability was compounded by the fact that Britain's actions not only took place one after another, indeed overlapping in the case of Britain's 1967 EEC application and the military withdrawal, but also within a relatively short period of time. Although this analysis confirms Ward's assertion that Australia's attachment to the idea of Britishness was profoundly shaken as a result of Britain's first application, it is contended that the 1961–3 Common Market crisis was by no means 'the end of the affair'. In fact, it is argued, as Goldsworthy has done in his analysis of Australian policy towards the British withdrawal from east of Suez, that 'if the Common Market dispute left race patriotism seriously wounded, the East of Suez dispute administered the coup de grace'. This book recognises, however, as did Goldsworthy, that this interpretation would be 'tempting', but 'no doubt simplistic'.[20] The examination here reveals that it was in fact the close succession of four crises and their cumulative impact that put an end to an era in Anglo-Australian relations.

The second contribution this book makes is its attempt to integrate politico-strategic and politico-economic factors.[21] Australian scholars have tended to emphasise either the first or the second of these. This has resulted in considerably different explanations for the fraying of the Anglo-Australian relationship. On the one hand, politico-strategic analyses have stressed the importance of strategic issues in shaping Australian post-war perceptions and policies towards Britain, and by extension, in weakening their bilateral relations. Scholars such as David Day and Coral Bell have focused on Britain's inability to defend the Singapore base, which was the focal point of the British defence system in the Far East. They have argued that the fall of Singapore in 1942 dealt a mortal blow to the assumption that London retained the military capacity to protect the far-flung outposts of its empire.[22] Day and Bell are not alone in making this claim. Others have drawn similar conclusions. While not focusing primarily on defence, historians such as Stuart Macintyre, Geoffrey Bolton, Brian Farrell

---

[20] Goldsworthy, 'Point of departure'.

[21] To date David Lee's *Search for security* remains the only other attempt to integrate economic and strategic factors in the study of Australia's post-war foreign policy.

[22] Day, *Great betrayal*; Coral Bell, *Dependent ally: a study in Australian foreign policy*, Sydney 1988, 18.

8

and T. B. Millar have all unfailingly emphasised the crucial implications of the fall of Singapore for the future of Anglo-Australian relations.[23] Robert O'Neill has taken this conclusion further and indeed regards the fact that neither the Chiefly nor Menzies governments 'saw Britain as a comparable ally to the United States' as contributing to Britain's post-war problems and its declining power.[24] This Australian attitude to ensuring protection had begun immediately after the war. As Gregory Pemberton has argued, 'Australia's external relations remained overwhelmingly oriented towards Britain' in the initial post-war period,[25] but this was done out of necessity rather than by choice. With the United States unwilling to commit itself to the security of Australia's neighbourhood, it was evident that Canberra had nowhere else to look than to Britain. However, the signing of the ANZUS Treaty in 1951 clearly revealed the belief of the Menzies government that Australia's 'long term security interests would be best served by a direct alliance with the United States, whether this alliance included Britain or not'.[26] From this point Australia increasingly sought to rely on American power for its own security. Those who have dwelt on defence issues have concluded that Anglo-Australian relations never recovered from the politico-strategic implications of the fall of Singapore and the harsh realities of post-war world politics, which witnessed the steady decline of British power.

This view, however, has been challenged recently, and ultimately rejected, by Wayne Reynolds in his original study of Australia's bid for the atomic bomb. Reynolds has sharply criticised the tendency amongst Australian scholars to overstate 'the point of departure with respect to the empire caused by World War II' while not 'appreciating the elements of continuity'.[27] He has argued that a crucial but forgotten aspect of Australian defence policy between 1945 and 1957 was the attempt to develop a nuclear capability in partnership with Britain. Lacking the necessary resources to develop its own nuclear weapons Canberra became closely associated with Britain's nuclear programme in the belief that this would allow Australia to acquire a nuclear capability. In this context, therefore, the importance of Britain and the empire, far from declining, actually increased in Australian eyes in the immediate post-war years. As Reynolds himself has put it, between 1945 and 1957, 'British and Australian defence policies were closer then ever before'.[28] It is only with the

[23] Stuart Macintyre, *The Oxford history of Australia*, IV: *The succeeding age, 1901–1942*, Melbourne 1993, 335; Geoffrey Bolton, 'The United Kingdom', in W. J. Hudson (ed.), *Australia in world affairs, 1971–75*, Sydney 1980, 210; Brian Farrell, *The defence and fall of Singapore, 1940–1942*, Stroud 2005, 392; T. B. Millar, *Australia in peace and war: external relations since 1788*, Canberra 1991, 122.

[24] Robert O'Neill, *Australia in the Korean war, 1950–53*, I: *Strategy and diplomacy*, Canberra 1982, 21.

[25] Gregory Pemberton, *All the way: Australia's road to Vietnam*, Sydney 1987, 1.

[26] O'Neill, *Korean war*, 404.

[27] Wayne Reynolds, *Australia's bid for the atomic bomb*, Melbourne 2000, 26.

[28] Ibid. 6.

restoration of the Anglo-American atomic alliance, following the Bermuda agreement in 1957, that the nuclear partnership between Britain and Australia came gradually to an end.[29] In Reynolds's view, it was not the fall of Singapore which undermined Anglo-Australian relations, rather, it was the British decision to abandon nuclear co-operation with Australia which spelled the end of the close relationship.

Focusing on the politico-economic dimension on the other hand, some scholars have stressed the significance of economic and financial issues in undermining Anglo-Australian relations. Kosmas Tsokhas, for instance, has suggested that the Second World War played a crucial role in what he calls the 'dedominionisation' of Australia. In his view, Australia's drift away from its imperial moorings was caused not so much by the fall of Singapore, as by the economic and financial strains that came to beset Anglo-Australian relations during the war.[30] Beresford and Kerr have also focused on the economic implications of the Second World War for Anglo-Australian relations. They contend that Australia's acceptance of article VII of the wartime Mutual Aid Agreement and its decision to join the International Monetary Fund (IMF) in 1947 are to be seen as a rejection of the British connection in favour of an American-centred international economic system.[31]

However, the claim that the Second World War played a decisive role in weakening Anglo-Australian relations, has recently come under close scrutiny and, ultimately, has been dismissed by a number of scholars. In doing so they have drawn attention to the 1950s as the main catalyst for change in the relationship. Paul Robertson and John Singleton have attributed the diminution in importance of Australia's bilateral ties with Britain to the steady erosion of both the Commonwealth preference system and the sterling area during this period.[32]

---

[29] At the Bermuda summit of March 1957, the Eisenhower administration agreed to offer London a limited nuclear partnership. Under the agreement Britain was to receive sixty intermediate range ballistic missiles (IRBMs).

[30] Kosmas Tsokhas, 'Dedominionisation: the Anglo-Australian experience, 1935–45', *Historical Journal* xxxvii (1994), 861–83.

[31] M. Beresford and P. Kerr, 'A turning point for Australian capitalism, 1942–1952', in Edward Wheelwright and Kenneth Buckley (eds), *Essays in the political economy of Australian capitalism*, iv, Sydney 1980, 148–71. In February 1942 the United States and Britain signed the Mutual Aid Agreement, extending American 'Lend-Lease' material assistance to the British empire. Under the Lend-Lease Bill, passed by Congress in March 1941, the US made available war materials to their allies while leaving the financial value of the supplies unspecified until the end of the war. Alarmed by the British determination to retain tight preferential trade arrangements with the empire, Washington demanded in return the inclusion of article VII, calling for the 'elimination of all forms of discriminatory treatment in international commerce and to the reduction of tariffs and other trade barriers'.

[32] Paul Robertson and John Singleton, 'The Commonwealth as an economic network', *AEHR* xli (2001), 241–66. More recently, the authors have argued that while the Commonwealth economic nexus began to unravel during the 1950s, separation was not

Sandra Tweedie has gone even further, claiming that, despite Australia's reassertion of the ties of kinship and its continued reliance on British markets in the late 1940s, 'the sentiment, tradition and questionable economic advantage which had maintained Australia firmly in the UK orbit up until World War II were all ended by the mid-1950s'.[33] The turning point in what she has described as 'an overly long and painful weaning from the imperial connection' was the negotiation of a new Anglo-Australian trade agreement in 1956 through which the Menzies government sought to obtain better terms of trade than those contained in the old Ottawa Agreement of 1932.[34] In this context, Britain's attempts to join the EEC in the 1960s are treated as no more than mere signposts along the road of a steady decline in Anglo-Australian relations. The controversial nature of Tweedie's arguments could not go unchallenged, particularly by those who have regarded Britain's first EEC application as an important factor in undermining the bilateral relationship. Stuart Ward for instance has argued that the 1956 Anglo-Australian trade negotiations 'did not, in any fundamental sense, provoke a wider examination of the steadily widening gap between British commercial interests and Australian national aspirations'. He contends that 'both the Prime Minister's Department and External Affairs were opposed to any measures which would "derogate from the strength of British influence" in the world, while the Trade Department behaved as though a severe curtailment of British trade advantages was a simple matter of "restoring the balance" to a gentlemen's agreement'.[35] In contrast, while careful not to treat Britain's 1961–3 EEC bid as 'the fundamental cause of Australia's drift away from imperial moorings', he has not shied away from emphasising its important role in undermining post-war Anglo-Australian relations. In his view, Britain's 1961–3 bid shows 'how the disentangling of Australian and British cultural identities was directly informed by the disentangling of their political and economic interests'.[36] Others before Ward had also underlined the importance of the 1961–3 application. Henry Gelber, for instance, wrote in 1966 that the British bid presented Australia with a 'problem different in kind from the trade talks previously conducted with Britain or Japan or the conclusion of SEATO or the ANZUS Pact'.[37]

In the light of these contrasting views, it is important to take a balanced approach and to seek to bring both the politico-strategic and politico-economic aspects of the relationship into one study. This book has the merit of doing so. By looking at both dimensions, it avoids offering a partial explanation for

complete until Britain joined the EEC in 1973: Singleton and Robertson, *Britain and Australasia*, 215.

[33] Sandra Tweedie, *Trading partners: Australia and Asia, 1790–1993*, Sydney 1994, 97.

[34] Ibid. 105.

[35] Ward, *British embrace*, 36.

[36] Ibid. 254, 260.

[37] Gelber, *Australia, Britain and the EEC*, 258; J. D. B. Miller, *Survey of Commonwealth affairs: problems of expansion and attrition, 1953–69*, London 1974.

the erosion of Anglo-Australian relations. In so doing, it is also able to show how both the politico-economic and politico-strategic implications of Britain's turn to Europe interacted to deal a crucial blow to, and as a consequence to unravel, the once intimate Anglo-Australian relationship.

While a major engine of change in Anglo-Australian relations, it is worth noting that Britain's radical redefinition of its post-imperial role was also an important factor that affected global stability and impacted upon the structuring of international politics in the 1960s. This volume takes this aspect into account and places the erosion of Anglo-Australian ties into a wider international context. Not only does it explore Britain's end of empire as it impinged on the western alliance's strategic aims in Cold War Asia, it also examines in some detail British policy-making during those twilight years, discussing the role of Britain's end of empire in furthering Australia's ties with Asia and giving some consideration to south-east Asian reactions to the British decision to pull out of the region.

This book draws extensively on newly released archival material from the National Archives of Australia in Canberra and the National Archives in London. It also draws on various collections of Australian private papers, in particular those of John McEwen and Robert Menzies, held in the National Library of Australia in Canberra. These sources are supplemented by the various volumes of *Foreign Relations of the United States* and by a number of official sources including Australia's parliamentary debates and ministerial documents, and Britain's House of Commons debates. The book also makes use of contemporary material contained in Australian, British and European newspapers and magazines. Finally, some policy-makers, government officials and diplomats of the time were able to share their reminiscences.

This study is organised in three sections. The first briefly discusses Anglo-Australian relations in the early post-war period and examines, in more detail, Britain's 1961 application to join the EEC. Australia's post-war relations with Britain are discussed in chapter 1. Chapter 2 concentrates on the Macmillan bid for EEC membership and its impact on the bilateral relationship. The Menzies government's reactions are fully examined and the chapter argues that, in spite of leaving Anglo-Australian relations profoundly shaken, the 1961–3 Common Market crisis by no means represented 'the end of the affair'.

The second and central section analyses Anglo-Australian relations during Wilson's premiership (1964–70), looking at the combined effect of Britain's 1967 EEC application and its military withdrawal from south-east Asia. Chapter 3 looks briefly at Anglo-Australian defence relations in the early 1960s and at Australian perceptions of Britain's military role east of Suez. Australian reactions to British attempts to disengage between 1965 and 1966 are examined in chapter 4, while chapter 5 focuses on the period 1967–8 when the Wilson government took the decision to withdraw and considers Australian responses to it. To conclude this section, Britain's second EEC application and Australia's reactions are examined in chapters 6 and 7.

Analysis of this period shows that the Wilson government further reoriented Britain's foreign and defence policies towards Europe. It also shows that disengagement from east of Suez, and the resulting retrenchment into Europe, were carried out rapidly once the Malaysian-Indonesian *Konfrontasi* (Confrontation) ended in 1966. The withdrawal of all British forces from east of Suez by the mid-1970s was first announced in July 1967, but a subsequent announcement in January 1968 brought the date forward to 1971. The first announcement followed quickly upon the May 1967 launch of a new bid to join the EEC. Despite the fact that 'Wilson's "voyage into Europe" foundered, like Macmillan's, on the rocks of de Gaulle's intransigence' and his bid ended in a diplomatic debacle,[38] the British application was not withdrawn, but remained on the table. This signalled that, the temporary set-back notwithstanding, Britain did not intend to give up its quest for EEC membership. Or, as John Darwin argues, Wilson's bid 'marked the emergence of entry into the EEC, and the revival of British influence into Europe, as the first priority of foreign policy'.[39] It was hoped that entry was only postponed.

The book here contends that Wilson's marked turn to Europe vanquished any remaining Australian hopes that the bonds of empire would hold. It was evident to Australian policy-makers that together, the withdrawal and the EEC application clearly indicated that Britain's reorientation towards Europe, while not fully achieved, was none the less nearly a *fait accompli*. Wilson's determined reorientation towards Europe exacerbated differences between Canberra and London. Australian disappointment turned to indignation as the conflict of interest strengthened. This section highlights how far apart Australia and Britain had drifted within the few years since the 1961–3 Common Market crisis. It also reveals the extent to which the Wilson government was prepared to disregard Australian interests in order to secure Britain's foreign and defence policy objectives. Macmillan had sought painfully to reconcile the conflicting interests of Britain, Australia and the Commonwealth during the 1961 negotiations. Yet to Wilson, desperately trying to address Britain's economic deterioration, such consideration was of little interest. Unlike Macmillan, who had hoped that Britain would be able to continue to play an influential role in the Commonwealth, Wilson had no such hope. His turn to Europe was not so much an attempt to prop up Britain's declining influence in world affairs by other (read European) means, but the recognition that Europe was the only option available for a country with limited resources. In this context it was inevitable, and hardly surprising, that Australian interests were thought to be expendable.

The third section of the book discusses Australian responses to Britain's

[38] David Reynolds, *Britannia overruled: British policy and world power in the 20th century*, London 1991, 232.
[39] John Darwin, *Britain and decolonisation: the retreat from empire in the post-war world*, Basingstoke 1992, 295.

revived application to the EEC in 1970. Chapter 8 studies Anglo-Australian defence relations in the post-withdrawal period, and chapter 9 examines the impact of the 1970–2 application on Australian policy and the Anglo-Australian relationship. It is argued here that, although by the late 1960s transformed beyond recognition as a result of Britain's shift to Europe, it was only with British entry in January 1973 that change in the bilateral relationship was fully realised. While far from having the same impact as earlier applications, the 1970–2 bid had important symbolic and practical implications. British entry represented a formal abandonment of the close ties of empire that had characterised Anglo-Australian relations until the end of the 1950s. It also spelled the end of the imperial preference system. Last, but not least, it pushed Australia further to reorient its external and economic policies towards Asia. This section also analyses Australian reactions to the British withdrawal in the post-1968 period, and briefly examines Australian policy towards the negotiation of the Five Power Defence Arrangements. It shows that, despite welcoming the British decision to maintain a token military force in south-east Asia, the Australian government was initially rather cautious in its response. Far from accepting British proposals unreservedly, Canberra was careful to ensure that a continued British presence should accord with a more independent formulation of Australia's regional interests. This was an indication of how much Australian thinking had developed since the Wilson government's decision to withdraw from east of Suez. In less than three years of Wilson's announcement in January 1968 of an acceleration of withdrawal, Australia's defence policy was no longer dependent on a British military presence in Malaysia and Singapore.

PART I

ANGLO-AUSTRALIAN RELATIONS
AT A TURNING POINT

1

Australia and Britain at the End of the 1950s

'Great Britain, let me remind you, is only part of the British Empire, but it is the most important part. It is the centre of our history, the centre of our being. We have no illusions about it; when you stand we stand, and when you fall we are rudderless for the time being in a very strong sea': Robert Menzies, 1948.[1]

These were the words with which Robert Menzies, then opposition leader but soon to become Australia's longest-serving prime minister, endeavoured to capture the essence of the Anglo-Australian relationship when he addressed the Empire Parliament Association in London in 1948. Rhetoric notwithstanding, Menzies's words were a clear indication that, at the turn of the 1940s, Australia and Britain still enjoyed a unique relationship. Their relationship remained strong throughout the following decade in spite of changes which resulted in a weakening of Anglo-Australian ties. Proof of this was the fact that, at the end of the 1950s, Australia and Britain were still bound by a vast array of formal and informal links. These links were not confined to foreign policy, defence or trade. They also encompassed a wide range of issues – from constitutional arrangements to social connections. This chapter offers a snapshot of the Anglo-Australian relationship at this time. In so doing, it provides the context in which the changes which were taking place during the 1960s should be assessed. To substantiate the claim that these were radical, this chapter aims to provide a benchmark against which political shifts can be evaluated. This approach, however, does not imply that relations between Canberra and London remained static between the 1940s and the late 1950s.

A special relationship

The close relationship between Australia and Britain was of course the legacy of a shared historical experience that had begun in 1770 when Captain James Cook claimed the eastern part of Australia for King George III. By 1860 Britain had gradually consolidated its hold on the entire continent by establishing six colonies, which inherited political and social institutions, language and culture from Britain. In 1901 they federated into a single entity

[1] As quoted in John Arnold, Peter Spearritt and David Walker (eds), *Out of empire: the British dominion of Australia*, Melbourne 1993, 8.

17

– the Commonwealth of Australia, a dominion under the British crown.[2] It was only with the ratification of the Statute of Westminster in 1942 that Australia became in every respect a sovereign state.

Australia nevertheless remained closely bound within the British imperial nexus. The most visible link between the two countries was constitutional, since the British monarch was also Australia's head of state. The British monarch, who acted only on the advice of the Australian government, was represented in Australia by the governor-general, and it is noteworthy that, with the exception of Isaac Isaacs (1931–6) and William McKell (1947–53), governors-general had up to the period under study been British. Yet, for all its importance, the monarchy was not the only symbolic link between Britain and Australia. For instance, Australians travelling abroad carried a passport stamped on the front 'British passport'. In fact, even though the concept of Australian citizenship was for the first time formalised in the Nationality and Citizenship Act of 1948, Australian citizens were required, until the late 1960s, to declare their nationality as British.[3] Furthermore the Australian national anthem was still 'God Save the Queen' (or 'King') despite the fact that various commercial and official competitions were held over the years to find a substitute.[4]

Significant links existed at the economic level. Throughout the 1950s Britain remained Australia's largest market taking, in 1950, 38 per cent of Australian exports. Ten years later, despite a noticeable decline, Australia still sent 26 per cent of its total exports to Britain (see table 1). In the 1950s Australia's prosperity was still perceived as being dependent upon the country's ability to retain Britain as a substantial export market. The reverse, of course, was hardly true, yet it would be wrong to assume that the economic significance of the commercial relationship was a one-way affair. For if it was true that Britain's foreign trade was much more diversified and,

2 Though never formally defined, the title 'dominion' applied to the self-governing territories of the British empire (renamed British Commonwealth of Nations in 1931, then Commonwealth of Nations in 1946), that is, Australia, Canada, New Zealand, South Africa, Eire and Newfoundland. During the first half of the twentieth century dominion status gradually changed to accommodate the dominions' demands for greater independence. The Statute of Westminster (1931) recognised the dominions as separate states under the British crown and granted them full legislative authority. After the Second World War the word 'dominion' was abandoned to be replaced by 'member of the Commonwealth'. For a detailed analysis see K.C. Wheare, *The Statute of Westminster and dominion status*, London 1953, especially pp. 6–17.

3 The concept of 'Australian nationality' gained official recognition only after the Nationality and Citizenship Act was amended in 1969. It is noteworthy that in August 1967 the Holt Cabinet approved the deletion of the word 'British' from the covers of Australian passports: Cabinet decision 517, 22 Aug. 1967, NAA, A5840/XM1, vol. 2. Nevertheless, the phrase 'British subject' remained in the inner pages of Australian passports until 1973.

4 Department of Foreign Affairs and Trade, 'The Australian national anthem', available at http://www.dfat.gov.au/facts/pdfs_2004/aust_national_anthem.pdf.

Table 1
Australia's main export markets, 1950–60

	1950	1960
	As % of total exports	As % of total exports
USA	8.09	8.10
Japan	3.91	14.36
Britain	38.70	26.38
France	6.63	6.43
West Germany	–	4.09

Source: E. M. Andrews, A history of Australian foreign policy, Melbourne 1988, 173.

therefore less dependent on one single market than Australia's, it was also true that throughout the 1950s Australia was still one of Britain's largest export outlets. In 1950, with nearly 11.8 per cent of its total exports going to Australia, the latter was Britain's largest export market that year. In 1959 Australia was still Britain's third largest export market after the EEC and the United States (see table 2).

This close trading relationship was based on a system of mutual trade concessions, known as the Ottawa Agreement, which Britain and its dominions negotiated at the Ottawa Imperial Economic Conference in 1932.[5] According to the agreement, Britain and Australia were committed to protecting their reciprocal trade interests in their respective economies and to according each other's exports preferential treatment in their own markets. By the mid-1950s, 40 per cent of Australian exports to Britain received preferences in comparison with 80 per cent of British exports to Australia.[6] Some Australian commodities such as lamb, mutton, wool and wheat, while receiving no preference at all, could still enter the British market freely.[7] In 1956, however, believing that the Ottawa Agreement was working significantly in Britain's favour, the Menzies government sought to renegotiate it, and in spite of falling short of Australia's expectations, a new agreement was signed in Canberra in November 1956. Its main features were the continuation of preferential trade between the two countries, an across-the-board cut in the margin of preference on British exports to Australia, a reiteration of the 1952 meat agreement committing Britain to purchase all

[5] The Ottawa Agreement was in reality a series of bilateral trade treaties between Britain and the dominions as well as between the dominions themselves.
[6] Tweedie, Trading partner, 99.
[7] Ibid. 100.

Table 2
Britain's main export markets, 1950–9

	1950			1959		
	Value of exports (£million)	As a % of total exports	Ranking	Value of exports (£million)	As a % of total exports	Ranking
USA	113.9	5.2	4	360.1	10.8	2
EEC*	243.3	11.1	2	446.3	13.4	1
Canada	125.9	5.8	3	207.4	6.2	4
Australia	255.8	11.7	1	223.6	6.7	3
South Africa	120.7	5.5	5	148.9	4.4	6
Eire	86.7	3.98	6	107	3.2	8
NZ	86.5	3.97	7	96.9	2.9	9

* As the EEC was established in 1957, the 1950 figures for the EEC are purely indicative

Source: Central Statistical Office, *Annual abstract of statistics, no. 96* (1959), *no. 97* (1960), London 1959–60.

Australian beef, and a non-binding clause whereby Britain endeavoured to buy 750,000 tonnes of Australian wheat each year.[8]

Yet, during the 1940s and the early 1950s there was another important, and perhaps even more effective, factor which contributed to binding Britain and Australia together economically – their common membership of the sterling area, a financial and economic network whose primary objective was to ease the effects on Commonwealth countries of the US dollar shortage. To this end, sterling area members were encouraged to economise on the use of hard currency by trading with and investing in each other. Robertson and Singleton point out that 'as the central purpose of the sterling area was the operation of currency controls, this necessitated the regulation of trade to ensure the protection of the currency pool'.[9] Members were in fact expected to deposit their US dollar earnings in a common pool. Their ability to draw on this pool varied from member to member. Britain, for instance, was the only country to have unlimited access to it as long as there were enough dollars in the pool. Australia and the other dominions (with the exception of Canada which was not a member) were allowed to convert their sterling holdings into dollars provided they did not abuse the system. In that case, Britain could have denied access. The colonies and big dollar earners such as

8 Ibid. 99–104, and Ward, *British embrace*, 35–7. For the text of the 1957 Trade Agreement see Cmnd. 91, *Trade agreement between the government of the United Kingdom and Northern Ireland and the government of the Commonwealth of Australia*, London 1957.
9 Robertson and Singleton, 'Commonwealth', 255.

Table 3
Australia's sterling balances, 1955–66

	Sterling (A$ m)	Sterling % of total reserves	US dollar % of total reserves
1955	679.4	80.4	4.5
1956	508.7	73.2	5.9
1957	965.9	86.5	4.6
1958	853.5	82.6	5
1959	832.6	82.3	6.1
1960	785.6	78.4	8.3
1961	881.5	81.8	5.6
1962	870.9	79.4	6
1963	936.1	76.4	8.8
1964	1346.2	80.5	7.6
1965	994.5	73.4	11.3
1966	980.6	71.3	14.1

Source: NAA, A1209/84, 1967/7734, attachment 2.

Malaya or Nigeria were generally not allowed to draw on the pool. In practice, only Britain and the old dominions were the real beneficiaries of this system as they 'were able to call on more dollars than they earned without upsetting the balance of the entire Sterling Area'.[10] However, following the outbreak of the Korean war this tight system began to loosen: dollars came to be more freely available in the early 1950s as the Americans increased their imports of strategic materials.[11] Australia also played a role in weakening the system by negotiating a dollar loan directly with the US and the International Bank for Reconstruction and Development (IRBD) in 1950.[12] Trade policy coordination was gradually abandoned after 1952.[13] With the restoration of sterling's convertibility in 1958, the dollar pool, which until then had remained an important source of foreign exchange, was terminated. By 1961 strict policy coordination, one of the hallmarks of the sterling area, was also over.[14] Yet the sterling area did not become of 'little significance' as has been contended.[15] Its members continued to hold their reserves in sterling and kept their currencies pegged to it. This meant that 'the reserve

[10] Paul Robertson, 'The decline of economic complementarity? Australia and Britain, 1945–1952', *AEHR* xxxvii (1997), 94.
[11] Robertson and Singleton, 'Commonwealth', 256–7.
[12] Lee, *Search for security*, 140–5. See also Robertson, 'Complementarity', 100–3.
[13] Schenk, 'Sterling area', 124.
[14] Ibid.
[15] Robertson and Singleton, 'Commonwealth', 260.

currency and transactions currency role of sterling in the international monetary system was tightly bound up with the sterling area'.[16] In practice, this also meant that Britain and the Commonwealth's big sterling holders, including Australia (*see* table 3), had a strong interest in managing the sterling exchange rate and co-operating on monetary issues. Last but not least, members of the sterling area continued to enjoy privileged access to the London capital market.[17] This was not an insignificant matter, particularly for a country like Australia, which since the early 1950s had been attempting to modernise and expand its economy, and to this end needed easy and ready access to foreign capital to finance its development programme. The London capital market was an important source of such finance. In 1961 Australia had a £342 million sterling debt outstanding in London.[18]

Political relations between Australia and Britain were also cemented by their joint membership of the Commonwealth. This informal association which, in the 1950s, consisted of Britain, the old dominions and a few former British dependencies, provided a valuable forum within which to co-ordinate policies of mutual interest.[19] Throughout the decade, the intimate relations which existed between Britain and its old dominions, and between the old dominions themselves, facilitated political consultations. Although by the turn of the decade it was 'clearly no longer the expression of British power that it had been before the war or even before the Suez crisis', the Commonwealth remained 'a highly significant vehicle of British influence'.[20] Likewise, despite Australian concerns at its gradual transformation from an essentially white man's club into a multi-ethnic association, the Commonwealth remained a valuable political asset for Australia.

Defence was another important area where close links existed between Australia and Britain. Although Australia had been seeking to establish close defence links with the United States since the end of the Second World War, Britain remained an indispensable partner throughout the decade, as will be discussed in chapter 3. The presence of sizeable British forces in south-east Asia ensured a certain degree of stability in an area of great strategic importance to Australia.[21] In Australian eyes it also symbol-

16 Schenk, 'Sterling area', 124–5.
17 David Kandiah and Gillian Staerck, 'Commonwealth international financial arrangements and Britain's first application to join the EEC', in Alex May (ed.), *Britain, the Commonwealth and Europe: the Commonwealth and Britain's application to join the European Communities*, Basingstoke 2001, 113.
18 Document passed to UK representative at a meeting in Treasury, 5 Oct. 1961, TNA, T 230/668, quoted in Schenk, 'Sterling area', 128.
19 India and Pakistan joined the Commonwealth in 1947 followed by Ceylon (1948), Malaya (1957) and Ghana (1957).
20 Alex May, '"Commonwealth or Europe?" Macmillan's dilemma, 1961–63', in May, *Britain, the Commonwealth and Europe*, 88.
21 For the number of British forces deployed in south-east Asia and their location see chapter 3 below.

ised Britain's continuing interest in the defence of Australia. For their part, British policy-makers indeed regarded the deployment of British forces in south-east Asia as a commitment to the security of Australia, but this was neither the primary, nor the sole, reason for British troops being in the region. Deployment depended essentially on Britain's imperial strategy and Cold War objectives. Yet, the commitment to Australia was real enough. While not formally enshrined in any defence treaty, it was undertaken by successive British governments as a genuine obligation. On the one hand, it was recognition of Australia's military contribution to the British war effort during the two world wars. On the other hand, it was the price to be paid for Australia's strategic co-operation in the region. Commonwealth co-operation had been formalised in 1949 with the establishment of the so-called ANZAM arrangements under which Australia, Britain and New Zealand had undertaken to co-ordinate their strategic planning for the conduct of military operation in a vast area which included the Australian and New Zealand homelands, and the British territories in Malaya and Borneo, along with the adjacent sea areas.[22] In the event of war, Commonwealth forces in the region would in fact come under the command of ANZAM Chiefs of Staff.[23] Anglo-Australian defence co-operation was given further meaning with the creation of the Commonwealth Strategic Reserve (CSR) in 1955. The concept of such a reserve had been proposed originally by Britain in 1953:[24] it would comprise British, Australian and New Zealand forces which could be deployed in Malaya as a deterrent against Communist aggression and, in situations short of war, would be available for counter-terrorist operations.[25] In 1955 the Menzies Cabinet agreed to commit ground, naval and air forces to the Strategic Reserve.[26]

Close links between Britain and Australia, however, went well beyond the realms of politics, economics and defence. Despite their undeniable importance, such ties were not the only significant aspects of the bilateral relationship. Social and cultural links had also a special relevance as they were in a sense the premise upon which close Anglo-Australian relations rested. In the 1950s the great majority of Australians were of British stock and Britain was still Australia's traditional source of migrants in spite of the increasing number of non-British citizens who had settled there since the

---

[22] Peter Edwards with Gregory Pemberton, *Crises and commitments: the politics and diplomacy of Australia's involvement in Southeast Asian conflicts, 1948–1965*, Sydney 1992, 61. The British, however, made it clear that they should have the sole responsibility for the internal defence of Malaya: O'Neill, *Korean war*, 39.

[23] This body consisted of the Australian Chiefs of Staff and the representatives of Britain and New Zealand.

[24] David Horner, *Defence supremo: Sir Frederick Shedden and the making of Australian defence policy*, Sydney 2000, 312. See also Edwards with Pemberton, *Crises and commitments*, 162–3.

[25] O'Neill, *Korean war*, 347.

[26] See chapter 3 below.

late 1940s. Between 1948 and 1957 Australia took nearly 414,000 British migrants, 33.9 per cent of Australia's total migrant intake.[27] Not surprisingly, Australia's predominantly British complexion was reflected in its cultural and social institutions. From radio to newspapers, from private schools to universities, from clubs to trade unions, Australian organisations were often modelled after their British equivalents. Traditions and social conventions, when not similar, were at least often reminiscent of those in the 'mother country'. Sporting connections were also strong, in cricket, tennis and rugby. A number of Australian commentators have remarked that Britain's cultural influence on Australian society was even more pervasive than mere facts would suggest. Donald Horne, for instance, has commented on the Australian habit of 'deriving inspiration from London'.[28] In 1966 J. D. B. Miller noted how 'much overseas news is filtered through London before it gets to the newspapers in the Old Dominions, and British issues are given much prominence'.[29] John Rickard has emphasised the Australian tendency to turn to Britain as the 'arbiter of high culture'.[30] Stuart Ward has spoken of 'British race patriotism' in Australia, and of the strongly held assumption that British and Australian interests ought to coincide. Yet, as the Australian novelist, Martin Boyd, noted in 1953, while 'the Australian is always aware of Britain ... the Englishman has not the same reasons to look towards us'.[31] Although true, this does not invalidate the fact that sentiments of kith and kin worked both ways given that many British families had relatives in Australia. Australian visitors to Britain were also numerous and visible. Between 1953 and 1960 and average of 10 per cent of Britain's total immigrants were Australian.[32] These social contacts and connections ensured a sense of familiarity between the two peoples, a familiarity reinforced by similar traditions, and similar cultural and social institutions, which also benefited from a shared common language.

'British race patriotism' – the idea that all British peoples, their differences notwithstanding, formed a single community through the ties of blood, language, history and culture – was in fact a British phenomenon and not confined exclusively to Australia. Yet it was in Australia that the phenomenon was particularly strong. For a country that still regarded itself as a far-flung outpost of British civilisation on the periphery of Asia, British race patriotism provided a reassuring ideology which helped Australians cope with disturbing perceptions of isolation and loneliness. When Britain turned to Europe, it was this notion of British race patriotism, and the underlying assumption that the interests of two British nations such as Australia and

27 J. D. B. Miller, *Britain and the old dominions*, London 1966, 237.
28 Donald Horne, *The lucky country*, Melbourne 1964, 97.
29 Miller, *Old dominions*, 240.
30 John Rickard, 'Loyalties', in Arnold, Spearritt and Walker, *Out of empire*, 51.
31 Martin Boyd, 'Their link with Britain', ibid. 207.
32 Miller, *Commonwealth affairs*, 455.

Britain should ultimately coincide, that was severely challenged. By introducing serious elements of discord between London and Canberra, Britain's 1961–3 application to the EEC marked the first step towards the demise of British race patriotism in Australia, and the unravelling of the bonds of empire.

2

The Common Market Crisis, 1961–1963

'I beg of you to realise that there is great uneasiness in my own country, which may lead to some weakening of our historic and invaluable ties': Robert Menzies to Harold Macmillan, 15 January 1962.[1]

Between late 1959 and 1961, spurred by concerns that the emergence of a powerful political and economic bloc, such as the EEC, jeopardised Britain's position in Europe and the world, the Conservative government of Harold Macmillan began a thorough reappraisal of its policy towards the Six.[2] Gradually, British thinking – among both Whitehall officials and ministers – shifted in favour of a closer association with the EEC. In 1959 the Foreign Office began to advocate closer links with the Six on the ground that, by remaining outside the EEC, Britain would not only risk damaging its special relationship with the United States, but also see its influence in both Europe and NATO curtailed.[3] By July 1960 ministers recognised that a new approach to the EEC question was needed.[4] Between late 1960 and early 1961 exploratory talks were held with the Italians, Germans and French.[5] By then, most British policy-makers accepted that membership on special terms would bring more advantages than disadvantages.[6] In April 1961 Cabinet moved a step closer to EEC membership by agreeing that Britain should seek 'to join with the countries of the Six in forming a wider political and economic association of Europe'.[7] Finally, in July 1961, Cabinet took the historic decision to open negotiations with the Six with a view to seeking entry into the EEC.[8] Within less than two years the Macmillan government had accomplished a complete reversal of policy. After a decade in which it had shunned all continental attempts to establish a more integrated Europe,

---

[1] As quoted in Goldsworthy, *Losing the blanket*, 125–6.
[2] The term, 'the Six', commonly refers to the six European countries (Belgium, France, Italy, Luxembourg, the Netherlands and West Germany) which established the EEC and Euratom by signing the Treaty of Rome on 25 March 1957.
[3] Frank Heinlein, *British government policy and decolonisation, 1945–1963: scrutinising the official mind*, London 2002, 275.
[4] TNA, CAB 128/34, CC(60)41st, 13 July 1960.
[5] See Piers Ludlow, *Dealing with Britain: the Six and the first UK application to the EEC*, Cambridge 1997, 32–7.
[6] Heinlein, *British policy and decolonisation*, 278.
[7] CAB 128/35 pt 1, CC(61)24th, 26 Apr. 1961.
[8] CAB 128/35, CC(61)44th, 27 July 1961.

the British government was now ready to seek EEC membership provided that a satisfactory accommodation of certain British, EFTA and Commonwealth interests could be found.

A large body of scholarship exists on the reasons for this reversal of policy.[9] Here it suffices to say that, following the failure of the Free Trade Area (FTA) initiative in 1958 – by which Macmillan had sought to link Britain and the Six economically without giving away Commonwealth agricultural preferences – outright EEC membership seemed to be the only viable option.[10] British policy-makers recognised that Britain still enjoyed significant economic benefits from its Commonwealth connection which was still a 'very important source of political influence which buttresses our standing as a Power with world-wide interests'.[11] Yet they were not blind to the fact that the Commonwealth's transformation into a large and heterogeneous association made it difficult for Britain to use it as an effective vehicle for its influence. They also saw that Britain's trade with the Commonwealth was growing much less rapidly than its trade with the EEC – the latter providing such 'a vigorous and rapidly expanding market' that 'there would be good grounds for hoping that [British] commerce and industry would benefit' from it.[12] Understandably, policy-makers in London were concerned that, by remaining outside an increasingly prosperous and influential European bloc, Britain would not only suffer economically, but would also 'be greatly damaged politically', and its 'influence in world affairs ... bound to wane'.[13] In this respect Washington's desire for greater European integration posed a further problem. British policy-makers were apprehensive that if the Six continued to grow in both economic and political stature, as Washington clearly hoped that they would, the US government would inevitably attach a higher priority to its relations with the Six than to those with London. Should this occur, the Anglo-American 'special relationship' would be irreparably damaged, with negative consequences for Britain's ability to remain a global player. As the British regarded the special relationship as instrumental in enabling their country to perform such a role, it was imperative that Britain should remain America's principal ally.[14] To do so it needed not only

9 See, for example, Miriam Camps, *Britain and the European Community, 1955–63*, London 1964, 274–376; Wolfram Kaiser, *Using Europe, abusing the Europeans: Britain and European integration, 1945–63*, London 1996, ch. v; Jaqueline Tratt, *The Macmillan government and Europe: a study in the process of development*, Basingstoke 1996, chs iv–xii; and Alan Milward, *The rise and fall of a national strategy*, London 2002, ch. xi.

10 For the FTA initiative see John Young, *Britain and European unity, 1945–1992*, Basingstoke 1993, 55–66, and Milward, *National strategy*, ch. x.

11 CAB 129/100, C(60)35, 29 Feb. 1960. In 1960 approximately 40% of Britain's exports went to the Commonwealth, three times as much as to the EEC: May, 'Commonwealth or Europe?', 89.

12 CAB 129/100, C(60)35, 29 Feb. 1960.

13 CAB 129/102, C(60)107, 6 July 1960.

14 Heinlein, *British policy and decolonisation*, 275–8.

to join, but also to seek to lead this influential group of European nations. Thus, far from being an abdication of Britain's great-power ambitions, EEC membership was seen in London as the only possible means of pursuing them. As British officials put it, 'if we try to remain aloof from [the Six] ... we shall run the risk of ... ceasing to be able to exercise any claim to be a world power'.[15]

Alarm in Canberra

Australia responded to British moves with deep concern. 'Throughout the 1950s', as Stuart Ward has noted, 'the official Australian attitude towards European integration had been predicated on repeated British assurances that Commonwealth interests would never be sacrificed in a trade deal with the European Community.'[16] The Australian government, parliament and the press had tended to take British assurances at face value, and, as a result, European integration had hitherto played only a marginal role in Australian political debates. Australian complacency, however, was soon to be shaken. There had already been an appreciable change of attitude in Canberra throughout 1960 and early 1961 as the Liberal-Country Party coalition government, led by ardent anglophile Robert Menzies, grew apprehensive of London's developing interest in EEC membership.[17] Australian concerns grew even stronger in the spring of 1961 when Macmillan began to disclose British plans. In late May he informed Menzies that as his government was ready to negotiate with the Six, he intended to dispatch the Commonwealth Secretary, Duncan Sandys, to Australia, New Zealand and Canada to explain British policy on closer association with Europe.[18]

Prior to Sandys's arrival in Australia, the Menzies government carried out a thorough policy review to assess the implications for Australia of an eventual British entry into the EEC. In early May, John McEwen, the Minister for Trade, made a submission to Cabinet dealing with the economic implications of entry. He pointed out that, should Britain join without adequate safeguards for Commonwealth exports, the economic consequences for Australian trade could be disastrous. Some £140–150 million, or 55–60 per cent of Australia's exports to the British market, could be affected, depending on the nature of the agreement.[19] Australia's farm exports, in particular, stood to suffer serious damage as a result of the concomitant dismantling of imperial preferences and Britain's adoption of the Common External Tariff (CET),

---

15 CAB 129/102, C(60)107, 6 July 1960.
16 Ward, British embrace, 69.
17 Ibid. 69–70; Goldsworthy, Losing the blanket, 121–2.
18 Harold Macmillan to Robert Menzies, 31 May 1961, NAA, A1838/283, 727/4/2 pt 1.
19 Cabinet submission 1108, 5 May 1961, ibid.

which would establish a 'reverse preference' in favour of European farmers. A further problem was represented by the attempts made by the Six in the early 1960s to set up a common agricultural regime which, depending on the level of protection accorded to European farmers, could lead to the exclusion of Australian farm exports from British and European markets.[20] The Australian government, McEwen believed, could 'assume that the United Kingdom will go as far as she possibly can to avoid unqualified acceptance of the Treaty of Rome'. Yet it was far from certain that London would be able to do so. Thus, Australia should be prepared, McEwen warned, to 'face the contingency of the extreme'. He was under no illusion that this extreme case scenario 'would call for a complete re-orientation of all [Australian] trade policies'.[21]

While it is undeniable that British entry would force painful readjustments upon Australia's farming sector, it is also true that McEwen tended to over-emphasise the potential damage of entry on the Australian economy as a whole. Australia was less dependent on the British market than New Zealand, which sent to Britain 50.7 per cent of its total exports in 1960 (Australia sent 23.9 per cent, while Canada sent only 15.8 per cent).[22] But with its power-base in the countryside, McEwen's Country Party had traditionally championed the interests of rural Australia. He and his party were therefore resolved to do whatever it took to ensure that Australian rural concerns be heard both in Canberra and in London. As deputy prime minister and head of the influential Department of Trade, McEwen would successfully claim a central role in Australian policy-making on the EEC issue. This, in turn, ensured that Canberra would adopt a tough stance on the question of Britain's entry into the EEC.

The political consequences of entry were examined by the Department of External Affairs in a submission to Cabinet at the end of June. While recognising that it could give Britain 'the opportunity of a new period of growth and vigour' sufficient to slow down its decline as a world power, the DEA believed that British entry would, on the whole, have a negative impact on Australia. In the view of the department, it was clear that if the Macmillan government decided to join the Community, Britain would not be able 'to escape the trend towards progressive European integration'. This, in turn, could curtail its freedom of action as a world power and leader of the Commonwealth. In this context, the DEA was concerned that London's accession to the EEC could have far-reaching repercussions for the British defence posture east of Suez. Policy-makers in Canberra feared that entry would undermine Britain's resolve to play a politico-military role in south-east

---

[20] On the possible implications of a common agricultural policy for Australian primary produce see Piers Ludlow, 'Too far away, too rich and too stable: the EEC and trade with Australia during the 1960s', *AEHR* xli (2001), 283–4.

[21] Cabinet submission 1108, 5 May 1961, NAA, A1838/283, 727/4/2 pt 1.

[22] May, 'Commonwealth or Europe?', 92.

Asia where Australia's main strategic interests lay. Officials in the DEA also saw that British entry would have wider political ramifications. In their view, these threatened to disturb 'the whole complex of relationships, including the Commonwealth, on which Australia's traditional outlook and politics rest, and [to] compel us to make important adjustments in consequence'. The DEA was not unmindful of the fact that Britain's economic and political influence in the world would further decline if the country remained outside the EEC, a fact that would certainly inhibit Britain's ability to remain a major world power and an effective leader of the Commonwealth. As for the latter, it was true that the Commonwealth was 'no longer the close group' it used to be, yet it was evident that 'to the extent that the Commonwealth draws its vitality from some common political and economic interests it would be weakened by the United Kingdom's entry into Europe'. From an economic standpoint, there was little doubt that 'the existing structure of Commonwealth economic cooperation', as the DEA put it, 'would lose much of its relevance'. Finally, the DEA was also much concerned about the impact that entry would have on the strong ties of 'kith and kin' which had traditionally bound the old dominions to Britain. The DEA believed that 'the countries which are likely to be hardest hit economically if the United Kingdom joins the E.E.C. are those which have traditionally placed most importance on their attachment of sentiment to the United Kingdom'. 'How would', External Affairs speculated, 'these attachments be affected by a decision which resulted in serious hardship?'[23] As the DEA submission made clear, British entry was bound to introduce a serious element of discord in Anglo-Australian relations.

Australia's strong concerns were conveyed forcefully to Sandys when he began talks with the Menzies government in Canberra on 8 July 1961. Sandys explained to the Australian ministers that Britain faced one of the most difficult decisions in its history. Despite his claim that the British government had not yet taken the decision to apply, the thrust of his argument left the Australian ministers in no doubt that London had already made up its mind. As he told the Australians, '[it] is quite clear to us that, if we stay outside this new grouping our influence in the world will be reduced ...This diminution in our international position combined with an inevitable economic decline in our economic strength, would gravely reduce our value to the Commonwealth.' Sandys expressed his belief that a new association with Europe would in no way be incompatible with Britain's traditional ties with the Commonwealth. He was also confident that there was no reason to believe that EEC membership would significantly alter London's attitude towards world problems. On the contrary, British membership might help

---

[23] Cabinet submission 1183, 26 June 1961, NAA, A1838/269, TS899/1/4 pt 2.

prevent the Community from developing into an inward-looking association.[24]

On the economic aspects of British entry, Sandys emphasised that 'in recent years the share of our exports going to the Commonwealth markets has declined, while the share going to Europe has increased'. He also pointed out that entry would provide 'great opportunities' which would otherwise not be open to Britain. In recognising the negative impact of entry on some Australian agricultural commodities, he thought it possible to secure some means of 'ensuring in Britain, or in Europe as a whole, an outlet for Commonwealth produce comparable to that which it now enjoys'.[25]

Sandys's arguments cut no ice in Canberra. According to the *Economist*, he faced an 'onslaught of Australian objections'. 'When the time came for Australia to make its reply', the *Economist* noted, 'this turned out to be a veritable blast.'[26] The Australian ministers found it frustrating that 'while constantly asserting that no decision had been taken, Duncan [Sandys] devoted a great deal of time to demonstrating the absolutely unanswerable nature of the arguments for going in'.[27] As Menzies pointed out to him, the 'move into Europe, represents a complete reversal of ... policy. It may disclose in time great results. But if it turns out that the results are bad, it will be too late to reverse the policy'.[28] Menzies and his ministers, therefore, 'engaged in a good deal of cross-examination' and subjected Sandys to intense questioning.[29] Menzies dealt with the political aspects of entry, emphasising 'the risk that Europe would develop under the Treaty of Rome into a tight system'. He felt that should Britain join the EEC, 'it would be caught up in the system'. Successful entry would lead to 'greater absorption with [the EEC] and less with the Commonwealth'.[30] The economic aspects of entry were mostly dealt with by McEwen who argued that entry could have 'serious' effects on Australia. He instanced some of the problems that might arise for several Australian farm commodities including wheat, dairy products, meat, sugar and dried fruits, and expressed disappointment that Australia had not as yet been given any indication of how its interests would be protected.[31] Treasurer Harold Holt pointed out that 'an examination should be made not only of the trade effects, but also the financial [ones]'. He

---

[24] Duncan Sandys to the Australian government, 8 July 1961, NAA, A1838/283, 727/4/2 pt 1.

[25] Ibid.

[26] *Economist*, 15 July 1961.

[27] Menzies to Eric Harrison, 21 Aug. 1961, R. G. Menzies papers, NLA, Canberra, MS 4936 series 1, box 14, folder 122.

[28] Menzies quoted in A.W. Martin, *Robert Menzies: a life*, I: *1944–1978*, Melbourne 1999, 439.

[29] Menzies to Harrison, 21 Aug. 1961, Menzies papers, MS 4936 series 1, box 14, folder 122.

[30] UK-EEC consultations: 1st meeting, 8 July 1961, NAA, A1838/283, 727/4/2 pt 1.

[31] UK-EEC consultations: 3rd meeting, 9 July 1961, ibid.

was concerned about some trends that were already in evidence and quoted the operation of the European Monetary Agreement which, he claimed, put Australia's sterling reserves on a footing of 'second class' sterling.[32]

In the end, Sandys 'managed to irritate almost every Australian in sight'.[33] The gap between the Australian and British positions was not bridged. As David Goldsworthy has noted, 'the overall outcome was a sense of standoff',[34] a situation reflected in the final *communiqué* which was the result of hours of drafting and controversy.[35] In it, the Australian government made it clear that, while not entitled to object to the opening of negotiations by the British government, it did not regard the absence of objection as implying approval.[36]

Protecting Australian interests

Negotiations between Britain and the Six opened in October 1961. In August the Department of Trade had begun to work on Australia's position. In a submission to Cabinet, McEwen realistically assessed the problems Australia would encounter in trying to safeguard its interests. He conceded that 'however liberal the United Kingdom might be induced to be in her interpretation of our interests we cannot be optimistic of getting what we want'. He pointed out that Britain's negotiating position was extremely difficult and, given EEC resistance to any exceptions to the Treaty of Rome, its ability to secure major concessions was anything but certain. McEwen realised that a further complication lay in Australia's 'dubious' bargaining power *vis-à-vis* Britain and the Six. Despite these drawbacks, he none the less believed that Australia should ensure that both the British government and the British public fully understood the Australian predicament and went on to note how this should be accomplished. In the first place, any discussion and comment should emphasise that Australia's stability depended significantly on its capacity to trade. Additionally, Australia should act in concert with New Zealand and Canada – two other Commonwealth countries with important interests in the negotiations. It should also ensure that the Six understood the Australian case. Last but not least, it should attempt to enlist American support. Here McEwen was treading a difficult path given Washington's opposition to Commonwealth preferences and to their extension to

---

[32] UK-EEC consultations: 2nd meeting, 8 July 1961, ibid.

[33] Gelber, *Australia, Britain*, 81.

[34] Goldsworthy, *Losing the blanket*, 125. See also UK-EEC consultations: 4th, 5th and 6th meetings, 10–11 July 1961, NAA, A1838/283, 727/4/2 pt 1.

[35] *Economist*, 15 July 1961.

[36] See Common Market *communiqué*, 11 July 1961, NAA, A1838/283, 727/4/2 pt 1.

the Common Market. Yet, he was hopeful that the Kennedy administration would be sympathetic to Australia's plight.[37]

McEwen's view was that Australia should aim to gain the protection of its trade on a continuing basis in the forthcoming negotiations. Australia should not accept transitional arrangements as a means of safeguarding its trade interests in the British market. Nor should it accept a final settlement based on vague understandings that the Commonwealth trade problem would be subject to further negotiations, which would leave Australia at 'the mercy of the Six'. Trade officials in Canberra were asked to examine a number of possible permanent arrangements to protect Australian exports to Europe. Of these, officials favoured the concept of 'comparable outlets', whereby trade losses deriving from the phasing out of Commonwealth preferences in the British market should be made up by 'comparable' gains in an enlarged EEC market. In the end, however, as McEwen himself recognised, it was for Britain to decide whether the terms under which it would be prepared to join the Community met Commonwealth demands. Australia 'could, of course, refrain from approving a particular kind of settlement', it 'could no doubt deplore it', but no one 'should be under the illusion that [Australia] could veto it'.[38]

Subsequent preliminary talks between Australian and British officials in September 1961 revealed that, despite British attempts not to upset the Commonwealth, Australian and British interests remained difficult to reconcile. Both British and Australian officials agreed on 'comparable outlets' as a guiding principle for the forthcoming Brussels negotiations, but differences remained on the extent to which Australian interests could be realistically safeguarded.[39] Australian officials in London had gained the impression that the British government regarded some items in Australia's trade with Britain as expendable and, as a result, might not seek safeguards for them. In response, Australian ministers agreed in October that 'Australia could not regard any of her trade items as expendable' and conveyed Australia's firm stance on this point. Ministers also reiterated demands for direct representation in the Brussels negotiations, provided that 'Australia was able to participate at the critical point of time with full authority'.[40]

Negotiations with the Six proceeded slowly as Britain's opening bid was

37 Cabinet submission 1327, 28 Aug. 1961, NAA, A3917/1, vol. 9. For the Kennedy administration's stance on Commonwealth preferences see George Ball to John Kennedy, 23 Aug. 1961, *Foreign relations of the United States, 1961–63*, XIII: *West Europe and Canada*, Washington 1994, doc. 16.

38 Cabinet submission 1327, 28 Aug. 1961, NAA, A3917/1, vol. 9.

39 Common Market consultations: note for ministers, 4 Oct. 1961, NAA, A3917/1, vol. 9.

40 Cabinet decision 1620, 4 Oct. 1961, ibid. The Australians had originally put this request to Sandys in July. Their demands were partially met on 26 April 1962 when Alan Westerman, the Secretary of the Department of Trade, was able to put Australia's case directly to the Committee of Deputies in Brussels.

burdened with a lengthy list of requests to protect Commonwealth inter-ests.[41] In practice, the British started by demanding that virtually all Austral-ia's trade with Britain be shielded from the likely impact of the CET and the Common Agricultural Policy.[42] In early 1962 the British delegation in Brussels began to explore possible solutions for threatened Commonwealth exports with the Six with a view to securing the EEC's agreement on the principle of comparable outlets. However, it soon became clear that the Six were not particularly receptive. They were concerned that, by accepting the concept of comparable outlets, they would end up allowing for too many exceptions to the Treaty of Rome.[43] Instead, the Six showed a clear preference for tran-sitional rather than permanent arrangements to safeguard Commonwealth interests. As a consequence, in April 1962, the British government began to scale down its demands and to abandon its opening bid.[44]

Worried that Australian problems were now not being sufficiently taken into consideration by the British, McEwen flew to London in the early spring of 1962. His visit was part of a wider overseas tour which also had taken him to the United States and to the capitals of the Six. In Washington McEwen pleaded Australia's case forcefully, emphasising the potentially negative impact of entry on Australian exports. His arguments fell on deaf ears. His hopes of enlisting American support were quashed as he came to understand the extent to which the Kennedy administration supported British entry into the EEC. He also came to realise the strength of American opposi-tion to the continuance of the imperial preference system in an enlarged EEC.[45] In his talks with the Six, McEwen was again disappointed. Although he found the Europeans sympathetic to Australia's plight, he secured no assurances.[46] Now in London, McEwen criticised the British government for not doing enough to protect Australian interests and complained about the lack of clarity in British negotiating aims.[47] He was so unimpressed by the British ministers' response that he remarked irately that if London wished to 'treat the Australian government as opponents, well and good; but we would like to know'.[48] Towards the end of his London visit, McEwen summed

[41] Anne Deighton and Piers Ludlow, '"A conditional application": British manage-ment of the first attempt to seek membership of the EEC, 1961–63', in Anne Deighton (ed.), Building postwar Europe: national decision-makers and European institutions, 1948–63, London 1995, 110.

[42] Ludlow, 'Too far away', 275.

[43] Idem, Dealing with Britain, 94–6.

[44] Deighton and Ludlow, 'Conditional application', 110.

[45] John McEwen to Menzies, cablegram 83, 15 Mar. 1962, NAA, A1838/275, 727/4/1/4 pt 1; Ward, British embrace, 123–5.

[46] McEwen to Menzies, cablegram 386, 28 Mar. 1962; cablegram 211, 2 Apr. 1962; cablegram 1535, 7 Apr. 1962; cablegram 1536, 7 Apr.1962, NAA, A3917/1, vol. 7. For the EEC's attitude towards the Australian case see Ludlow, 'Too far away', 267–86.

[47] McEwen to Menzies, cablegram 1745, 19 Apr. 1962, NAA, A3917/1, vol. 7.

[48] McEwen quoted in Ward, British embrace, 127.

up Australia's case by reminding his British hosts of what was at stake in the Brussels negotiations. In a speech to the Australia Club in London, he emphasised that Australia's 'buying from the United Kingdom over the last forty years had been greater than her sales to any other country', and that no one in Britain 'could afford lightheartedly to ignore this fact'. The Anglo-Australian partnership, he added, had been 'so close that no-one ever thought to question its continuance until the United Kingdom commenced her negotiations with the Common Market countries'. Yet, the British application put the very continuation of close Anglo-Australian relations at risk, unless Australian concerns were addressed. 'Trade relations and political relations', he warned, 'go hand in hand. A weakening in the one cannot but help weaken the other ... Serious trade damage, and the sense of disillusionment which would inevitably go with it, would impair the very foundations upon which our Commonwealth association rests.'[49]

A few weeks later, it was Menzies's turn to fly to London for talks with Macmillan and his ministers. While McEwen had concentrated on trade issues, Menzies focused on the political implications of British entry. His aim was to appeal to 'Britain's loyalty to the old Commonwealth' and 'to intervene in the British policy process on behalf of Australian and Commonwealth interests before Britain had gone so far down the European road that these interests were effectively marginalized'.[50] The Menzies visit, however, did not enjoy favourable auspices. On the day of his arrival, British negotiators in Brussels reached a settlement with the EEC on the phasing out of preferences for manufactured goods from Australia, Canada and New Zealand by 1970. While bound to affect Australian exports only marginally, the UK-EEC agreement on industrial goods none the less caused concern in Australia. The settlement seemed in fact to delineate the type of arrangements that the British might negotiate with the Six in order to deal with the problem of Commonwealth temperate zone agricultural produce. In a joint statement with the New Zealand deputy prime minister, John Marshall, Menzies strongly criticised the deal and made it clear that it could not 'in any circumstances be taken as a pattern for the type of settlement which might be reached in other products of even greater concern to Australia and New Zealand'.[51]

In the course of his visit, Menzies consistently highlighted the political implications of entry for Commonwealth ties. He pointed out that membership of 'an actual European federation involving ... great change in the Commonwealth ... would be a great mistake'.[52] Despite adopting a more conciliatory tone than McEwen, Menzies also reiterated his government's stance that '"solutions" under which Commonwealth preferences and other

49 McEwen to Australia Club, 17 Apr. 1962, NAA, A3917/1, vol. 7.
50 Goldsworthy, *Losing the blanket*, 129–30.
51 The Menzies-Marshall joint statement quoted in Ward, *British embrace*, 162.
52 Menzies to Australia Club, 12 June 1962, NAA, A1838/275, 727/4/2 pt 2.

special trading arrangements [would be] phased out by 1970' were unacceptable to Australia.[53] Finally, Menzies sought to pressure the Macmillan government by resorting to sentimental arguments of kith and kin. In a speech to the Australia Club, he reminded Macmillan of the close ties which bound Australia and Britain together. He spoke at length of the Commonwealth, 'whose roots have been nurtured in the soil of co-operation and affection and loyalty'. These were 'wonderful things' and should not be 'lightly disregarded'. In appealing to the British sense of loyalty to the Commonwealth, he declared that he was the leader of 'a country which is British to the boot heels'. While recognising that Britain faced a difficult choice, between the Commonwealth and the EEC, Menzies believed that the only possible solution was '[b]etter the devil you know than the devil you don't know'.[54]

Rethinking Australian policy

By mid-1962, it was evident that Britain would enter the EEC on terms that would end the imperial preference system and establish new reverse preferences in favour of the EEC member states.[55] In early August 1962 British and European negotiators reached a tentative agreement on a temperate zone foodstuff package. Britain accepted that Commonwealth preferences would have to be phased out over a transitional period. The Six were willing in fact to contemplate special arrangements for New Zealand given its high dependence on the British market, but no special arrangements were envisaged for Australia and Canada. Furthermore, an understanding was reached on the necessity for worldwide commodity agreements as a long-term solution for Commonwealth producers of temperate zone foodstuffs.[56] The package, however, was only a partial settlement. No decision, for example, was taken on the length of the transitional period, which meant that Macmillan would have to face Commonwealth leaders in September without having secured a final settlement on Commonwealth farm exports.[57] Yet, according to the British leader, the package offered 'a realistic basis for discussion with the Commonwealth Governments concerned'.[58] Piers Ludlow has noted that nothing was to be gained from pressing further on this issue.[59] As Macmillan himself told Menzies back in August 1961, 'when negotiations are resumed

---

[53] Cabinet decision 275, 25 June 1962, NAA, A3917/1, vol. 9.
[54] Menzies to Australia Club, 12 June 1962, NAA, A1838/275, 727/4/2 pt 2.
[55] Stuart Ward, 'Sentiment and self-interest: the imperial ideal in Anglo-Australian commercial culture', AHS xxxii (2001), 103.
[56] The British negotiations with the EEC, British paper, August 1962, NAA, A3917/1, vol. 9.
[57] Ludlow, Dealing with Britain, 94.
[58] Macmillan quoted ibid. 169.
[59] Ibid.

our room for manoeuvre will be limited. The Six will not be prepared to make radical changes to their existing proposals'.[60]

In the spring of 1962 Macmillan had agreed to convene a Commonwealth Prime Ministers' Conference in London for the following September.[61] In British eyes, the aim of the conference was to enable the government to present a final UK-EEC deal to the Commonwealth governments and then to the British parliament with a view to formal accession to the Treaty of Rome in January 1963. Negotiations in Brussels had not proceeded as speedily as the British had originally wished, and were behind schedule when Commonwealth leaders gathered in London that September. Worse, an outline agreement on temperate zone agricultural produce had begun to materialise and this seemed indicative of what could realistically be expected from the Six. It made gloomy reading for Australia. Predictably, the Australian press was strongly critical, yet newspaper headlines 'lacked the sting of the previous months' and 'there were signs of a shift of emphasis toward the question of how Australia might adjust to these new trading circumstances'.[62] A change of emphasis was also noticeable at government level. In the summer of 1962 policy-makers in Canberra were increasingly concerned about the risks of pushing the Australian case too far. With Canada and New Zealand toning down their criticism of Britain, and the United States encouraging Australia to help Macmillan at the forthcoming conference, Australian ministers did not want Australia to be singled out as the chief opponent of the British bid.[63] At a time of increasing political turmoil in south-east Asia, any serious damage to Australia's traditional strategic alliances could be far more harmful than the economic harm deriving from British entry into the EEC.[64]

The DEA, in particular, was opposed to any initiative which could be interpreted as having 'the effect of blocking British entry'.[65] While keeping up pressure on Britain, the Six, and the United States, Australia had to avoid 'getting out on a limb'. The DEA recognised that at some point Australia would have to accept Britain's entry.[66] According to the department, the political implications of British entry were not as negative as it had itself previously assumed. British entry could ensure, for example, that the EEC would adopt liberal and outward-looking policies in the political sphere. It could also 'help to avoid the prospect of further decline in Britain's interna-

---

60 Macmillan quoted in Common Market negotiations, paper by the inter-departmental committee, 29 Aug. 1962, NAA, A3917/1, vol. 9.

61 Martin, *Menzies*, 443.

62 Ward, *British embrace*, 191.

63 For American pressure see ibid. 203.

64 Stuart Ward, 'A matter of preference: the EEC and the erosion of the old Commonwealth relationship', in May, *Britain, the Commonwealth and Europe*, 169–70.

65 Ralph Harry to Garfield Barwick, 17 Aug. 1962, NAA, A1838/275, 727/4/2 pt 3.

66 Harry to Barwick, 30 Aug. 1962; possible points for Cabinet: Common Market negotiations, 30 Aug. 1962, ibid. pt 4A.

tional standing'.[67] It was true that 'Britain's entry into the Community would accelerate the tendency towards the transformation of Britain into a European rather than a world power and towards a decline in its commitments east of Suez', yet these tendencies already existed. At the core of the DEA's change of emphasis was the fact that the Kennedy administration regarded 'the development of an integrated Western Europe through Britain's entry into the E.E.C. as essential for both its political and strategic objectives and as important for its more liberal trade policies'.[68] The Americans, in particular, were concerned that, outside the Community, Britain would remain 'an element of disintegration', whereas British entry would 'ensure European cohesion', which, in turn, would strengthen the Atlantic alliance and tie West Germany irreversibly to the West.[69] If Britain did not enter the Community, the DEA concluded that American objectives might be frustrated. The departmental view was therefore that Australia had nothing to gain from upsetting the Americans, particularly when their politico-strategic support might be needed in south-east Asia.[70]

The attitude of the Department of Trade was rather different. Officials were aggrieved that 'not one of their many proposals had been incorporated into the emerging package'. According to them, 'the Brussels negotiations had resulted in a complete capitulation by the British to the will of the Six'. Realistically, they accepted that the time had come for Australia to lower its demands. None the less, anxious to salvage what they could for Australian markets, they wanted the government to keep up pressure on the British to prevent them from settling for even less advantageous terms.[71]

Recognising the need to provide ministers with an agreed negotiating brief for the forthcoming Commonwealth Prime Ministers' Conference, the Departments of External Affairs and of Trade reconciled their differences in an Inter-Departmental Common Market Cabinet Committee paper dated 29 August 1962. In it, officials advised ministers that at the Commonwealth summit Australia should 'tread a very circumspect course between two extremes in the case she puts and the image she creates'. 'On the one hand', officials emphasised, 'Australia must avoid putting herself in the position of appearing obstructive and yet, for the sake of her own trade and political interests, she must make it quite clear whether or not Britain's entry into the Common Market under the terms likely to be agreed by the Six would, in fact, pose serious problems and not provide reasonable safeguards'. It was essential, however, that 'Britain makes – and appears to make

---

67 Harry to Barwick, 17 Aug. 1962, ibid. pt 3.
68 Common Market negotiations, 29 Aug. 1962, ibid.
69 Ball and Maurice Couve de Murville, memcon, 21 May 1962, *FRUS, 1961–63*, xiii, doc. 39. See also Pascaline Winand, *Eisenhower, Kennedy and the United States of Europe*, Basingstoke 1993, ch. x.
70 Common Market negotiations, 29 Aug. 1962, NAA, A1838/275, 727/4/2 pt 4A.
71 Ward, *British embrace*, 196–7.

– her own decision whether to enter'. The conclusion was that 'neither the British people, nor the Six, nor the United States should be able to point to Australia alone (or principally) as the effective cause of a decision by Britain not to enter'.[72] In making a case for restraint, officials were hoping to carry the prime minister with them as they knew that without his backing their tactics would remain a dead letter.

In the end, Menzies heeded his officials' advice. The Australian attitude at the Commonwealth Prime Ministers' Conference was indeed restrained. It was Canada, not Australia, that was singled out for its strident disapproval of Britain's European policy.[73] While critical towards the British, Menzies shied away from voicing his criticism too loudly. He told the conference that 'he understood the deeply-felt reasons that had lead to a decision which, if carried to a conclusion, would be revolutionary in its effects and would mark a new era in British history'. He 'would not wish to record an objection in principle', yet 'the Commonwealth had an obvious interest in the price that was to be paid for all this'. Menzies pointed out that as far as Australia was concerned the safeguards seemed a little sketchy. Britain's entry would cause some damage to Australian interests. There had to be compensating factors. Of these, however, there was little sign. Menzies also reminded the British of the risk that joining the EEC might pose to the future of the Commonwealth. If the EEC were to emerge as 'a sort of federation', then 'the nature of the Commonwealth would of necessity be dramatically changed'.[74] In the end Menzies adhered to the line that 'no objection in principle to Britain's entry should be expressed, and that no general benediction upon Britain's entry could be considered, let alone given'.[75]

The Commonwealth Prime Ministers' Conference left the Menzies government in no doubt about Britain's determination to join the EEC. It was clear that Britain was prepared to do so on terms that would be highly unsatisfactory for countries like Australia and Canada. As Miriam Camps has pointed out, the conference 'marked a turning-point in Commonwealth affairs and … even if negotiations in Brussels failed, a phase in Commonwealth relationships was over and a new uncharted relationship was beginning'.[76] This certainly describes the prevailing attitude in Australia at the time. At government level, a sense of resignation set in. Policy-makers in Canberra believed that the government had done all in its power to press the

---

72 Cabinet submission 380, 29 Aug. 1962, NAA, A1838/275, 727/4/2 pt 4A. The committee was established in June 1961 and included officials from the Departments of External Affairs, Trade, Primary Industry, Treasury, National Development and from the Prime Minister's Department.
73 Andrea Benvenuti and Stuart Ward, 'Britain, Europe and the "other quiet revolution" in Canada', in Phil Buckner (ed.), *Canada and the end of empire*, Vancouver 2005, 165–82.
74 NAA, A3917/1, vol. 11, PMM(62)5th, 11 Sept. 1962.
75 Cabinet decision 476, 2 Oct. 1962, ibid. vol. 9.
76 Camps, *Britain and the Community*, 444.

Australian case and to seek satisfactory safeguards for Australia's threatened exports. Even the Department of Trade, which, under McEwen's leadership, had emerged as the fiercest defender of Australian trade interests, seemed to be giving up the game.[77] Editorial opinion throughout the country expressed resignation. A mid-October debate on the EEC question in the House of Representatives recorded a general acceptance of the inevitability of British entry into the EEC.[78] After all the sound and fury, Australians were finally resigned to the fact that Britain would join the EEC, with Commonwealth interests the inevitable casualty.

Events in Europe, however, were to take an unexpected turn. In late January 1963 the French president, Charles de Gaulle, shattered Macmillan's hopes of joining the EEC by vetoing the British application. While giving Australian producers time to diversify their export markets, the French veto did not turn the clock back in Anglo-Australian relations. The fifteen-month long negotiations between the Six and Britain had been a traumatic experience for both the Australian government and public. It had not only shown that Britain would sooner or later join the Community but also that, in order to achieve this objective, London would allow no Commonwealth interest to stand in its way. In addition, the Brussels negotiations had shown the extent to which Australian and British interests were at variance, and how illusory were Canberra's hopes of seeing them reconciled. It was now clear that British entry into a closely-knit group of nations outside the Commonwealth would bring about an unprecedented conflict of interests between Australia and Britain. The Australian belief that British and Australian interests could and should be reconciled was profoundly shaken. After all, as Stuart Ward has argued, 'for much of the twentieth century Australian economic interests were imagined as a mere facet of a wider network of trade, financial and business links with the British empire'.[79] Political interests, too, were seen through the prism of traditional ties of kith and kin and a sense of belonging to a wider British community. In the end, the French veto ensured that no immediate material change to the Anglo-Australian relationship occurred, but Macmillan's unsuccessful bid had created a widespread feeling in Australia that relations between the two countries had changed for ever. John Crawford, former Secretary at the Department of Trade, encapsulated the prevailing mood when he pointed out that 'our psychology has been changed. We will never be the same as we were before we were given a shake-up by Britain's application'.[80]

The French veto threw Macmillan's policy on closer engagement with Europe into disarray and made entry into the EEC impossible in the short term. Facing up to this harsh reality, Sir Alec Douglas-Home – who had

[77] Treasury sources quoted in Singleton and Robertson, *Britain and Australasia*, 188.
[78] Ward, *British embrace*, 219–21.
[79] Idem, 'Sentiment', 93.
[80] John Crawford quoted ibid. 106.

replaced Macmillan in Downing Street in October 1963 – ruled out closer co-operation with the Community for the foreseeable future. The question of EEC membership virtually disappeared from British politics, and the Labour Party opposition, which remained opposed to entry, had no interest in reviving it in the run-up to the October 1964 general election.[81] The question of a possible British entry would resurface amidst the economic crises of 1966–7, but before then Anglo-Australian relations would have been placed under further strain by changes in Britain's global defence commitments. Ward is therefore mistaken in suggesting that the Common Market crisis of 1961–3 put an end to the traditionally close relationship between London and Canberra.[82] As the following chapter shows, Britain's plans for military disengagement from east of Suez would soon introduce a further element of discord into relations between London and Canberra. In due course, this would deal yet another blow to an already damaged relationship.

---

81 Clive Ponting, *A breach of promise: Labour in power, 1964–1970*, London 1989, 204–5.
82 Ward, *British embrace*, passim.

PART II

ANGLO-AUSTRALIAN RELATIONS UNDER STRESS

3

On the Road to East of Suez

'The British strategic presence is like a cake of which we are required to guess the weight. There is some reason to suspect that the heavy icing might cover a lack of fruit': Hooten, 5 September 1967.[1]

Although the French veto put the question of Britain's EEC membership temporarily in abeyance, policy-makers in Canberra were under no illusion that after the 1961–3 bid Britain would be drawn further into the European orbit. They recognised that Australia's relations with Britain were destined to undergo radical change as, sooner or later, Britain would make a renewed, and ultimately successful, attempt to join the EEC. However Britain's reorientation towards Europe was far from following a linear path. First, French opposition to British membership of the EEC drew out the process until the end of the decade, thereby making Britain's entry appear an elusive goal. Second, Britain's increasing engagement with the EEC overlapped with its attempts to readjust its global and imperial roles to the realities of decline. This became particularly evident in the painful process of military retrenchment undertaken by Harold Wilson's Labour government in the second half of the 1960s. In seeking to disengage from onerous politico-military commitments in the Far East, Britain set itself on a collision course with its loyal ally, Australia. As a consequence, Britain's military withdrawal from east of Suez – in particular, from south-east Asia – added a further source of serious friction between London and Canberra only few years after the 1961–3 bid. As a prelude to an examination of the impact of British withdrawal on Anglo-Australian relations, this chapter sets the question of the withdrawal in the broader historical context, and analyses long-held Australian fears and increasing doubts about Britain's ability to maintain a meaningful military presence in south-east Asia. It also examines the issue of Britain's membership of the EEC as an emerging problem in Australia's strategic thinking. This chapter therefore sets the scene for the subsequent analysis that blends politico-military thinking with the better-known economic dimension.

---

[1]   Hooten to Harold Holt, 5 Sept. 1967, NAA, A1209/80, 1966/7335 pt 7.

The British military presence in south-east Asia in the 1950s

At the end of the 1950s Britain still maintained a significant military presence in south-east Asia centred on well-established bases in Singapore and Malaya. Singapore was Britain's largest military establishment in the Far East and underpinned the British military presence there. In 1957 British forces in the south-east Asian theatre included 21,000 troops, ten Royal Air Force squadrons, and the two cruisers, four destroyers and five frigates that formed the Royal Navy Far East station.[2] In addition to defending Britain's remaining colonial possessions in the region (Singapore, the Borneo territories and Brunei), and protecting Malaya against external aggression, British forces fulfilled a broader strategic purpose.[3] As part of Britain's commitment to the South East Asian Treaty Organisation (SEATO), they could be deployed in SEATO military operations in support of western military objectives in south-east Asia.

Britain's military presence was important to Australia. It served to give substance to Australia's defence strategy, developed in the early 1950s around the concept of 'forward defence'. This postulated that the defence of Australia was best achieved 'in depth', through forward deployments on the rim of the Asian continent. In the 1950s Australian military planners saw 'forward defence' as a policy aimed at containing the perceived threat of Communist expansionism, in particular Chinese penetration in Asia: any such penetration was to be kept at maximum distance from Australian territory. To this end Australian combat forces had been deployed in Malaya since 1955 as part of the CSR, which also included British and New Zealand troops.[4] Between 1952 and 1953, a perceived growing Communist threat in Asia had in fact persuaded both London and Canberra to revise their early Cold War planning which had been centred on the Middle East as a Commonwealth priority for wartime reinforcement in case of global war and to attach greater importance to the Malayan region as an area of possible confrontation with the Communist powers.[5] In this context, memories of the fall of Singapore in February 1942, and of Japan's wartime advances

[2]   JPC report 34/1957, July 1957, NAA, A1838/269, TS692/2 pt 1.
[3]   Despite granting independence to Malaya in 1957, Britain remained responsible for the security of its former colony against external aggression under the Anglo-Malayan Defence Agreement (1957). For an examination of the AMDA see Karl Hack, *Defence and decolonisation in Southeast Asia, 1941–1968*, London 2001, 223–33.
[4]   The Australian contribution to the CSR consisted of naval, ground and air forces. Naval forces included two destroyers or frigates and one aircraft carrier on annual visits of six to eight weeks. The ground contribution amounted to a battalion group. The air force component consisted of a bomber wing of two squadrons (Canberras), a fighter wing of two squadrons (Avon Sabres) and an airfield construction squadron.
[5]   Horner, *Defence supremo*, 309–15. On the importance of the Middle East in British Cold War strategy in the years following the Second World War see David Lowe, *Menzies and the 'great world struggle': Australia's Cold War, 1948–1954*, Sydney 1999, 33.

through south-east Asia, reinforced Australian fears that the Malayan region functioned as a pontoon bridge, rather than as a barrier, between Australia and Asia, and served to confirm the importance of this region as a forward base for the containment of Communism in south-east Asia.[6] Lacking the necessary military capacity to undertake an autonomous defence role in the region – Australia had very limited military forces – Canberra relied upon a close military partnership with Britain since the United States throughout this period regarded the Malayan region as a Commonwealth responsibility and avoided any involvement there.

Britain's military presence was also seen in Canberra as a prerequisite to furthering western strategic objectives in the wider south-east Asian area through SEATO – namely, resisting Communist aggression and providing weak front-line Asian states with much-needed diplomatic and military reassurances. In the 1950s the Menzies government set great store by SEATO as a politico-military framework within which British and American defence efforts in the region could be co-ordinated. Since the early 1950s, the overriding strategic aim of the Menzies government had been to gain a firm commitment from the United States to the security of Australia and to harness American power to the protection of Australian and western interests in Asia. The first aim had, by and large, been achieved with the signing in 1951 of the ANZUS Treaty – which was to become the cornerstone of Australia's defence policy in the post-World War II era.[7] The Menzies government had been only too aware of the dramatic rise of American power in post-war international affairs and the relative decline of Britain as a great power.[8] The Australian view – shared by policy-makers and the general public alike – was that the presence of American military power in Asia and its assurances of support in the event of Communist aggression were 'the two most vital factors in maintaining the security of the countries in the region'.[9] Yet, despite Australia's growing reliance upon the United States, Australian policy-makers did not perceive a more intimate partnership with Washington as being incompatible with a continuing close defence relationship with London. On the contrary, they regarded SEATO as the means of combining the sizeable military capabilities of the United States with those of Britain for the sake of regional, as well as its own, security.[10] The Australian position was that SEATO could provide a useful strategic

6 Hack, *Defence and decolonisation*, 74.
7 A vast literature exists on the origins of the ANZUS Treaty and its significance in Australia's foreign and defence policies. See, for instance, David McLean, 'ANZUS origin: a reassessment', *AHS* xxiv (1990), 64–82, and O'Neill, *Korean war*, 185–200.
8 David Goldsworthy, 'Australian external policy and the end of Britain's empire', unpublished conference paper, London, July 2002.
9 Strategic basis of Australian defence policy, DC report, Jan. 1959, NAA, A2031/8, 4/1959.
10 For Australia's response to the establishment of SEATO see Lowe, *Menzies and the 'great world struggle'*, 172–7.

link between the Malayan region and the rest of south-east Asia – the area of more direct American interest.

Strategic considerations aside, there was a further reason for Australia's support for a continuing military presence in south-east Asia. Canberra viewed it as an essential stabilising influence in an unstable, and potentially volatile, region. In Singapore, the Borneo territories and Brunei, British rule and military commitment helped to maintain internal security and deter anti-British unrest. In Malaya, British forces not only provided a useful military backing for Kuala Lumpur's weak defence forces, but were also an important psychological prop for a newly-established state. It was also to this end that in the late 1950s the Australian ground component of the CSR was made available for anti-insurgency operations in the so-called Malayan Emergency.[11]

Given the importance attributed to a British military presence in south-east Asia, the Menzies government sought to ensure that Britain remain engaged in the region for as long as possible. The Australian defence view even stressed the need for Britain's capacity for effective military action in the Far East to be maintained 'at the highest possible level'.[12]

Anglo-Australian strategic tensions

By the early 1960s, however, this goal was becoming more difficult to attain. One problem was that Britain found its military presence in south-east Asia increasingly burdensome to sustain as it no longer possessed the economic and financial resources required to play a global role in an age of Cold War superpower rivalry. Moreover, its precarious economic situation, characterised by rising domestic costs and recurrent balance of payments difficulties, made it hard for successive British governments to maintain global defence commitments on a large scale.[13] Another problem was that decolonisation was gradually undermining the British colonial order in Asia. Since the war London had relinquished control over a sizeable area of its Asian empire – India, Pakistan, Ceylon, Burma and Malaya. With no empire to defend, the rationale for a British military presence east of Suez was becoming harder to justify.

[11] Hack, *Defence and decolonisation*, 184. In June 1948 the British colonial authorities in Malaya declared a state of emergency (hence 'Malayan Emergency') to quell an insurgency led by the Malayan Communist Party. This was not lifted until 1960. For Australia's involvement in the Malayan Emergency see Peter Dennis and Jeffrey Grey, *Emergency and confrontation: Australian military operations in Malaya and Borneo, 1950–1966*, Sydney 1996.

[12] Future of the CSR in relation to the AMDA, DC report, July 1957, NAA, A4926/XM1, vol. 28.

[13] On Britain's economic situation see Tony Judt, *Postwar: a history of Europe since 1945*, London 2005, 357–8.

Against this backdrop, the Menzies government became increasingly apprehensive about the future of Britain's military presence. In 1960 Sir William Oliver, the British High Commissioner in Canberra, could not fail to notice 'doubts in certain quarters in Australia ... about [the] United Kingdom's intentions to hold on in Singapore'.[14] The Australian Commission in Singapore, for instance, reported to the DEA in June 1961 that the Australian Services *attachés* 'had gained an impression of U.K. desire for non-involvement and disengagement' in south-east Asia.[15] These concerns were reinforced by the Australian perception of Britain's attitude within SEATO, which a DEA officer observed in early 1962 'has acted as a "brake" ... we have the feeling the United Kingdom is simply unwilling to agree to others acting because she is unable to act'.[16] Given Australian doubts about the way Britain's Far East strategic policy could be heading, it was not surprising that 'Canberra was sensitive to the slightest warning signals that British resolve to stay in the region might eventually falter'.[17] As these warning signals became more frequent in the early 1960s, the Menzies government's sense of unease heightened. Such signals served to confirm fears over Britain's intentions that had arisen in Canberra following Macmillan's earlier meeting with Menzies and the prime ministers of Canada (John Diefenbaker) and New Zealand (Walter Nash) on 13 May 1960.

This meeting was particularly significant as Macmillan used it to discuss a British official paper, 'Study of future policy (1960–1970)' with Britain's major Commonwealth allies.[18] This, also known as the 'Brook Committee Report', painted a gloomy picture of Britain's declining power in the world, which was expected to diminish even further in the decade ahead. The paper was downcast about the prospects for Britain maintaining a military role east of Suez, particularly in Singapore. In the committee's view, there was a danger 'that in future the effort involved in maintaining [Britain's] position in Singapore [could] be out of proportion to our interest in doing so particularly if developments in Singapore or Malaya were to lead to serious restrictions on the full use of the base facilities'. While it was in the country's interest to stay in Singapore 'for as long as possible', the authors of the report warned that Britain could be forced 'to abandon it as a base' before the end of the decade.[19] Earl Mountbatten, chairman of the Chiefs of Staff, was also present at the meeting and confirmed the seriousness with which Whitehall

---

14 D. W. McNicol to Arthur Tange, 30 Jan. 1960, NAA, A1838/280, 3004/12/11 pt 1.
15 John Ryan to Tange, 15 July 1961, NAA, A1838/277, 3004/12/11 pt 2.
16 Ralf Harry to Tange, 12 Mar. 1962, NAA, A1838/2, 67/1/3 pt 2.
17 Goldsworthy, *Losing the blanket*, 158.
18 CAB 129/100, FP(60)1, 24 Jan. 1961. For the genesis of the 'Study of future policy (1960–1970)' see Jeffrey Pickering, *Britain's withdrawal from east of Suez: the politics of retrenchment*, Basingstoke 1998, 108–14, and Ronald Hyam and William Roger Louis (eds), *The Conservative government and the end of empire, 1957–1964*, i, London 2000, 38.
19 CAB 129/100, FP(60)1, 24 Jan. 1961.

was treating this report, telling the Commonwealth leaders that 'the United Kingdom Chiefs were [already] reviewing some of their main military problems in the light of this ten-year study'. In particular, he pointed out that the Chiefs of Staff 'felt that they might not be able to rely indefinitely on all the existing bases – for instance, the security of tenure of the base at Singapore was uncertain'.[20]

The points made in London were well understood in Canberra and the reaction was one of obvious concern. According to officials in the DEA, 'the paper serves notice on Australia in a more direct way than has so far been apparent that the United Kingdom effort in the Far East is bound to taper off'.[21] In their view, 'the cost of the United Kingdom's activities will continue to be a main factor in her own calculation of what she can do in the future. She is primarily concerned with the defence of the British Isles and is clearly looking for a way of reducing the cost of her colonial possessions'. Consequently, Australia had to 'avoid the false assumption that the United Kingdom has substantial resources to deploy in the area between China and Australia, even in an emergency'.[22]

Macmillan's decision to broach awkward foreign policy issues, such as those articulated in the Brook Report, with his Commonwealth partners was not taken lightly. The report was in essence a 'crystal ball-gazing' exercise and revealed important trends in British foreign policy thinking. However, as John Subritzky has argued in his study of this period, 'Macmillan was no revolutionary in foreign affairs, still essentially believing in British global influence'.[23] Despite the seeming implications of Macmillan's message to the Commonwealth leaders, he was not in fact telling them that he was about to change Britain's imperial defence strategy. He might have chosen to focus in his talks with the three Commonwealth leaders on certain aspects of the paper – Britain's 'precarious economic strength', its weak external financial position, its 'limited material capacity' and the uncertainty of tenure of Britain's south-east Asian military bases – but for Macmillan the British presence east of Suez was one of the pillars of Britain's world role. As such it demanded that, in the face of British economic and colonial woes, every effort be made to preserve it. Thus, in June 1960, the important signal Macmillan was sending to the dominions was the other topic he raised with the prime ministers – the increasing need for the burden to be shared among the allies.[24] This message was not lost on Australian policy-makers, who

---

[20] Brief account of discussion between the four prime ministers, n.d, NAA, A1209/142, 1961/544.

[21] Notes on the Brook paper, n.d. NAA, A1838/269, TS899/6/6/4.

[22] UK study of future policy (1960–70): observations by DEA, 12 Jan. 1961, NAA, A1209/142, 1961/544.

[23] John Subritzky, 'Britain, *Konfrontasi*, and the end of empire in Southeast Asia, 1961–65', *JICH* xxvii (2000), 212.

[24] John Bunting (note for file), 14 May 1960; note of a meeting between Macmillan, Menzies, John Diefenbaker and Walter Nash, 13 May 1960, NAA, A1209/142, 1961/544.

noted that 'the United Kingdom expects Australia (and also New Zealand) to accept an increasing role and responsibility in South East Asia'.[25]

Still, in spite of policy-makers recognising that Macmillan's main preoccupation was with allied burden-sharing, Australian concerns that the British were moving towards a more realistic approach to defence policy were not put to rest. Rightly or wrongly, 'the feeling among senior officials in Canberra was that Britain would in due course be looking for a way out'. '[T]his was a feeling', Goldsworthy has observed,

> that the British did not yet wish actively to encourage. They stressed rather that no decisions had been taken. The danger, as British officials put it in a brief for Mountbatten, was that if the Australians came to believe 'that we were losing faith in the tenure of our bases', the consequences could include 'the breakup of ANZAM and further orientation towards America' – neither of which, evidently, the British wished to see.[26]

The problem was that, while London was seeking to reconcile the conflicting aims of maintaining an active role in south-east Asia and securing significant defence savings, Canberra regarded Britain's attempts to lessen its defence burden as a prelude to disengagement. Once again, the Australian response combined caution and mistrust. When in 1961–3 the Macmillan government pushed for the establishment of 'Greater Malaysia' (subsequently Malaysia) – the grouping of Malaya, Singapore, Brunei and the Borneo territories of Sabah and Sarawak into an independent federation – concerns resurfaced in Canberra.[27] Yet, Macmillan's decision to pursue the 'Greater Malaysia' plan was an attempt to find a solution to a different set of problems. First, Greater Malaysia would provide a viable political entity for the Borneo colonies, regarded as too small and underdeveloped to survive by themselves as independent states.[28] Second, it would accommodate Singaporean demands for independence and transfer responsibility for the internal security of the colony to the future federation. Third, incorporating Singapore into Greater Malaysia would ease British concerns over its tenure of the Singapore military base. These concerns arose from the fact that in 1961 the Barisan Sosialis (Socialist Front), which opposed the British presence in Singapore, emerged as a menacing force in Singapore's political life.[29] With national elections

---

[25] UK study of future policy (1960–70): observations by DEA, 12 Jan. 1961, ibid.

[26] Goldsworthy, *Losing the blanket*, 159.

[27] For the 'Greater Malaysia' plan see Matthew Jones, *Conflict and confrontation in south east Asia, 1961–1965*, Cambridge 2002, 61–97, and John Subritzky, *Confronting Sukarno: British, American, Australian and New Zealand diplomacy in the Malaysian-Indonesian confrontation, 1961–5*, Basingstoke 2000, 25–40.

[28] Subritzky, 'Britain, *Konfrontasi*', 210.

[29] In early 1961 Lee Kuan Yew, prime minister of Singapore and leader of the People's Action Party, expelled Communist sympathisers from his party. As a result, they established the *Barisan Sosialis*, which had a political platform centred on Singapore's complete independence from Britain and the adoption of a socialist constitution. In the summer of

due to take place by mid-1963, 'many observers were predicting the victory of the Opposition Barisan Sosialis ... at the polls, and an end to the British presence'.[30] The view in London was that, if Singapore joined a larger, pro-British federation, this Communist-led party would represent a lesser danger.[31] Strategically, the Greater Malaysia plan would enable Britain to maintain its bases in the region, while its responsibility for internal security in the colonies would be passed to the new Malaysian Federation. This would relieve Britain of an onerous political and military task. Historians have differed as to Macmillan's ultimate aims in pursuing decolonisation through Greater Malaysia. Some have argued that, far from wanting to disengage from southeast Asia, Macmillan was seeking to replace formal rule with a more subtle and indirect form of influence.[32] Others have regarded the Greater Malaysia project as an important step towards British disengagement.[33] Yet, as John Subritzky has rightly observed, 'evidence clearly suggests that British intentions at the time in creating Malaysia were to maintain rather than end Britain's historic interests in the region'.[34]

The Australian response was mixed.[35] While recognising that the Greater Malaysia project 'could make an important contribution to the stability of the region', Menzies had qualms about its defence implications. In particular, he warned the British authorities that 'serious and sustained efforts would be necessary to obtain from the new central government of Greater Malaysia defence arrangements to meet the requirements of the Commonwealth Strategic Reserve'. Thus, he wanted to ensure that the new defence agreement, which had to be negotiated with the government of Malaya, 'provided for the continued presence of the Strategic Reserve in its primary role of deterring communist aggression in the area'.[36] In other words, he was concerned

1961, following a by-election victory, the *Barisan Sosialis* held the same number of seats as the ruling PAP in the legislative assembly. Lee Kuan Yew could only govern thanks to the speaker's vote.

[30] Matthew Jones, 'A decision delayed: Britain's withdrawal from South East Asia reconsidered, 1961–68', *English Historical Review* cxvii (2002), 572.

[31] Incidentally, Australian policy-makers were concerned that were Singapore to become independent as a single entity, 'it might gravitate towards China and provide an effective base for subversion, not only of Malaya but the whole of Southeast Asia': David Lee and Moreen Dee, 'Southeast Asian conflicts', in David Goldsworthy (ed.), *Facing north: a century of Australian engagement with Asia, I: 1901 to the 1970s*, Melbourne 2001, 265.

[32] Darwin, *Britain and decolonisation*, 290; A. J. Stockwell, 'Malaysia: the making of a neo-colony?', *JICH* xxvi (1998), 138–56.

[33] Kin Wah Chin, *The defence of Malaysia and Singapore: the transformation of a security system, 1957–71*, Cambridge 1983, 179; Jones, 'Conflict and confrontation', 27–8.

[34] Subritzky, 'Britain, *Konfrontasi*', 211.

[35] For the differences over the creation of a Greater Malaysia between the Prime Minister's Department, traditionally more receptive to British views, and the Department of External Affairs, under Garfield Barwick (Dec. 1961–Apr. 1964) see Goldsworthy, *Losing the blanket*, 145; Subritzky, *Confronting Sukarno*, 13–4; and Edwards with Pemberton, *Crises and commitments*, 262.

[36] Menzies to William Oliver, 28 Aug. 1961, NAA, A6706/1, 61.

that the new federation government might place restrictions on the Singapore base. Without unrestricted access to the base, British, Australian and New Zealand forces would find their ability to operate in their SEATO roles curtailed.[37] Macmillan's reply to Menzies in October 1961 was far from reassuring. He advised the Australians that over the next ten years, due to local susceptibilities, it could become

> extremely difficult to use Singapore as a base for active operations in the region – whether or not a Greater Malaysia can be established ... If we cannot rely in the long run on those facilities what in the long term should be the nature of our military role in SEATO? How far will a new seaborne-airborne strategy enable us to make an effective military contribution without having to rely on old-style bases?

According to Macmillan, these were 'all major and far reaching questions' which would have to be discussed with Australia, New Zealand and the United States in due course.[38]

They were, indeed, far-reaching questions and, from an Australian viewpoint, deeply disquieting. As seen from Canberra, the problem was that, if the British harboured serious doubts about their ability to play a strategic role in south-east Asia, then the Greater Malaysia project seemed a good pretext for negotiating a release (albeit gradual) from unwelcome defence commitments. Hence, Australia's main objective became to 'secure ... a fuller account ... of United Kingdom aims in the forthcoming discussions with the Tunku', the prime minister of Malaya.[39]

Doubts over the Singapore base, however, were not the Australian government's only concern. In the same October message to Menzies, Macmillan also informed him that, with the transfer of responsibility for internal security to the federation, all British land forces earmarked for that role, would be withdrawn once Malaysia was established. Macmillan referred to 'certain specific and urgent problems' – that is, the financial situation and acute manpower problems – which made it imperative to 'secure substantial savings in our [Britain's] overseas expenditure including military expenditure'.[40] In a note to Menzies, John Bunting, Secretary of the Prime Minister's Department, alerted his prime minister that Macmillan's message more or less foreshadowed a British rundown in south-east Asia. He added: 'The time-scales for such a review and other details are not given, but we cannot take his hint too lightly. He [Macmillan] indicates that the desire to make

---

[37] Menzies's concerns were justified. Since 1957 the Malayan government had been opposed to the use of British bases on its soil in support of SEATO operations in the region. This problem had hitherto been overcome by relocating CSR forces from Malaya to Singapore from whence they could then be deployed in SEATO operations.
[38] Macmillan to Menzies, 20 Oct. 1961, NAA, A6706/1, 61.
[39] Bunting to Menzies, 1 Nov. 1961, ibid.
[40] Macmillan to Menzies, 20 Oct. 1961, ibid.

manpower and money savings will be an important influence in the United Kingdom decisions'.[41]

In the event, Australian worries about Britain's intentions in south-east Asia abated somewhat – if only temporarily. In January 1963 the Indonesian foreign minister, Raden Subandrio, declared that Indonesia's policy towards the proposed federation of Malaysia (then scheduled to be established in August 1963) would be one of *Konfrontasi* (Confrontation).[42] Subsequently, between 1963 and 1966, *Konfrontasi* would see Britain involved in a low-level conflict with Indonesia in the defence of Malaysia. If one of Macmillan's motives behind the establishment of Greater Malaysia in 1963 had been to reduce Britain's military burden in south-east Asia, Indonesia's military campaign 'turned British plans on their head'.[43] In Macmillan's own words, Malaysia risked becoming a 'formidable liability'.[44] Despite this, his government was bound to honour Britain's commitment to defend the federation under its new defence arrangements. Thus, far from being able to cut its forces in the Far East, Britain was forced to strengthen its military presence in Malaysia in order to resist Indonesian aggression: a potentially open-ended military commitment to its former colonies. At the height of Indonesia's campaign, John Darwin contends that 'some 68,000 British servicemen were deployed in the Far East, together with a fleet of 80 ships including 2 aircraft carriers and a commando ship'.[45] From late 1963 and throughout 1964, the British strove to persuade the Australian and New Zealand governments to commit troops to Malaysia. By seeking to draw its two Australasian partners into the conflict, London hoped to reduce the burden of defending Malaysia, while raising the possibility of an American intervention in support of Australia and New Zealand, should they become involved in Malaysia.[46] Despite British pressure, it was not until February 1965 that the Menzies government committed a battalion and an SAS unit to operations in the Borneo territories in support of the British effort – and then only in response to a Malaysian request.[47] There were strong external political reasons for

---

41 Bunting to Menzies, 1 Nov. 1961, ibid.
42 In February 1963, at a quadripartite meeting in Washington between the representatives of the United States, Britain, New Zealand and Australia, the Australians voiced the concern that the British decision to establish Malaysia at all costs – that is, with or without Indonesian or Filipino concurrence – would certainly lead to Jakarta's (if not Manila's) long-term hostility towards the new state. Australia wanted to avoid being drawn into a conflict with its closest Asian neighbour: Subritzky, *Confronting Sukarno*, 50–1.
43 Idem, 'Britain, *Konfrontasi*', 209.
44 Macmillan, quoted in Jones, 'Decision delayed', 576.
45 Darwin, *Britain and decolonisation*, 290.
46 Subritzky, *Confronting Sukarno*, 63, 79.
47 For the commitment of Australian troops to *Konfrontasi* see Edwards with Pemberton, *Crises and commitments*, 340–4. For a detailed analysis of Australia's policy in response to *Konfrontasi* see Moreen Dee, 'In Australia's own interests: Australian foreign policy during Confrontation, 1963–1966', unpubl. PhD diss. New England, NSW 2000.

their apparent unwillingness. *Konfrontasi* brought Australia into an unwelcome position of conflict with Indonesia – its closest neighbour. In the end, however, Australian policy-makers, especially those in the traditionally pro-British Prime Minister's Department, could not afford to ignore British pleas for help. 'To do so', Subrizky has rightly claimed, 'would only have aided those ministers and advisers in London who wanted to phase out British commitments east of Suez.'[48]

Australian policy-makers may have felt reassured about Britain's short-term intentions, particularly as Britain in fact became bogged down in a costly and difficult fighting exercise in the jungles on the border of Indonesian Kalimantan, with little prospect of a swift victory. While *Konfrontasi* lasted, British disengagement from the area was out of question.[49] However, as Australian planners pointed out in a policy study dated August 1963, Britain's involvement in *Konfrontasi* was best seen as 'a temporary levelling off in the gradual downward curve of British influence and activity in Asia'.[50] Against this backdrop, the decision to commit troops to the defence of Malaysia has also to be seen as one of Australia's last attempts to keep Britain involved in south-east Asia for as long as possible.

The turn to Europe and strategic tensions

In the early 1960s Australia's lingering doubts about Britain's ability to remain east of Suez were further heightened by Britain's decision to seek entry into the EEC. Such a prospect, which had hitherto been absent from Australian politico-strategic considerations, emerged with force in 1961 and was to be a nagging concern for most of the decade. This is not to say that Australian policy-makers had overlooked the importance of a 'European' dimension to British defence thinking. They had long recognised that London's most vital strategic interests lay in Europe and did not necessarily regard the primacy of the European theatre in British military strategy as incompatible with Britain's role as a world power or with its Commonwealth commitments. Yet, there was little doubt that the prospect of British entry into the Community was an entirely different proposition. The view was that Britain's membership of a tightly knit group of European nations would lead to a significant reorientation towards Europe in London's external policies.

The Macmillan government announced its decision to apply for EEC membership in July 1961. In June and early July 1961, calculating that the

---

48 Subritzky, *Confronting Sukarno*, 139.
49 None the less, in April 1963, Macmillan wondered whether 'the security of Malaysia would be more effectively safeguarded in the long term by the negotiation of a political understanding with Indonesia than by the maintenance of British forces in Singapore': quoted in Jones, 'Decision delayed', 576.
50 DEA policy planning study 1/63, 30 Aug. 1963, NAA, A1838/346, TS691/1 pt 3.

British bid was imminent, the Menzies Cabinet met to assess the political and economic consequences of an eventual British entry. The members had before them a detailed DEA submission. The Department of External Affairs argued that, while not entailing 'specific commitments in the fields of foreign affairs and defence', British membership of the EEC could none the less 'have far-reaching effects' in the long term, which it described in the following terms:

> Our concern is that by [Britain's] entry into a European community which within twenty years could become so unified as to compel, at the least, harmonious extra-European policies on the part of its members, such freedom of action as the United Kingdom now enjoys as a world power and employs as leader of the Commonwealth could be further reduced; and, in particular, that it might lose both the interest in maintaining and the ability to maintain, an effective strategic role in the world beyond Suez, where Australia's defence interests lie.[51]

The paper also pointed out that while British entry was likely to have negative implications for Australia's strategic interests in south-east Asia, Britain's failure to join the EEC would, by the same token, bring problems. If Macmillan's bid were to prove unsuccessful, the DEA contended that the prospect facing Britain would be 'one of further decline' in its 'political and economic strength, relative to that of other major powers and the continental group'. The department argued that Britain's position in the world had already been eroded, and that, in a sense, 'the very decision with which the United Kingdom is now confronted is evidence of the decline in its independent power'. To support this contention it was noted in the submission that Britain was in fact essentially dependent on the United States and on its various alliances, especially NATO. This was not surprising since Britain clearly no longer possessed the basic economic and financial resources which alone could sustain its former position. The DEA concluded that in these circumstances the restoration of Britain's previous influence was no longer feasible. Furthermore, it maintained that, even if London remained outside the EEC, Britain's future was one of continuing decline as a world power. The predicament for Australia was that, in the long run, Britain's decline would inevitably weaken not only its resolve, but also its ability, to play a meaningful political and strategic role in south-east Asia.

On balance, however, the DEA regarded British entry into the EEC as the course of action more harmful to Australia's politico-strategic interests. The main reason was that British entry 'would accelerate tendencies which are already established towards the transformation of the United Kingdom into a European rather than a world power and towards a decline in its commitments beyond Suez'. There was also a second reason. According to

---

51 Cabinet submission 1183, 26 June 1961, NAA, A1838/269, TS899/1/4 pt 2.

the DEA, British membership 'would make plainer than before the existing and accepted fact that Australia is essentially dependent for effective physical resistance to aggressive powers in Asia, for national survival, not on the United Kingdom but on the goodwill, self-interest and strength of the United States'. Hence, Britain's turn to Europe, the department warned, 'could require of us [Australia] earlier adjustments than if the United Kingdom remained outside Europe'. In conclusion, it argued that

> [t]he pace of European integration cannot be assessed. But even the most rapid timetable would be likely to give us ten or twenty years in which to adjust ourselves politically and strategically in the developing situation and there should be no immediate or dramatic changes in these fields if compared with what we may expect in any case. But we might suffer an initial period of increasing isolation from United Kingdom and European support, while the Community takes shape and the United Kingdom is proving itself as a European power.[52]

In August 1962 the DEA temporarily became somewhat more relaxed about the politico-strategic risks posed by Britain's membership of the EEC. On the whole, however, Australian policy-makers remained apprehensive about possible repercussions on Australian defence interests and felt little relief when President de Gaulle vetoed the British application. They viewed Macmillan's failure to join the EEC as a minor set-back for the British, believing that Britain in fact 'may well have reached a full political and economic accommodation with Western Europe' by the early 1970s. Hence, while the acceleration of tendencies towards the transformation of Britain into a 'European power' – as Australian policy-makers saw it – was temporarily averted, the problem of British entry was not. And this fact was intertwined with Australian concerns about Britain's willingness to maintain a military presence in south-east Asia, which refused to fade away. Given that Britain's primary political interests increasingly lay in Europe, the Australians argued that 'British military resources are unlikely to be maintained at their present levels'. Britain's renewed attempt to join the EEC in 1966–7 therefore raised strong concerns in Canberra that British entry would further weaken the faltering resolve of the Wilson government to remain east of Suez.[53]

The EEC issue and its defence implications aside, Australian policy-makers remained aware of the constant economic pressures on the British government domestically to rein in defence expenditure and to thin out British overseas commitments.[54] The beginning of *Konfrontasi* in January 1963, by forcing Britain to honour its arrangements to remain responsible for the defence of the proposed Federation of Malaysia, increased Britain's defence

---

[52] Ibid.
[53] DEA policy planning study 1/63, 30 Aug. 1963, NAA, A1838/346, TS691/1 pt 3.
[54] Ibid.

burden. Plagued with economic problems at home and faced not only by the rising costs of Britain's military presence in the Far East but also with the prospect of a protracted conflict with Indonesia, British policy-makers of necessity had to find ways to lighten Britain's burden in the region. Matters came to a head under Harold Wilson's Labour government. All Australia's fears and concerns were fully realised when this government decided in 1967–8 to end Britain's military presence east of Suez.

4

The British Taking to the Boat, 1964–1966

'The priority of Britain's commitments in Europe and NATO, financial considerations, difficulties in the way of her communications to
the area, and opposition to bases appear certain to affect Britain's
future military capability in the area. The separation of Singapore
from Malaysia has given additional urgency to the question of the
future of the Singapore base. ... It would therefore be prudent to
assume that Britain will start to run down the Singapore bases as
soon as military confrontation ceases. Thereafter the period of effective occupation of the bases may not extend beyond [a] few years':
Joint Intelligence Committee, 12 October 1965.[1]

Privately, then, the Menzies government long harboured doubts about
Britain's long-term willingness and ability to maintain a significant military
presence in south-east Asia. Australian suspicions were soon to be vindicated. In 1965, as its resolve to remain east of Suez weakened, the Wilson
government began to consider plans for a much reduced military presence
in south-east Asia. Although the British were careful to present their plans
not only as part of a broad settlement aimed at ending the Indonesian-
Malaysian *Konfrontasi*, but also as an exercise in contingency planning in
the event that they were asked to vacate their bases in Malaysia and Singapore, the Australian government sensed a noticeable change of emphasis
in British defence thinking and became apprehensive about British intentions. What policy-makers in Canberra feared at this point was that the
British, despite their reassurances, were seeking a way out of south-east Asia
at the very time when Australia was stepping up its involvement in regional
crises. In early 1965 Australia had committed troops to South Vietnam and
to the Borneo territories, where British and Malaysian forces were facing
Konfrontasi. Fundamentally though, Canberra was concerned that a British
disengagement would undermine Australia's forward defence strategy, leave
a political and military vacuum in a highly volatile region, and weaken the
American determination to retain a military capability in south-east Asia.
Under strong pressure from Australia, the United States and New Zealand
– all worried about increased instability in south-east Asia – London was
forced to defer its plans, albeit temporarily. Throughout 1966 Australia and
its ANZUS partners sought to stiffen Britain's resolve to maintain a significant military presence in south-east Asia. But while Britain's plans to with-

[1] JIC (AUST) (65) (61) Final, 12 Oct. 1965, NAA, A1209/80, 1965/6595 pt 1.

draw had seemingly been shelved, Australia was unable to secure a strong British commitment to regional defence. Nor did it gain British support for a common strategic plan for the area. The gulf between Australian and British politico-strategic interests was widening, and Australian policy towards Britain gradually hardened. As its suspicions grew stronger, Canberra became less forthcoming lest an overtly helpful attitude towards Britain's defence predicament facilitated a British pull-out. Moreover the re-emergence of 'the EEC question' in British policy-making played a major part in reinforcing Australian suspicions of British intentions. It is in this context that this chapter shows how the Wilson government's renewed interest in EEC membership impinged upon Australia's strategic concerns.

Labour's strategic thinking, 1964–5

The strong possibility of a change of government in Britain after a decade of Conservative rule was viewed with some anxiety in Canberra given Labour's well-known desire for far-reaching changes to British defence policy. 'Such indications as one has about Labour attitudes', Australian policy-makers remarked in 1963, 'are not altogether encouraging.' Australians were concerned that a future Labour government might feel under less of an obligation to provide for the defence of Australia and New Zealand and, as a result, might be more assertive in demanding that its Australasian allies do more in their own defence.[2] Yet, despite Australian misgivings, Labour's initial moves in defence and foreign affairs following Wilson's election victory in October 1964 were remarkably cautious. On 16 December 1964 the new prime minister informed the House of Commons that whatever his government 'may do in the field of cost effectiveness, value for money, and a stringent review of expenditure, we cannot afford to relinquish our world role, our role which, for shorthand purposes, is sometimes called our "east of Suez" role'.[3]

None the less, a mere six months later, British ministers were considering plans for a gradual disengagement from south-east Asia. These encompassed the withdrawal of British forces from their bases in Malaysia and Singapore (*see* table 4) and their redeployment on a much reduced scale in northern Australia. Until recently, historians have maintained that British senior ministers remained committed to Britain's role east of Suez until withdrawal was forced upon them by a combination of economic problems and party pressure.[4] According to traditional scholarship, policy-makers in London

2   DEA policy planning study 1/63, 30 Aug. 1963, NAA, A1838/346, TS691/1 pt 3.
3   Britain, *PD*, HC, 1964–5, dcciv.423–4.
4   See Phillip Darby, *British defence policy east of Suez*, London 1973, passim; Darwin, *Britain and decolonisation*, 291; Robert Holland, *The pursuit of greatness: Britain and the world role, 1900–1970*, London 1991, 320–1; Pickering, *Withdrawal*; and Chin, *Defence*, 106, 126.

only began to look at ways of withdrawing from south-east Asia between late 1966 and early 1967. For instance, Phillip Darby has argued that 'in the period to July 1966 there was no official consideration of the possibility of a British withdrawal from the Far East'.[5] John Darwin has added that 'in the first year of the Labour government concern for the economy had little effect on strategic policy'.[6] Lately, as new archival material has become accessible, these assumptions have been challenged by a number of revisionist historians. Saki Dockrill, David Easter, Phuong Pham, John Subriztky and Matthew Jones have convincingly argued that British ministers had in fact begun to consider plans for a gradual disengagement from south-east Asia as early as mid-1965.[7] As Subritzky has pointed out, the Wilson government 'was more willing to accept a radical reappraisal of Britain's position east of Suez than has previously been recognized by most historians'.[8]

It is beyond the scope of this book to analyse the complex and tortuous steps taken by the Defence Review, which the Wilson government initiated in early 1965 and brought to completion in early 1966. Nor is it possible to examine in detail the reasons for Wilson's early revision of Britain's defence posture in south-east Asia. The original works of Pham and Dockrill have provided an illuminating account of the 1965 Defence Review. Here it suffices to outline British planning as it evolved throughout 1965.

Upon taking office, the Labour government was resolved to maintain Britain's role east of Suez while fully appreciating the urgent need to reduce spiralling defence spending and large overseas commitments in the light of a precarious economic situation.[9] At Chequers, on 21–22 November 1964, Wilson and his senior ministers agreed 'not to seek to maintain in the future [Britain's] three roles on their present scale'.[10] Yet they expressed considerable support for the view that the country's first priority should be the maintenance of the east of Suez commitments.[11] This policy, Wilson stressed to

---

5 Darby, *British defence policy*, 312.
6 Darwin, *Britain and decolonisation*, 291.
7 Saki Dockrill, *Britain's retreat from east of Suez: the choice between Europe and the world?*, London 2002; Phuong Pham, 'The end to "east of Suez": the British decision to withdraw from Malaysia and Singapore, 1964 to 1968', unpubl. PhD diss. Oxford 2001, ch. i; David Easter, 'British defence policy in South East Asia and the Confrontation, 1960–66', unpubl. PhD diss. London 1998, ch. vii; Jones, 'Decision delayed', 569–95; Subritzky, *Confronting Sukarno*, 146–9.
8 Subriztky, 'Britain, *Konfrontasi*', 220.
9 For the economic problems facing Wilson in his early days in office see Ponting, *Breach of promise*, 61–84.
10 The three roles were the defence of Europe under NATO, the continuation of Britain's nuclear power status and the maintenance of a world-wide military presence based on overseas commitments.
11 CAB 130/213, MISC 17/1st, 21 Nov. 1964.

Table 4
British military presence in Malaysia and Singapore, 1965

Royal Navy	Army	Royal Air Force
2 aircraft carriers	19 infantry battalions	19 flying squadrons, approximately 224 aircraft
1 commando carrier	10 other major units	
1 guided missile destroyer	Total strength approx. 50,000	
18 escorts		
5 submarines		
minesweepers		

Source: British defence review, report by the Defence Committee on matters for discussion between British, Australian and New Zealand ministers, Jan. 1966, NAA, A1209/80, 1965/6595 pt 3.

his full Cabinet a week later, was 'desirable, both in principle and as a means of maintaining the Commonwealth connection'.[12]

At Chequers, ministers decided to initiate a process of reassessment of British defence policy. They agreed to keep the annual defence budget below a £2,000 million ceiling (at 1964 constant prices) for the next decade.[13] The Defence Review was set in motion on this basis. In order to put a brake on defence spending, ministers planned to cut reserve forces and soon decided to scrap certain arms projects, including the HS681 medium transport aircraft, the fifth Polaris submarine, and the P1154 Hunter replacement.[14] At the same time, the White Paper of February 1965 ruled out any abandonment of Britain's world role. While conceding that British forces were 'seriously over-stretched', it contended that it would be 'politically irresponsible' to abandon commitments east of Suez.[15]

While senior ministers emphasised the importance of the east of Suez role, this attitude was not fully shared within Whitehall.[16] At Chequers, top officials had presented ministers with an agreed interdepartmental paper which, while rejecting 'a sudden and wholesale withdrawal', suggested 'a controlled reduction of [Britain's] commitments'. Reductions in Europe were ruled out on the ground that Britain had 'a major interest in increasing British political influence in Europe'. This required the maintenance of British 'military influence within NATO'. Thus, the paper argued that 'if

12 CAB 128/39, CC(64)11, 26 Nov. 1964.
13 CAB 130/213, MISC 17/4th, 22 Nov. 1964.
14 Pickering, *Withdrawal*, 141; Darby, *British defence policy*, 287.
15 Cmnd. 2592, *Statement on defence estimates, 1965*, London 1965, paras 11–12.
16 Pham, 'Suez', ch. i. According to Subritzky, not all senior ministers supported the east of Suez role: *Confronting Sukarno*, 146.

economic considerations force on [*sic*] the decision to reduce our overseas military expenditure and if there is a choice between the Far East and the Middle East we should seek to make the reduction in the Far East'. According to the paper, Britain's military presence in the Far East was not material to its economic interests. Rather, Britain's interests in the area were defined as politico-strategic: that is, defending, and upholding the links with Australia and New Zealand, containing Communism and making a contribution to the Anglo-American alliance in protecting western interests around the globe. If commitments were to be reduced in the Far East, the report warned, it would need 'careful planning'. It would also have to be done 'in utmost secrecy' if 'damage to British interests is to be kept to a minimum'. The paper emphasised, however, that 'in taking decisions, time is thus ... the essence of this process; and time is not on our side'.[17]

Within Whitehall, the Treasury was inclined to question Britain's role east of Suez. The Foreign Office, while in general favouring the maintenance of a military role, seemed sceptical about the value of retaining a strong British military presence in south-east Asia, and in particular, the Far Eastern military hub of Singapore.[18] The Singapore base controlled the deployment of approximately fifteen land forces units with substantial naval and air forces as well as another six major units outside the area in Hong Kong. Such a commitment entailed a cost of £300 million, which amounted to roughly 15 per cent of Britain's total defence budget.[19] In a planning paper, 'British policy towards Southeast Asia', Foreign Office officials emphasised that, while Britain retained substantial politico-strategic interests there, the region now had 'relatively little economic importance to Britain'. Moreover, Britain's colonial possessions in the region had, with the exception of Brunei, all been relinquished. None the less, FO planners conceded that the Singapore base remained important to the protection of Britain's politico-strategic interests. They specifically noted that, as long as a military presence allowed Britain to 'exercise a major influence on United States policies', Singapore was 'worth retaining for that reason alone'. Yet it was also argued that not only was the military value of the base 'declining', but the base itself was becoming a 'liability'. This, of course, begged the question as to how, other than by the retention of the Singapore base, Britain's politico-strategic interests in the region could best be protected. For Foreign Office planners the answer was to

---

[17] British interests and commitments overseas, 23 Oct. 1964, CAB 148/40.

[18] Revisionist scholarship is divided on how to assess the attitude of the Foreign Office towards a British presence in that area. According to Saki Dockrill, it favoured the maintenance of commitments east of Suez: *Retreat*, 53, 57, and 'Britain's power and influence: dealing with three roles and the Wilson government's defence debate at Chequers in November 1964', *Diplomacy and Statecraft* xi (2000), passim. Pham, Subritzky and Jones have instead argued that the FO was moving towards a position of support for a British gradual disengagement from the area: Pham, 'Suez', ch. i; Subritzky, 'Britain, *Konfrontasi*', 217–19; Jones, *Conflict and confrontation*, 282–3.

[19] TNA, FO 371/177824, SC(64)46, PLA18/9, 31 Dec. 1964.

be found in a formal, or even tacit, understanding between the West and the Communist powers for the 'neutralisation' of south-east Asia. In practice, neutralisation meant the establishment of a non-aligned area where neither the West nor the Communist camp would be the predominant force. This in turn entailed the removal of the western military presence from the area. However, with Britain involved in *Konfrontasi*, neutralisation was necessarily a long-term objective. Conflict with Indonesia required a strong British military presence in Singapore and Malaysia. Despite this, FO planners observed that 'a delicate balance has to be struck between the dangers of staying too long and the opposite dangers of withdrawing too fast'.[20] As John Subritzky has noted, the ideas expressed in the Foreign Office paper clearly betrayed unease over Britain's role in south-east Asia.[21]

The FO paper was an important indication of the direction in which official (though not yet ministerial) thinking on Britain's future role in the region was moving. None the less, during the first half of 1965 ministerial thinking began to shift. It was in fact becoming clear from the ongoing Defence Review that reductions in weapon systems were in themselves not sufficient to ensure a £2,000 million budgetary ceiling. Troop commitments would inevitably have to be reduced.[22] Britain's economic and financial situation was far from reassuring.[23] Under pressure from the economic departments to bring defence spending under control, ministerial support for the east of Suez role began to weaken. In June 1965 Wilson and his senior ministers met at Chequers once again. They endorsed plans for a withdrawal from south-east Asia and subsequent redeployment on a much reduced scale to bases in northern Australia and/or in the Indian Ocean.[24] In the Far East Britain would retain only the Hong Kong garrison.[25] The Chequers meeting significantly transformed Britain's defence strategy in the Far Eastern theatre: from a strategy centred on south-east Asian deployments, British ministers opted for a much leaner defence posture based on out-of-area deployments. As Phuong Pham has observed, 'a new direction for policy had been set. The question for the next few months would be to see if these plans could be made viable'.[26] In other words, the task for British policy-makers was to encourage, through quiet diplomacy, circumstances in which disengagement

---

[20] Ibid.

[21] Subritzky, 'Britain, *Konfrontasi*', 218

[22] Pham, 'Suez', ch. i. For the progress of the Defence Review see also Dockrill, *Retreat*, 76–104.

[23] Ponting, *Breach of promise*, 72–9.

[24] Defence expenditure review, 10 June 1965, CAB 130/213, MISC 17/8, OPD(O); FO 953/2255/PLA 12/46, PC(65)28, 9 Aug. 1965.

[25] CAB 130/213, MISC 17/5th–7th, 13 June 1965.

[26] Pham, 'Suez', ch. i. On the Chequers meeting see also Easter, 'British defence policy', ch. vii.

could begin.[27] As Burke Trend, Wilson's Cabinet Secretary, told his prime minister:

> Even if we decide that, in the light of the Review, we will 'pull out of Germany' or 'give up Singapore' or 'abandon the East of Suez Role', we shall not be able to say so in public. All that we shall be able to do is to determine that, over the next few years to 1969–70, we will try to direct our external policy in such a way that we may be able to negotiate our way out of certain commitments. With luck, we may succeed; but we cannot be sure of this and it is quite certain that, if we announce in advance that we intend to take any of the steps which are conveniently (but very misleadingly) summarised in the catch phrases quoted above, we shall frustrate our whole purpose.[28]

For disengagement to be carried out successfully, Britain needed the co-operation of its ANZUS allies. Without Canberra's agreement to British bases on Australian soil, or without Washington's assent to joint naval and air facilities in the Indian Ocean, London's 'peripheral' strategy would fail. Yet, the importance of allied support went beyond mere technical and logistic matters. After all, Wilson's whole gambit consisted of seeking to reduce onerous Far Eastern commitments without jeopardising Britain's political links with the ANZUS countries. Was this a realistic objective? As far as Australia was concerned, it is worthy of note that, at the end of 1964, FO planners seemed to believe that Australian agreement would become easier to secure as Australia grew increasingly aware of the threat from the north.[29] And, in 1965, the Menzies government was indeed troubled by growing regional instability. The Vietnam war was escalating, *Konfrontasi* showed no signs of abating, and there were indications that growing internal political instability was threatening the very existence of the Malaysian Federation.[30] Under these circumstances, would Australian consent be forthcoming, as FO planners clearly expected?

The British were determined to pursue their plans with Australia and the other ANZUS partners, regardless. London calculated that – if negotiations were handled skilfully – Britain would retain some leverage *vis-à-vis* its allies. This view was based on the premise that, as these countries considered a continued British presence essential, they would probably acquiesce in British plans, provided London continued to play a military role in south-east Asia. In order to achieve this objective, however, a certain amount of deception was essential. As Trend told Wilson,

> there should be no premature disclosure of the way in which our minds are working if only because once it is thought that we are on the run, we have

27 Subritzky, *Confronting Sukarno*, 149.
28 Burke Trend to Wilson, 9 Apr. 1965, TNA, PREM 13/214.
29 FO 371/177824, SC(64)46, PLA18/9, 31 Dec. 1964, para 24.
30 For the growing political instability within Malaysia see Jones, *Conflict and confrontation*, 269–70, 273–4.

lost our main negotiating card, and a process which ought to be a phased and controlled contraction of commitments will degenerate into a disorderly and ignominious retreat.[31]

British plans, therefore, were to be presented in very careful language. Australia and the other allies would be told that, owing to economic and budgetary constraints, Britain was forced to cut defence expenditures. Manpower reductions were essential if the £2,000 million ceiling on defence spending were to be achieved. In this context, Australia, New Zealand and the United States were expected to help ease Britain's defence burden in the region. In addition, the allies were to be told that, while nationalist sentiment in Malaysia was less militantly opposed to foreign bases than in Aden and South Arabia, local political pressure might soon build to force British troops out of the Federation.[32] The implication was that if this occurred, and British forces did not have a fall-back position in the region, they would have to be pulled back to Europe. The hope was that Britain's allies would, given the circumstances, be willing to co-operate in British contingency planning.

Initial reactions

In the summer of 1965 the Wilson government cautiously introduced its ANZUS partners to some aspects of British defence thinking. Between May and July, British ministers and officials had several opportunities to canvass the east of Suez question with their American counterparts. Despite British caution, the Johnson administration gained the distinct impression that London was seeking significant troop reductions east of Suez. The Americans became so concerned about British intentions that, in late June, Defense Secretary Robert McNamara warned the visiting British Chancellor of the Exchequer, James Callaghan, that if London reduced its troops east of Suez, Washington would have to readjust its alliance obligations with 'deleterious effects' on relations with Britain. He also made it clear that American willingness to ease Britain's foreign exchange problems would be conditional upon London maintaining its world-wide commitments.[33]

Meanwhile, on the Australian front, the British enjoyed an easier ride as

---

[31] Trend to Wilson, 14 June 1965, PREM 13/215.

[32] Like Singapore, Aden was both a crown colony and an important military base. In 1963 Aden joined the Federation of South Arabia. Faced with growing nationalist unrest, the Wilson government began to consider withdrawal in mid-1965. See John Young, *The Labour governments, 1964–70, II: International policy*, Manchester, 2003, 89–98, and Stephen Ashton and William Roger Louis (eds), *British documents on the end of empire: east of Suez and the Commonwealth, 1964–71*, London 2004, pp. xliii–li.

[33] Memcon, UK defence review, 30 June 1965, in *Foreign relations of the United States, 1964–68, XII: Western Europe*, Washington 2002, doc. 244. See also Jonathan Tepper,

the Menzies government appeared more receptive to British ideas. When Wilson and his Defence Secretary, Denis Healey, met Menzies in London on 1 July, they drew his attention to the urgent need for defence economies. Wilson told Menzies that, in the current Defence Review, a major problem was the burden east of Suez. Healey added that the £2,000 million target would not be achieved unless commitments were shared or cut. While professing that Britain still 'had a job to do East of Suez', Wilson expressed doubts about the long-term viability of the Singapore base. Referring to the climate of political instability within Malaysia, Wilson maintained that 'we could not stay for long in bases if we were not welcome'. 'This', he pointed out, 'raised the question of how we retained a presence east of Suez if both Aden and Singapore became not viable'. The urgency of defence economies and the uncertain life of present bases, he concluded, had led the British government to consider sharing commitments east of Suez on a quadripartite basis, in partnership with Australia, New Zealand and the United States.[34]

Menzies's reaction was surprisingly positive. He told the British ministers that 'he quite understood that [Britain] did not wish to abandon South-East Asia and the defence of the free world'.[35] He agreed that 'it could be most unwise to depend for long' on the Singapore base, although it should be maintained 'as long as could be managed'. He also welcomed joint allied co-operation on military matters, including the collaborative use of defence facilities in Australia.[36] He 'thought there would be no difficulties about staging and bases' in Australia.[37] Menzies also 'saw value and promise in contingency planning'. 'The sooner we got together on planning, the better', he argued.[38] The only cautionary note he introduced into the proceedings was that Australia was 'severely stretched in terms of manpower', despite the fact that the government had recently introduced compulsory military service and doubled the defence budget.[39] Australia's increasing involvement in south-east Asian crises was taking its toll. In February 1965 Canberra committed an infantry battalion and a squadron of SAS to combat Indonesian infiltrators in Borneo. In April 1965 it decided to deploy a battalion

'The dollar, the pound and British policy "east of Suez, 1964–67": deals and understandings between Wilson and Johnson', unpubl. MLitt diss. Oxford 2004, ch. ii.
[34] Wilson, Denis Healey and Menzies, memcon, 1 July 1965, PREM 13/889.
[35] Ibid.
[36] Menzies to McEwen, cablegram 5688, 3 July 1965, NAA, A1209/80, 1965/6595 pt 2.
[37] Wilson, Healey and Menzies, memcon, 1 July 1965, PREM 13/889.
[38] Menzies to McEwen, cablegram 5688, 3 July 1965, NAA, A1209/80, 1965/6595 pt 2.
[39] Wilson, Healey and Menzies, memcon, 1 July 1965, PREM 13/889. Between 1962 and 1966, the defence budget doubled from approximately A£200 million to about A£400 million. See Hewitt to William McMahon, 4 Jan. 1966, NAA, A1209/80, 1965/6595 attachment 2.

to Vietnam. As a result, Australia 'was about to enter its largest military commitment apart from the two world wars'.[40]

Menzies, of course, misjudged British intentions. This was rather surprising given Australia's long-standing misgivings about the British resolve to remain east of Suez. Had he full knowledge of the way British thinking was evolving, it is doubtful that Menzies would have been so forthcoming. He probably believed that, while under pressure to cut defence spending, Wilson remained committed to the east of Suez role. Menzies was not alone in believing this. In May his Minister for External Affairs, Paul Hasluck, had conveyed to Healey Australia's 'great satisfaction with the robustness of defence decisions and attitudes of his [the British] Government'.[41] Yet, despite Hasluck's protestations, the Australian government could not fail to see Wilson's resolve to make defence cuts. Consequently, 'a situation might arise', the Department of Defence warned, 'where the U.K. Government might wonder to what extent they are under obligation to Australia to retain forces in the Indian Ocean area'. In stressing the importance of retaining a British presence in the area, the DOD indicated that 'there might be a need for some deliberate action on Australia's part to bring this about'.[42] Menzies's support for increased allied co-operation and contingency planning is best understood against this background. Yet other considerations, too, would have influenced Menzies's response. First, there was on Australia's part, as he had told Wilson in February 1965, 'the almost instinctive obligation, unwritten but there nonetheless, to do all in [our] power to help Britain'.[43] Second, Menzies probably regarded British proposals as an opportunity to fulfil Australia's long-held aim of getting London and Washington to co-ordinate their military efforts in the region. He was acutely aware that as Australia became increasingly involved on two south-east Asian fronts (Borneo and Vietnam), more allied co-ordination was needed to ensure an effective defence of western interests in Asia.

Singapore and the London quadripartite talks

The Australian attitude towards Wilson's proposals, however, was bound to change, as British determination to remain in south-east Asia appeared to falter. Unbeknownst to the Australians, British plans for military disengagement received new impetus in the summer of 1965 with the separation of

---

[40] Peter Edwards, A nation at war: Australian politics, society and diplomacy during the Vietnam war, 1965–1975, Sydney 1996, 28. For Australia's commitment to Borneo see Dennis and Grey, Emergency and confrontation, ch. xiii.

[41] Paul Hasluck to DEA, cablegram 3665, 7 May 1965, NAA, A1838/346, TS691/1 pt 3.

[42] UK defence review, DOD note, June 1965, NAA, A1209/80, 1965/6124.

[43] Menzies quoted in Goldsworthy, Losing the blanket, 157.

Singapore from the Malaysian Federation on 9 August.[44] The break-up of the Federation heightened British concerns for the future of Britain's military bases there. In an emergency meeting on 15 August, the British Cabinet acknowledged that London's tenure of its bases was unlikely to extend 'beyond the next three or four years at most'. Senior ministers felt that the likelihood of 'increasing friction' between Malaysia and Singapore would in the end undermine 'the security and effectiveness of [British] bases'. The government, therefore, should seize the initiative and 'use the freedom of action which recent events had accorded to us'.[45]

Freedom of action did not mean that Britain could simply offload its responsibilities onto its allies. *Konfrontasi* had to be ended first. Under AMDA, Britain was responsible for the security of its former colony against external aggression. It was for this reason that London had come to Kuala Lumpur's rescue in 1963 following Indonesian attempts to destabilise the proposed Federation of Malaysia. To end *Konfrontasi*, British ministers were willing to consider a negotiated settlement with Indonesia. But to do this, and to implement its plans for disengagement, Britain needed the acquiescence of its ANZUS allies. The Cabinet therefore agreed to secret quadripartite talks to be held in London in early September. It also decided that the talks should be used to warn the allies that Britain's 'ability to contribute to the defence of Western interests in the Far East would be contingent on suitable facilities in Australia'. In particular, ministers were of the view that Britain 'should press for the cost of construction of a base to be met from Australian funds'. After all, Australia not only 'spent a much smaller proportion of her gross national product on defence', but 'had a higher standard of living' than Britain. Hence, Australia should be encouraged to do more.[46]

These points were further elaborated in an interdepartmental paper which was to serve as a brief for the quadripartite talks and which ministers endorsed on 31 August.[47] This recommended that the government seek to convince Britain's allies that recent developments in south-east Asia had significantly reduced Britain's prospects of retaining a military presence there. It reaffirmed the need for an early end to *Konfrontasi* provided that 'minimum terms' acceptable to Britain could be obtained.[48] While rejecting the idea of a unilateral and complete withdrawal from the Far East – for this 'would have most serious repercussions, especially on [Britain's] relations with Australia, New Zealand and the United States, including the willing-

---

44 For the reasons for the separation of Singapore from Malaysia see Nicholas Tarling (ed.), *The Cambridge history of Southeast Asia*, II: *The nineteenth and twentieth centuries*, Cambridge 1992, 409–15.
45 CAB 130/239, MISC 76/1st, 15 Aug. 1965.
46 Ibid.
47 CAB 148/18, OPD(65)37th, 31 Aug. 1965.
48 For these minimum terms see Repercussions on British policy of the secession of Singapore from Malaysia, 26 Aug. 1965, CAB 130/239, MISC 75/6.

ness of the last-mentioned to support [British] interests elsewhere' – the paper recommended a phased withdrawal from Singapore (and Malaysia) to bases in Australia. However, as the paper made clear, a continuing British contribution to western defence arrangements in south-east Asia could only be maintained on condition that 'the economic and financial burden can be substantially reduced with the help of [Britain's] allies'.[49]

Australian policy-makers approached the talks with considerable anxiety. By now they had received hints that London was contemplating a negotiated end to *Konfrontasi* and also regarded the tenure of the Singapore base as being on a strictly short-term basis. They wondered whether the British were genuinely worried about the prospect of being forced out of Singapore or were preparing the ground for a planned withdrawal from south-east Asia.[50] Despatches from London revealed that 'the idea of "taking to the boat" was not being entirely overlooked in current British Review'.[51] Such indications, if confirmed, clearly foreshadowed a serious politico-strategic problem for Australia. A British departure from south-east Asia could destabilise Malaysia and Singapore further, and increase Indonesian influence in the region.[52] It could also have a negative impact on the United States' resolve to retain a forward military capability in south-east Asia.[53] Finally, it could create a strategic vacuum in the area at a time when Australia was under pressure to step up its involvement in the Vietnam war.[54]

Australian concerns were justified when the talks opened on 3 September.[55] The British tabled a memorandum that called for a negotiated end to *Konfrontasi* and reiterated that the separation of Singapore had had 'severe and serious implications as regards to the tenure of bases in Singapore and … Malaysia (Terendak camp and Butterworth airfield)'.[56] Even more disturbing from an Australian viewpoint was the assertion that

---

[49] Ibid.

[50] K. H. Rogers to Lewis Border, 3 Sept. 1965, NAA, A1838/346, TS3006/10/4/1 pt 1.

[51] Allan Eastman to DEA, cablegram 7037, 14 Aug. 1965, NAA, A1209/80, 1965/6595 pt 1. See also Eastman to DEA, cablegram 7230, 20 Aug. 1965, NAA, A1838/280, 3006/10/4/1 pt 2.

[52] Quadripartite talks on Malaysia and Singapore, DEA paper, 26 Aug. 1965, NAA, A1945/39, 248/10/17.

[53] British position in the Far East, DOD paper, Aug. 1965, NAA, A1838/346, TS3006/10/4/1 pt 1.

[54] For Australia's growing commitment to Vietnam see P. G. Edwards, 'Singapore and Malaysia, 1965', in Lowe, *Australia and the end of empires*, 193–4.

[55] For a record of the quadripartite discussions see FO 371/181529, IM 1193/161/G, QT(65)2nd, 7 Sept. 1965; and Edwin Hicks and Laurence McIntyre to DEA, cablegram 7674, 3 Sept. 1965, and cablegram 7756, 7 Sept. 1965, NAA, A1209/80, 1965/6595 pt 1. For an exhaustive account of the quadripartite talks see Pham, 'Suez', ch. ii.

[56] The text of the British memorandum, 'The repercussions in South East Asia of the separation of Singapore', can be found in London to DEA, cablegrams 7578, 7579, 2 Sept. 1965, NAA, A1838/346, TS3006/10/4/1 pt 1.

in the twelve months before Singapore's separation from Malaysia the British Government had been considering the long term future of the military bases in Malaysia. It was then apparent that ... the time would come when, for a variety of reasons ... there would be increasing pressure on Britain and her Commonwealth Allies to withdraw militarily from Malaysia.[57]

The memorandum also argued that 'Britain should continue, although on a reduced scale, to make a military contribution to the defence of Australasia and South East Asia'.[58]

The Australian reaction was extremely critical. John Bunting, the PMD Secretary, described the British document as 'a paper with prefabricated decisions of a kind which we would want to contest'.[59] A DEA official regarded the memorandum as 'a blueprint for disengagement rather than a basis for a common policy to maintain the Malaysian area against Indonesian aggression'.[60] On 3 September Menzies informed Wilson that the 'proposals contained in the memorandum are very far-reaching and in some ways *rather surprising*'.[61] In particular, he complained that the memorandum appeared to involve acceptance of the demands inherent in the Indonesian policy of *Konfrontasi* – namely, the break-up of Malaysia and the removal of British bases from the area. Consequently, he concluded, 'these are matters of high moment requiring Ministerial consideration on the basis of full knowledge'. On these grounds, the Australian government should 'remain uncommitted in respect of the assumptions and aims of your paper'.[62]

'A stiff-ish message', commented Oliver Wright, Wilson's Private Secretary.[63] Stiff was also the reaction of Britain's other allies – the United States and New Zealand. Wellington let the British know that there was no alternative to 'soldiering on'.[64] Washington was even more forceful. It told London that the talks had not only been 'misconceived', but also 'premature and hazardous'.[65] Samuel Berger, US Deputy Assistant Secretary of State for East Asian Affairs and American representative at the talks, told the British that their memorandum had registered 'seismic grade 8 in Washington'.[66] More important, in the hours following the end of the talks, the Deputy Secretary of State, George Ball, arrived in London to discuss American-led multi-

57 London to DEA, cablegram 7578, 2 Sept. 1965, ibid.
58 Ibid.
59 Bunting to Menzies, 3 Sept. 1965, NAA, A1209/80, 6595 pt 1.
60 Rogers to Border, 3 Sept. 1965, NAA, A1838/346, TS3006/10/4/1 pt 1.
61 Author's emphasis. Menzies to Wilson, 3 Sept. 1965, NAA, A6706/1, 6.
62 Ibid.
63 Oliver Wright to Wilson, n.d., PREM 13/431.
64 FO 371/181529, IM 1193/161/G, QT(65)2nd, 7 Sept 1965.
65 Bundy to Lyndon Johnson, 9 Sept. 1965, FRUS, 1964–68, xii, doc. 250.
66 Edward Peck to H. Rumbold, 30 Sept. 1965, FO 371/181529, IM 1193/155/G.

lateral support for sterling.[67] On 8–9 August President Johnson's emissary impressed upon Wilson that the American effort 'to relieve Sterling was inextricably related to the commitment of the United Kingdom to maintain its commitments around the world'. Although 'it took two talks' to nail Wilson down, Ball managed to extract a secret understanding whereby the British government 'agrees to the association between [American] defense of the pound and [British] overseas commitments'.[68]

The Johnson administration wanted no reductions in British military deployments east of Suez. Washington considered a continuing British presence there vital to the stability of the Indian Ocean and Malaysian regions where the United States retained no military capability. American strategic planning regarded these areas as coming under direct British responsibility: over the years the United States had come to rely on British forces there. London's military role east of Suez not only allowed the United States to give priority to the Atlantic and Pacific Ocean regions, where America's strategic and economic interests had traditionally been greater, but also made a significant contribution to western efforts to contain Communism in Asia. With America's deepening involvement in Vietnam, a continuing British presence in Asia acquired greater political value in Washington as the Johnson administration was reluctant to take up new defence commitments there. Like the Australians, the Americans feared that a British withdrawal would create a dangerous political vacuum which would be difficult and costly for the United States to fill.[69] If the West's efforts to hold back Chinese and Soviet influence in Asia were to succeed, the Johnson administration argued, the British would have to retain their worldwide commitments.[70]

Given the strength of allied opposition, the British backtracked. On 6 September Wilson informed the Cabinet that Britain would have to 'acquiesce' in not seeking an early conclusion to *Konfrontasi*. He also decided to hold off any plans for early disengagement from Singapore and Malaysia, while reiterating the need for further quadripartite consultations and increased allied burden-sharing.[71] Hence, on 7 September, British officials informed

---

[67] In August 1965 US and British officials had begun negotiations on a multilateral package (valued between US$900 million and US$1 billion) designed to support sterling. The US contribution would amount to US$ 400 million. See Joseph W. Barr to Johnson, 10 Sept. 1965, *FRUS, 1964–68*, xii, doc. 249.

[68] Bundy to Johnson, 9 Sept. 1965, ibid. doc. 250. For the Anglo-American understanding on sterling and east of Suez see Tepper, 'The dollar, the pound', ch. iii, and Pham, 'Suez', ch. ii. See also Diane Kunz, '"Somewhat mixed up together": Anglo-American defence and financial policy during the 1960s', in Robert King and Robin Kilson (eds), *The statecraft of British imperialism*, London 1999, 214–18.

[69] Tepper, 'The dollar, the pound', ch. i; Thomas Alan Schwartz, *Lyndon Johnson and Europe: in the shadow of Vietnam*, Cambridge, MA 2003, 71; Victor Kaufman, *Confronting Communism: U.S. and British policies toward China*, Columbia, MI 2001, 184.

[70] See, for instance, UK defence review, memcon, 27 Jan. 1966, *FRUS, 1964–68*, xii, doc. 255.

[71] CAB 130/239, MISC 78/1st, 6 Sept. 1965.

their ANZUS allies that Britain would not initiate any negotiations to end *Konfrontasi* and that, as long as it continued, there would be no reduction of British forces in the Malaysian area.[72] In the following weeks, British policy-makers sought to distance themselves from the views expressed in their memorandum.[73] Healey even told the Australian High Commissioner, Alexander Downer, that 'he had not seen the paper around which the Quad-ripartite Talks revolved but he knew something about it'.[74]

While 'effective in pulling the British up short on their "give away" proposals', the ANZUS countries were much less successful in changing British minds.[75] This was evident in a message sent by Wilson to Menzies in late September. In it, Wilson reiterated Britain's commitment to playing its part in defence arrangements in the Far East area, but he repeatedly returned to old ideas such as the uncertain future of the Singapore base. Wilson argued that 'time was not on our side' and that Britain 'had no intention of being forced out of Singapore in a humiliating manner'. He also informed Menzies that 'we have in the course of our current Defence Review taken into account that by 1970 we might no longer be able to count on the use of the Singapore base once the Confrontation has been ended'.[76] The import of Wilson's words was not lost on Australian policy-makers. 'There is an unrepentant and unconvinced note in Wilson's message', commented Alan Renouf, a DEA First Assistant Secretary, while, to Bunting, the message betrayed 'a policy of getting out when the getting out is good'.[77] 'We have [not] achieved anything other than a change in British tactics and presentation', argued Allan Griffith, PMD Assistant Secretary.[78] All were correct in their assessment. As the British Defence Review progressed through the final months of 1965, policy-makers in Whitehall 'continued to develop their arguments and ideas for a partial withdrawal from Singapore to Australia'. Far from being discarded, these plans remained the working assumption of the Defence Review in its final stages.[79] The momentum for disengagement was now too strong.[80]

72 Hicks and McIntyre to FAD, 3, 7 Sept. 1965, NAA, A4940/1, C4266.
73 Alexander Downer to Menzies, cablegram 7866, 10 Sept. 1965, ibid.
74 Downer to Menzies, 20 Sept. 1965, NAA, A1209/80, 1965/6595 pt 1.
75 Eastman to McIntyre, 22 Sept. 1965, NAA, A1838/346, 682/4 pt 5A.
76 CRO to Canberra, telegram 2521, 24 Sept. 1965, PREM 13/889.
77 Wilson's message to prime minister, note by Renouf, 29 Sept. 1965, NAA, A1838/346, TS3006/10/4/1 pt 1; Bunting to Menzies, 19 Oct. 1965, A1945/39, 248/10/19.
78 British presence in South-East Asia, note by Allan Griffith, 6 Oct. 1965, NAA, A1209/80, 1965/6595 pt 1.
79 Pham, 'Suez', ch. iii. See also Dockrill, *Retreat*, 129–31.
80 Subritzky, *Confronting Sukarno*, 179.

Australian policy following the quadripartite talks

Although British disengagement had been momentarily averted, concerns in Canberra over Wilson's long-term plans remained acute. In September and October 1965, the Menzies government, therefore, set out to devise the most appropriate course of action in order to stiffen Britain's resolve to stay. In October, the Defence Committee, a group of top-ranking officials advising the Minister of Defence, examined Australia's policy options.[81] It suggested that Australia's policy should be to warn the British of the serious implications of a withdrawal for the West's position in south-east Asia. Not only would withdrawal have a detrimental effect on the political and military stability of the whole area, but it would most certainly place Australia's forward defence policy in jeopardy. As if this were not disturbing enough, withdrawal could unsettle the United States at a time when the Johnson administration was showing firm resolution in the defence of south-east Asia. It could also encourage Indonesian expansionist policies and subversion throughout the area. Consequently, it was essential that Britain maintain an adequate presence in south-east Asia for as long as possible, even though this could potentially lead to a withdrawal under less favourable conditions. Members of the Defence Committee were aware, however, that efforts to induce Britain to stay would only succeed if they were backed by some form of concrete assistance. Hence, they recommended an early examination of the form of assistance that Australia could offer Britain: it could include the provision of additional Australian forces, or in some circumstances, a financial contribution towards the maintenance of the Singapore/ Malaysian bases. It could also involve Australian purchases of British civil aircraft (BAC 111 and AVRO 748). In addition, the committee stressed the importance of agreeing to contingency planning and to the examination of possible base facilities in Australia as this would 'help to convince the United Kingdom that [Australia] understands [its] problems'.[82]

On 19 October 1965 the Defence Committee's report was examined by the Cabinet's Foreign Affairs and Defence Committee (FAD), membership of which was restricted to senior Cabinet ministers.[83] While sharing the DC's view that it should be a primary objective of Australian policy to encourage

---

[81] The DC comprised the permanent heads of the DOD, the DEA, the Treasury and the PMD. It also included the chairman of the COS Committee and the three Chiefs of Staff.

[82] It should be noted, however, that the DC also emphasised that 'the development of additional facilities in Australia which could be used by United Kingdom forces is not … a satisfactory alternative to the maintenance by the United Kingdom … of a physical presence in Singapore/Malaysia for as long as possible': FAD submission 1095, 18 Oct. 1965, NAA, A1945/39, 248/10/20.

[83] This FAD was established by the Australian Cabinet in late 1963. Its aim was to handle questions of national security. With the increased instability of south-east Asia it soon took on an extremely important role within Australian policy-making.

the British to continue to play a major part in the defence of south-east Asia, ministers did not endorse its recommendations on matters such as assistance to Britain, contingency planning and bases in Australia.[84] On the latter issue the FAD 'felt that this sort of offer should be reserved until [the government] reached the stage of Ministerial consultations and entered into negotiations' with the British.[85] Ministers appeared uncertain and divided as to what course of action Australia should take in its dealings with the British. According to Peter Howson, a junior minister in the Menzies administration, ministers were split into three different schools of thought. Menzies, for instance, held the view that Britain 'needed help and encouragement to stay in Singapore as long as possible'. To this end, Australia 'should offer increased aid'. By contrast, Harold Holt, the Treasurer, and William McMahon, the Minister for Labour, thought that Britain 'was bluffing' in order to induce Australia, the United States and New Zealand to increase their burden-sharing in south-east Asia. Thus they urged that the government be 'tougher than ever with [Britain] and get [the] USA to help [Australia]'. Ultimately, according to John Gorton, Minister of Works, and Allen Fairhall, Minister for Supply, Britain was 'going to get out of Singapore in any event'. Australia, therefore, 'had better plan accordingly either to stay there with US help – or retreat to "Fortress Australia"'.[86] In the end, all ministers could agree on was to get Menzies to send a message to Wilson.[87]

Menzies's message was sent on 22 October. In it, he refuted British concerns about the viability of the Singapore base and urged Wilson to 'look towards means of staying, even in adversity'. He also called for quadripartite consultations at ministerial level.[88] His intent was clear. Menzies wished to achieve a long-standing Australian aim – the co-ordination of allied strategy in the Far East. In so doing, he hoped to tie the British to a common strategic concept by which Britain and its ANZUS allies would earmark their forces for the region. Furthermore, he sought to ensure that strong pressure would be brought to bear on the British in order to dissuade them from leaving.

Menzies's suggestion that Britain should remain in Singapore 'even in adversity' was not well received in London. Healey complained that 'it was one thing for our allies to think that we should not get out of Singapore merely to save money; it is another for them to imply that we ought to stay there ... regardless of the practical and political difficulties which will mount up against us if current trends continue'.[89] He urged Wilson 'to take [Menzies]

---

84 Cabinet decision 1330 (FAD), 19 Oct. 1965, NAA, A5821/1, vol. 4.
85 Hicks to acting minister, 23 Nov. 1965, NAA, A1945/39, 248/10/20.
86 Peter Howson, *The Howson diaries: the life of politics*, Ringwood 1984, 181, and personal communication with the author. The concept of 'Fortress Australia' postulated that Australia's military efforts should centre on the defence of the Australian mainland rather than on forward deployments in south-east Asia.
87 Cabinet decision 1330 (FAD), 19 Oct. 1965, NAA, A5821/1, vol. 4.
88 Menzies to Wilson, 22 Oct. 1965, PREM 13/889.
89 Healey to Wilson, 1 Nov. 1965, ibid.

up on this and force him to think it through'. However, Commonwealth Secretary Arthur Bottomley advised caution, warning Wilson to 'avoid coming to a premature confrontation with [Menzies] on this central issue'.[90] In the end, Wilson took Bottomley's line. In his reply to Menzies, Wilson asked the Australian leader to 'elaborate your views further to our High Commissioner'. Wilson claimed not to be 'sure what kind of circumstances you [Menzies] envisage when you express the view that we should look towards means of staying in Singapore "even in adversity"'.[91] The Australians remained steadfast. When Menzies met the British High Commissioner on 24 November, he paraphrased Churchill and said that Britain should 'plan for victory and not for defeat'. Hasluck added that the British should 'stay on until the last possible moment "and then some"'.[92]

Australian and American pressure appeared to have been effective when the Wilson government finally concluded its year-long Defence Review in January 1966. Yet, with only a few weeks remaining before the results of the review was to be made public, British policy-makers still had not tackled the difficult question of how to gain allied support for their policy for south-east Asia. They had instead continued to focus on plans for a post-*Konfrontasi* withdrawal from the area. 'In its studies and costings of Britain's projected force structure', the Ministry of Defence (MOD) still assumed that 'its Southeast Asian forces would be based in Northern Australia, with the capital cost paid by the Australian Government'.[93] This assumption operated despite evidence that – given ANZUS opposition to a withdrawal from Singapore to Australia – the British would never obtain allied support unless they were prepared to cede some ground. On 23 January, ministers on the Defence and Overseas Policy Committee (OPD) apparently changed tack and opted for a different approach. They decided that British forces would remain in Singapore for as long as the local government wished them to stay, hoping thereby to reassure the allies that Britain was not leaving Singapore. Yet, in reality, British policy was unchanged as there were no plans to hold on to Singapore indefinitely. Ministers were relying on their conviction that withdrawal would soon be forced upon them.[94] This being the case, there was no point confronting the allies over the issue of an early disengagement. In the meantime, it had to be made clear to the allies that should British forces be

---

90 Bottomley to Wilson, 9 Nov. 1965, ibid.
91 CRO to Canberra, telegram 2978, 19 Nov. 1965, ibid.
92 Canberra to CRO, telegram 1428, 24 Nov. 1965, ibid.
93 Pham, 'Suez', ch. iii. See also Easter, 'British defence policy', ch. vii.
94 The British had serious concerns that in the Singapore general election scheduled for 1968 the *Barisan Sosialis* might gain office. In that case, given their opposition to the British bases, they were likely to put an end to Britain's military presence in Singapore. London was also worried that permanent tensions between Malaysia and Singapore could lead to a situation in which it would be problematic to keep the Singapore base operational.

forced out of Singapore, they would have to return to the United Kingdom unless alternative facilities were made available in Australia.[95]

The British ploy threw the ball back into the allies' court. As a British eviction from Singapore could not be entirely ruled out, the allies were effectively put under pressure to accede to London's requests for greater burden-sharing and contingency planning as reluctance to do so would have increased the risk of an early withdrawal. Yet, the British ploy had its shortcomings. Were events to prove the British wrong, Britain would end up committed in Singapore for longer than expected. None the less, it was with this new game plan in hand that Wilson despatched his emissaries to Washington and Canberra, with Healey flying to Australia in late January 1966.

London recognised that these negotiations would not be easy. As Healey himself told the OPD, indications were that 'discussions with the Australians would be difficult'. He summarised the Australian attitude as 'a desire to keep any fighting in the Far East as far as possible from Australia, and a suspicion that [Britain] wanted Australia to finance a change in our defence posture which was not in her interest'. Consequently, Britain's aim in the talks 'should be to commit the Australians as far as we could towards joint defence arrangements ... and to urge our case upon Mr. Holt before he became further committed to other views on defence'.[96]

The Healey visit was preceded by an important change of leadership in Australia. In late January 1966 Menzies retired from politics after sixteen years in office. He was replaced on 26 January by his Treasurer, Harold Holt, who, unlike his predecessor, was much less of an anglophile. Holt was an experienced politician who had entered parliament in 1935 and had held various ministerial posts since 1949.[97] In terms of foreign and defence policy, however, he was relatively inexperienced and certainly untested. The Healey visit, therefore, could not have taken place in more demanding circumstances for the new Australian prime minister.

In view of the forthcoming talks with Healey, the Australian government had been considering the problems arising from the ongoing British Defence Review from early January. Noting that London 'seems to have accepted in principle the fact of withdrawing, with only the question of timing remaining', the Australian government became increasingly suspicious.[98] Unsurprisingly, its position hardened. In mid-January Menzies challenged Britain's 'need for an alternative posture in the Far East'. There were, he told Wilson, 'overwhelming strategic considerations why British defence bases in the Far East ... should be held where they are ... A new develop-

95 CAB 148/25, OPD(65)8th, 23 Jan. 1966.
96 Ibid.
97 Immigration (1949–56), Labour and National Service (1949–58) and Treasury (1958–66).
98 British defence review, DOD paper, 4 Jan. 1966, NAA, A1209/80, 1965/6595 pt 2.

ment of bases and facilities in Australia would be no adequate substitute for the present British defence structure in the region'.[99]

Canberra's worries were not assuaged when, a few days before Healey's arrival, the Wilson government gave the Australians an outline of the proposals the Defence Secretary intended to put before them.[100] 'We must resist the "leave Singapore" complex', Bunting urged his new prime minister.[101] His Assistant Secretary, Allan Griffith, also felt that the British proposals still indicated a desire to 'avoid being in a situation of primary commitment in South East Asia'. He noted that for Britain, 'the best way of doing this is to remove the bases from inside the area'. However, Australia's forward defence strategy required 'a continuing effective defence commitment by Britain within South East Asia against the erosion by subversion and military pressure of the Western position in the area'. Canberra, therefore, could not 'assist Britain to establish a new strategy for [the] defence of the area which abandons or makes impracticable in the course of time, legitimate allied effort for the forward defence in the region'.[102]

In seeking to understand Wilson's apparent willingness to disengage, Australian policy-makers were of course alert to Britain's financial and economic problems. They were also aware of party pressure within Labour to end the country's military commitments east of Suez. Moreover, they knew that the south-east Asian political landscape remained potentially unstable and the tenure of the Singapore base uncertain. Above all, they vividly remembered the question of a new British application to the EEC. As Griffith noted:

> Britain will most certainly look to the movement towards Europe as a source of long term opportunity. Although the subject is differently treated in public pronouncements as between the Conservative and Labour Parties, the tendency to look to Europe is bound to be very strong in British government policy councils. As part of this trend, Britain will give priority to European commitments over Far Eastern commitments. The pressure to do this are now very strong in England [sic].[103]

Here Australian officials were correct for by early 1966 the Wilson government seemed to be warming to the idea of a renewed bid to join the EEC. Griffith had earlier suggested that Australia should 'consider the thesis that Mr. Wilson is just as keen on getting a position with Europe as the Conservatives, but is using more concealed methods'. In essence he was arguing that,

---

[99] Menzies to Wilson, 19 Jan. 1966, ibid. pt 4.
[100] This outline was contained in two papers which the Australian government received on 26 January: UK defence review, HMG *aide-mémoire*, Jan. 1966; UK memorandum, Four power defence arrangements in the Indo-Pacific area, Jan. 1966, ibid.
[101] Bunting to Holt, 31 Jan. 1966, ibid. pt 3.
[102] British defence review, note by Griffith, 26 Jan. 1966, ibid.
[103] Ibid.

in planning for disengagement from the Far East, Wilson was attempting to raise his credentials as a good European with President de Gaulle. His advice therefore was clear: 'We have to achieve a real confrontation in the defence sector with British Eurocentric thinking.'[104] The Defence Committee later reached the same conclusion, recognising that it was not 'merely a question of diminution of British forces in the area'. It was 'a whole shift of approach'.[105]

On 26 January Australian senior ministers endorsed the DC's view that 'the centre of possible general war has now moved from Europe to Asia and the emergence of China will probably present the main political and military problem for the world in the next few decades'.[106] It was on this premise that policy-makers in Canberra developed their strategy. In their opinion it was in south-east Asia that Britain's military presence was most needed. Any British attempt to move forces out of the area and into Australia should be resisted. If British forces were to play a useful strategic role in SEATO and Commonwealth forward strategy, they had to remain deployed on the mainland of Asia. None the less, the FAD recognised that the government could not avoid co-operating in contingency planning against the possibility of a forced British withdrawal from the Singapore and Malaysian bases.[107] The dilemma for the Australians lay in the fact that by accepting contingency planning, Australia would facilitate a British pull-out. To avoid this, Cabinet agreed that 'any detailed contingencies studies should arise out of quadripartite discussions'.[108] In other words, it was the Australian view that contingency planning should only be 'a subsequent step to quadripartite talks and the definition of strategic objectives'.[109] The Australian aim was evident. Australia sought to encourage the British to clarify their strategic thinking and to agree on a common strategic approach for the region. The quadripartite initiative would prove a useful tool in achieving this, as it would put Britain under strong allied pressure. Only when Britain and its allies had agreed on a common strategic approach, could the issue of possible British bases in Australia be properly assessed. Then, and only then, would Australia be willing 'to involve herself further in commitments towards the security of the region'.[110]

At the end of January 1966 Healey arrived in Canberra from Washington where he and the Foreign Secretary, Michael Stewart, had secured American agreement to quadripartite arrangements, despite Washington's continuing misgivings about British intentions. The Johnson administration was

---

104 Griffith to Bunting, 19 Jan. 1966, ibid.
105 DC agendum 2/1966, 20 Jan. 1966, ibid.
106 Ibid; Cabinet decision 3(F), 26 Jan. 1966, NAA, A5839, vol. 1.
107 Cabinet decision 3(F), 26 Jan. 1966, NAA, A5839, vol. 1.
108 Cabinet decision 108 (FAD), 31 Jan. 1966, ibid.
109 DC agendum 2/1966, 20 Jan. 1966, NAA, A1209/80, 1965/6595 pt 3.
110 Cabinet decision 108 (FAD), 31 Jan. 1966, NAA, A5839, vol. 1.

concerned that, by espousing the aim of greater quadripartite coordination, the British were seeking 'as firm an institutionalised grip as they can manage on US policy in the Far East' while at the same time trying to offload some of their defence burden onto their allies.[111] Yet Washington was careful not to reject British ideas for greater allied strategic cooperation in Asia for fear that, without American strategic and financial support, the Wilson government might be encouraged to seek greater cuts to British defence forces east of Suez.[112]

In Canberra, Healey had two days of intensive talks with the Australian Cabinet and a small New Zealand delegation, led by the Minister of Defence, Dean Eyre, on 1 and 2 February. On his own admission, 'the talks were hard going at times'.[113] He began by illustrating the provisional conclusions of the Defence Review. True to his plan, Healey said that London 'entirely shared' the Australian (and American) desire to see British forces deployed 'as far north as possible' although 'there was a difference in our assessment of the possibility of being able to do so'. He went on to say that Britain had no intention of making any reduction in its forces in south-east Asia so long as *Konfrontasi* continued. Healey's presentation was a combination of reassurance and admonition. While seeking to reassure Australian ministers of Britain's resolve to remain east of Suez, he also warned them of the 'considerable amount of political opposition in both parties in England [*sic*], to our retaining forces in the Far East'. It was therefore imperative that his government be able to show that Britain's military contribution east of Suez 'was vital to an effective and collective force'. He made it clear that his country's intention was to seek 'better co-operation' with its allies. He called for greater burden-sharing as well as increased co-operation in defence planning in the Far East. In relation to the first point, Healey told the Australian Cabinet that 'Australia at present had the chance of committing two very powerful Allies to the defence of Australia for many years to come'. 'To induce them to do this', Healey continued, 'might necessitate Australia raising its expenditure on defence to a level which would in other circumstances have been reached after several years'. As for co-operation in defence planning, the Defence Secretary sought Australian consent to explore the possibility of alternative facilities on Australian soil in the event of a hasty departure from Singapore or Malaysia. He reiterated the British view that, if no alternative facilities were found, 'then our forces would have to return to the United Kingdom and it would thereafter be extremely difficult for them ever to return'.[114]

---

[111] Walt Rostow to Johnson, 20 Jan. 1966, *FRUS, 1964–68*, xii, doc. 253.

[112] On this point, as well as on American concerns about British intentions, see Pham, 'Suez', ch. iii, and Tepper, 'The dollar, the pound', ch. iv.

[113] Healey to Wilson, 3 Feb. 1966, PREM 13/889. See also Subritzky, *Confronting Sukarno*, 182–3.

[114] Defence in the Far East, memcon, 1–2 Feb. 1966, PREM 13/889.

The Australian response was guarded. McEwen 'questioned whether the basic British/Australian relationship was such that the possibility of ultimate disengagement ... was conceivable'. 'Surely', McEwen argued, 'the historic relationship between our countries was such that it was unthinkable that Britain would relinquish all further responsibility towards Australia.' The Australian government, Holt warned, 'would deprecate a British departure from the mainland of Asia'. This would in fact 'lead to the very real danger of an American withdrawal' and would also encourage 'further troubles in Asia'. Holt 'could not believe that, whatever successor Governments came to power [in Singapore and Malaysia], they would wish to eject the British since their own existence and economic well-being was largely dependent on the British bases'. In relation to burden-sharing, Holt claimed that with its defence budget already overstretched, Australia was in no position to make a larger contribution. As for the question of alternative facilities, Holt candidly confessed that 'if Australia seemed too forthcoming ... this might be interpreted as giving the United Kingdom too much incentive to leave Singapore'. 'Australia', he hastened to point out, 'was willing to make a practical contribution', but 'did not want to move in this matter except in concert with the United States'. Holt made it clear that, in relation to the defence of south-east Asia, 'decision-making would be a matter for quadripartite discussions'. In this context the Australians asked Healey 'whether there would be some talks on basic strategic concepts in Asia'. As Hasluck put it, 'having made its defence review the United Kingdom needed to rethink its contribution in Asia and its first result was the need for a co-operative effort, but this postulated broad agreement on the facts of the situation and on the aims'.[115]

In the end, Australian ministers gave some ground on the issue of alternative facilities. They accepted that 'military representatives ... should meet together, without commitment, to examine what might be involved, physically and in terms of costs and timing, in any proposal to base British forces in Australia'. In return, Healey accepted further talks whose 'primary objective ... would be to secure agreement on the strategic concept and aims for allied co-operation'.[116] The British thought that they had made good progress in easing Australian suspicions.[117] The Australians also appeared satisfied. 'We were pleased that the British would continue to maintain substantial forces in the Far East', James Plimssoll, the DEA Secretary, told the US Embassy in Canberra.[118] 'One job [in the Canberra talks]', Bunting observed, 'was to get the UK to give assurance of firm adherence to the mainland bases. This

---

115 Ibid.
116 Defence consultations, memcon, 1–2 Feb. 1966, NAA, A1209/80, 1965/6595 pt 3.
117 Healey to Wilson, 3 Feb. 1966, and Canberra to CRO, telegram 150, 2 Feb. 1966, PREM 13/889.
118 DEA to Washington, cablegram 295, 8 Feb. 1966, NAA, A1209/80, 1965/6595 pt 6.

was being achieved'.[119] 'We were', Holt wrote to Wilson in late February, 'delighted that your Government has decided firmly to maintain a global role' and 'we strongly commend your decision to remain in Singapore as long as acceptable conditions persist'.[120] That the Australians felt, at least temporarily, less apprehensive about British intentions after these talks became evident in early March when the Holt government increased Australia's commitment to Vietnam.[121] Interestingly, however, temporary Australian optimism was not shared by New Zealand. Indeed, Prime Minister Holyoake 'seemed to think that the British were bluffing with the view to getting Australia and New Zealand to foot more of the bill'.[122]

In the months following the Canberra talks, Australian policy sought to ensure that the British would not backtrack on their stated aims. To this end, throughout 1966, the Holt government made every effort to bring about quadripartite negotiations and to secure agreement on a common strategy as well as on the aims of allied co-operation in the area. Australia's task was not without difficulty. Canberra was aware that, while accepting the idea of four-power talks, the American administration was 'loath to enter into four power planning and command arrangements of the sort envisaged by the British'.[123] Given its growing involvement in Vietnam, Washington wanted to avoid shouldering Britain's defence burden in Asia.[124] The Wilson government, meanwhile, was in no hurry to commit itself to quadripartite consultations; indeed British officials 'were still finding it difficult to frame a position for the quadripartite talks that would be effective with their allies'.[125] This was not surprising as British thinking had until then focused on disengagement, rather than on working out co-operative arrangements with a view to maintaining Britain's position in south-east Asia. In these circumstances, officials in Whitehall recommended that the quadripartite talks concentrate on short-term tactics and concrete measures, such as the question of alternative facilities in Australia.[126]

---

[119] Bunting's minuted comments to DC agendum 7/1966, 17 Feb. 1966, ibid.

[120] Holt to Wilson, 25 Feb. 1966, ibid. See also Holt to Wilson, 8 Feb. 1966, PREM 13/890.

[121] Cabinet decision 60, 2 Mar. 1966, NAA, A5839, vol. 1. Cabinet agreed to replace the existing battalion group of 1,400 men with a task force of two infantry battalions, an SAS squadron, and combat and logistic support units. Eight Iroquois helicopters were also earmarked for Vietnam. In total, the Australian contribution increased to approximately 4,500 men. See Edwards, Nation at war, 93–6.

[122] Wellington to DEA, cablegram 93, 10 Feb. 1966, NAA, A1209/80, 1965/6595 pt 6.

[123] Keith Waller to DEA, cablegram 534, 14 Feb. 1966, ibid. Four-power planning and command arrangements as envisaged by the British are outlined in Four-power defence arrangements in the Indo-Pacific area, Jan. 1966, ibid. pt 4, paras 4–6.

[124] See, for instance, UK defence review, memcon, 27 Jan. 1966, FRUS, 1964–68, xii, doc. 255.

[125] Pham, 'Suez', ch. iv.

[126] Ibid.

And it was indeed on these issues that British ministers concentrated when Hasluck arrived in London in April 1966. In discussing quadripartite arrangements, British ministers informed the Australian that, at this stage, London was only seeking 'four-power discussions' and not 'four-power planning or command'.[127] As was to be expected, the British also raised the issue of alternative facilities. Healey told Hasluck that 'in seeking facilities in Australia, Britain was committed to a new stake in the Far East, despite considerable opposition to this policy both among the people of Britain and in all political parties'. For Australia, Healey warned, this was 'an opportunity which might not recur and might not last long'. Australians should be aware, Healey continued, that the British government 'was also making this commitment when other factors were leading Britain towards closer associations with Western Europe'. It is doubtful whether the British were really serious about their base proposal. As Michael Palliser, Wilson's Private Secretary at the time, has revealed in a recent interview, a base in Australia was an option that was 'studied', but never 'seriously entertained'. Healey himself has recently admitted that the base proposal 'was all part of the bullshit of negotiations'.[128] None the less, in April 1966 Healey intimated that if Australia 'did not take this opportunity to tie with [sic] Britain down there could be second thoughts and, especially in view of financial considerations, [Australia] might lose [its] opportunity to keep Britain in Asia'. Hasluck, of course, denied that his government 'was opposed to providing facilities', but stressed 'the importance of maintaining forces further north'.[129]

Healey's words were a warning to Australia. If Canberra continued to be rigid in its approach towards Britain's defence problems, it could end up facilitating, rather than averting, a British pull-out. In this respect Healey's reference to 'closer associations with Europe' was a skilful attempt to exploit Britain's renewed interest in EEC membership to urge Canberra to soften its stance. Wilson was in fact to inform the Commons on 21 April of his government's readiness to seek EEC entry provided its essential interests were safeguarded. Yet Healey's words also underlined the existence of domestic pressures on his government to reduce world commitments and join the EEC. As Wilson pointed out to President Johnson in July, 'some people in his own party and most of the press thought [the] UK should cut its world role and go in'.[130]

Chapters 6 and 7 will explore in greater detail the links between the

---

127 Hasluck to Waller, cablegram 3755, 21 Apr. 1966, NAA, A1209/80, 1965/6595 pt 6.
128 Michael Palliser and Healey, quoted in Tepper, 'The dollar, the pound', ch. iv.
129 Hasluck to Holt, cablegram 3664, 20 Apr. 1966, NAA, A1838/280, 3006/10/4/1 pt 3.
130 Department of State to posts in NATO capitals, 30 June 1966, FRUS, 1964–68, xii, doc. 266. For Australian views on the problem see G. E. Hartnell to Hicks, 25 Feb. 1966, NAA, A1945/37, 287/3/22.

Wilson government's so-called 'approach to Europe' and the east of Suez question. They will also show how Wilson's renewed interest in the EEC reinforced Australian concerns that the quest for membership would have a harmful impact on Britain's resolve to remain in south-east Asia. Canberra was worried that Britain's reorientation towards Europe could ultimately lead to what Hasluck in London referred to as a retreat 'to isolation in Europe'.[131] Here it suffices to say that, throughout 1966, the Holt government remained concerned about Britain's closer engagement with the EEC and its possible strategic fallout. Despite its scepticism about Britain's chances of overcoming French opposition to British entry, Canberra could not entirely dismiss the possibility of a successful bid. Yet, to a certain extent, the outcome of an eventual British application was beside the point. The Holt government was in fact worried that, in an all-out attempt to enter the EEC, Britain might adopt policies detrimental to the maintenance of an effective defence role east of Suez. Canberra would come to see EEC entry as entailing a heavy short-term burden on Britain's balance of payments and feared that, as a result, pressure on London to reduce defence commitments east of Suez would mount even further. Moreover, Australian policy-makers felt that, since the risk of Cold War confrontation had receded in Europe, defence reductions could and should be made in that theatre rather than in the Far East. However, as they were soon to discover, reductions of the British Army on the Rhine in Germany were not politically feasible, as the British government needed German support for its EEC application. Furthermore, fears existed – and not only in Australia – that, as a condition for entry, the French could demand that Britain abandon its role east of Suez. Australians had not forgotten that one of the reasons given by de Gaulle for his veto of the British application in 1963 was that Britain's policies were not Eurocentric enough.[132] Although these fears proved unfounded, they were none the less very real in Canberra.

Australian ministers, recognising the link between the EEC and the east of Suez questions, even went so far as to contemplate the adoption of a 'soft' approach to Britain in the event of a renewed bid for entry.[133] The possibility of trade concessions was also mooted, but in mid-1966 the Wilson government was not yet ready to apply. Sensing, however, that British thinking was shifting towards Europe, the Holt government agreed to impress upon the British the fact that their presence in south-east Asia was not 'a liability but an asset'.[134] In a visit to London in July, Holt told Wilson that Britain should not look 'inwards but towards the East'.[135] Australia did not want Britain to turn its back on 'the exciting possibilities that were arising throughout Asia

131 Hasluck to DEA, savingram 9, 21 Apr. 1966, NAA, A1945/37, 287/3/22.
132 Camps, *Britain and the Community*, 474–5.
133 See chapter 6 below.
134 Canberra to CRO, telegram 886, 22 June 1966, PREM 13/729.
135 CAB 133/329, AMV(66)3rd, 11 July 1966.

in the realm of economic development, trade and international co-operation generally'.[136] After all, Canberra was not asking London to retain 'massive troop formations in the Far East'. Wilson, for his part, played down Holt's enthusiasm for Asia. He argued that, since Britain and Australia were 'in different parts of the world', it was natural that they had 'different ways of looking at things'. None the less, he reassured Holt that Britain was not 'thinking on a basis of "scuttle" but intended to remain east of Suez' even though it might not be able to stay indefinitely.[137]

Holt claimed to be satisfied with these reassurances, yet he told Wilson that 'current British Government attitudes' did not make him 'particularly cheerful'.[138] This became obvious during his next stop, Washington. In a speech at the White House, Holt expressed disappointment that the British seemed 'so oblivious to the existence of that area of the world [i.e. Asia], almost as if they had quite deliberately turned their back upon a large part of life, history, and experience in these modern times'.[139] Although Holt was referring to the attitudes of both press and public opinion in Britain, Wilson interpreted his remarks as criticism of British policies. He immediately let Holt know that he was 'personally hurt', and instructed the British High Commissioner to approach the Australian leader as soon as he returned to Australia.[140] Holt susequently justified himself by saying that he had had no intention of criticising the Wilson government.[141]

The Holt visit to London revealed the wide gap between Australian and British aims and interests. Britain had repeatedly reassured its ANZUS allies that it was willing to remain in south-east Asia, but had never seemed particularly convincing. This was not surprising as they were a necessary element of a rather deceitful strategy to push through controversial policies. While not yet willing to forsake its role east of Suez – since doing so would have amounted to abandoning Britain's world role and imperil its global partnership with the United States – the Wilson government had nevertheless come to the conclusion that Britain had gradually to pull out of the Far East. Australian policy, on the other hand, was clearly aimed at preventing that pull-out. A British presence was seen in Canberra not only as vital to the maintenance of Australia's forward defence strategy, but also as a stabilising factor in a turbulent region. Its presence had become even more urgent since Australia had increased its involvement in Vietnam alongside the United

---

136 Holt to McEwen, cablegram 6856, 11 July 1966, NAA, A1838/1, 792/1 pt 4.
137 CAB 133/329, AMV(66)3rd, 11 July 1966.
138 Holt to McEwen, cablegram 6855, 11 July 1966, NAA, A1838/346, 682/4 pt 10; Holt to McEwen, cablegram 6856, 11 July 1966, A1838/1, 792/1 pt 4.
139 Washington to FO, telegram 2089, 15 July 1966, PREM 13/729.
140 Holt to Downer, cablegram 4335, 18 July 1966, and Downer to Holt, cablegram 7008, 15 July 1966, NAA, A1209/38, 1966/7285 pt 2.
141 Canberra to CRO, telegram 1076, 17 July 1966, and Canberra to CRO, telegram 1088, 18 July 1966, PREM 13/729.

States. While involved there, Australia could ill afford instability in the wider region.

Indochina had been yet another source of disagreements between the British and their ANZUS allies. London and Washington had agreed in early 1964 on a division of labour whereby Britain's primary strategic task in south-east Asia would be to defend Malaysia from Indonesia while the United States would seek to contain Communism in Indochina, but Wilson's refusal in 1964–5 to make even a small military contribution to the US-led war effort in Vietnam had irritated President Johnson and created problems for the Australians and New Zealanders who, as a result of Anglo-Americans differences, were forced into making a difficult choice between their two main allies.[142] Both London and Washington had sought to enlist Australasian support for their own particular strategic objectives in Malaysia and Vietnam.[143] The Labour government's resolve to avoid any military involvement in Vietnam had exposed the widening gap between Britain's strategic aims in south-east Asia and the interests of its allies, thus raising additional doubts in the ANZUS capitals about London's willingness to remain involved in the region.

Given London's evident disinclination to play a larger role in south-east Asia, Australian attempts to gain a firm British commitment to regional security had very little hope of succeeding. Predictably, in the end, no such commitment was secured despite the fact that Australian diplomacy registered some success in tackling 'the Singapore complex'. The four-power initiative and quadripartite planning, by which the Holt government had set great store in trying to elicit a common strategic concept for the Far East from the British, foundered. The British remained in Malaysia and Singapore: but for how long? With the Holt government running out of options, the task of keeping the British engaged in south-east Asia appeared increasingly difficult, and ultimately forlorn.

---

[142] John Young, 'Britain's and "LBJ" war, 1964–68', Cold War History ii (2002), 64–6; Frederik Logevall, Choosing war: the lost chance for peace and the escalation of war in Vietnam, Berkeley 1999, 373; John Dumbrell and Sylvia Ellis, 'British involvement in Vietnam peace initiatives, 1966–67: Marigolds, Sunflower and "Kosygin week"', Diplomatic History xxvii (2003), 117–18; Subritzky, Confronting Sukarno, 190, 198; Dockrill, Retreat, 107.
[143] Subritzky, Confronting Sukarno, 190.

5

The East of Suez Crisis, 1966–1968

'Tell Holt ... he must trust us more. ... We will always look after you. You don't need undertakings from us signed on the dotted line. We won't let you down': George Brown, 3 May 1967.[1]

On 30 June 1966, two weeks before Holt visited London, the foreign ministers of Australia, Britain, the United States and New Zealand met in Canberra for what the Australian government hoped would be the first round of quadripartite talks on Far Eastern strategy.[2] Australia had set great store by the quadripartite initiative as a means of achieving a common strategic approach to Far Eastern defence; through it, it hoped to commit Britain more firmly to regional security. The goal of the talks, as Paul Hasluck, the Minister for External Affairs, put it, was to ensure that the four powers would all be 'going in the same direction and be of the same mind'.[3] Hasluck's aims were to be frustrated. The British Foreign Secretary, Michael Stewart, remained elusive as to the real nature of British strategic objectives in the area.[4] He reiterated his government's willingness to remain in Singapore and Malaysia for as long as possible and pledged that Britain would keep significant forces in south-east Asia once *Konfrontasi* ended. Yet he was quick to emphasise that the forces that would be redeployed from Eastern Malaysia at the end of *Konfrontasi* 'were not a complete bonus' – implying that they were unlikely to be used elsewhere outside the Malaysian area (i.e. in Indochina), and that some of them would be brought home.[5] Stewart also told his allies that 'an invitation to depart would of course be an ideal solution if it could be done securely'.[6] Hasluck objected to this, making it clear that 'it would be undesirable simply to remain acquiescent until asked to go'. It was, Hasluck added, 'for the British, Australian and New Zealand Governments to make

---

[1] As quoted in Downer to Holt, cablegram 5326, 3 May 1967, NAA, A1209/80, 1966/7335 pt 3.
[2] The Canberra meeting was followed by further quadripartite discussions in London in October 1966. These talks, at officials' level, ended inconclusively and were the last attempt to hold such talks: NAA, A1945/37, 82/1/37.
[3] Quadripartite talks, DEA note, 30 June 1966, NAA, A4940/1, C4266.
[4] Ibid.; memcon, quadripartite ministerial discussions, 30 June 1966, TNA, DO 169/470; memcon, quadripartite discussions, 30 June 1966, in *Foreign relations of the United States, 1964–68*, XXVII: *Mainland Southeast Asia: regional affairs*, Washington 2000, doc. 17.
[5] Memcon, quadripartite discussions, 30 June 1966, DO 169/470.
[6] Quadripartite talks, DEA note, 30 June 1966, NAA, A4940/1, C4266.

it their business to stay as long as possible and to try to create conditions in which they would be able to do so'.[7]

Sensing the widespread scepticism with which British long-term intentions would be received in Australia, Stewart had sought guidance from London on 26 June with a view to giving robust reassurance to Australia.[8] Ministers on the OPD agreed that Stewart should make a positive statement.[9] They argued that the prospect of Britain having to come to the rescue of Australia or New Zealand in the face of an external attack was 'unlikely'.[10] An assurance of this kind, therefore, 'could well facilitate our policy of major withdrawals of forces from the theatre'.[11] Intended as a rather innocuous means of dispelling Australian concerns, such a statement could none the less backfire. While offering seemingly stronger reassurance, the British were in fact leaving the door open for further force reductions, which would undermine Australia's defence policy. This clearly laid Britain open to a charge of untrustworthiness, if not outright dishonesty. Yet, on 30 June – a few hours after the end of the quadripartite talks – Stewart none the less declared in an address to the Australian Institute of International Affairs that

> there might even be people in Australia who have so misread the implications of the Defence Review, the ending of confrontation, and the possibility of our leaving Singapore, that they believe that if it came to the crunch we would let Australia down. But just as Australia and New Zealand came to the help of Great Britain in two world wars so it is unthinkable that if Australia and New Zealand were the victims of aggression Great Britain would not simply come to their assistance. This is not a matter of treaties or legal obligations. It is simply unthinkable that the British Government or people would act otherwise.[12]

'This', David Goldsworthy points out, 'was intended to be a statement of some significance.' Yet 'it failed to mollify Holt and his colleagues. The guarantee that they wanted was not a British expeditionary force, but a British regional presence'.[13] On 1 July Hasluck told the US Secretary of State, Dean Rusk, and the prime minister of New Zealand, Keith Holyoake that 'Stewart seemed under the impression that assurances that Britain would come to Australia's help made Australians happy'. If that were the case, Hasluck continued, 'Stewart was a little behind the times in telling an Australian public audience that Australia need not fear because Britain would always be with her'. In fact, 'if Australia were threatened', Hasluck contended, 'the

---

7 Memcon, quadripartite discussions, 30 June 1966, DO 169/470.
8 Crawford MacLehose to Palliser, telegram 915, 26 June 1966, ibid.
9 CAB 148/25, OPD(66)30th, 29 June 1966; Palliser to MacLehose, telegram 1889, 29 June 1966, DO 169/470.
10 CAB 148/25, OPD(66)30th, 29 June 1966.
11 Ibid.
12 Stewart to Australian Institute of International Affairs, 30 June 1966, DO 169/470.
13 Goldsworthy, Losing the blanket, 166.

scale of the British support which would be available would not make it a major factor in Australia's thinking. ANZUS and our confidence in it were the keystone of our continental security'.[14]

ANZUS had indeed assumed a central role in Australia's defence thinking: by the end of the 1950s Australia's primary strategic alliance was with the United States. Moreover, relations between Canberra and Washington had strengthened since the early 1960s. Concerns over Britain's willingness to remain in south-east Asia had certainly 'accelerated the process of closer Australian-US relations', but of even greater import was the Vietnam war.[15] The commitment of Australian troops to Vietnam by the Menzies and Holt governments between 1965 and 1966 had been undertaken with the decided intention of inducing Washington to maintain a military presence in south-east Asia.[16] As the Foreign Affairs and Defence Committee put it in January 1966, 'the vital thing for Australia was to have the United States remain in the area and everything else must be measured against this'.[17] Securing an American military commitment to the mainland of south-east Asia had been a long-standing goal of Australian post-war diplomacy and Cold War strategy. This was an important objective *per se* – quite independent of British actions and intentions in the area. However, it was incontestable that, to a certain extent, Australian involvement in Vietnam was also related to the growing uncertainty surrounding British plans. In this context it is not surprising that throughout 1966 Canberra had aligned itself more closely with Washington. The two visits made by Holt to Washington in June and July, and the visit of President Johnson to Australia in the autumn of 1966, further strengthened American-Australian relations. Holt played no inconsiderable part in aligning Australia more closely with the United States. It was he who, paraphrasing the Democratic Party's 1964 presidential campaign slogan, declared during his July 1966 address to the White House that Australia would go 'all the way with LBJ' – a catchphrase which, in Australian political life, soon became a byword for close and unwavering alignment with Washington. Holt's close relationship with Johnson was to be the defining feature of his short premiership. As Holt told the British High Commissioner, while 'he felt personally far closer to Harold Wilson', 'Johnson probably means more to me and my country'.[18]

[14] ANZUS council meeting, DEA note, 1 July 1966, NAA, A4940/1, C4266.
[15] Pemberton, *All the way*, 331.
[16] For Australia's involvement in Vietnam see ibid. chs x–xi; Edwards with Pemberton, *Crises and commitments*, ch. xviii; and Edwards, *Nation at war*, chs iii–iv.
[17] Cabinet decision 33 (FAD), 30 May 1966, NAA, A5839, vol. 1.
[18] Johnston to Pritchard, 8 Nov. 1966, DO 169/471.

Britain announces withdrawal

While veering towards Washington, Holt continued to urge London to
remain in south-east Asia. However, unforeseen economic developments
in Britain were soon to add a new momentum to the east of Suez question and would ultimately lead to a British withdrawal. In early July 1966
the position of sterling became increasingly untenable following a further
deterioration in the British economy. As speculative pressure mounted,
the pound plunged. On 12 July it reached its lowest level since November
1964.[19] Resolved to avoid devaluation at all costs, Wilson announced a set
of economic measures on 20 July that the *Economist* described as 'perhaps
the biggest deflationary package that any advanced industrial nation had
imposed on itself since Keynesian economics began'. Public expenditure was
to be reduced by £500 million, with the government's axe falling heavily
on defence. Wilson's package included cuts in overseas military and civil
expenditure of at least £100 million in the fiscal year 1967–8.[20] To this end,
Wilson instructed Healey to seek the largest possible troop reductions in
south-east Asia.[21] With *Konfrontasi* drawing to a close, the Indonesian threat
receded, removing the *raison d'être* for the large British military presence in
the Malaysian region. London was finally free to plan for the redeployment
of British forces. Thus, when the Indonesian-Malaysian conflict ended in
August 1966, Healey was able to declare that about 10,000 troops would
be withdrawn from Borneo. In October he announced that most of the rest
would be home by April 1967.[22]

Although it did not immediately bring about any major change of policy,
the sterling crisis was a 'significant turning point' in the east of Suez question,[23] for it would eventually spark a critical reassessment of Britain's overseas commitments.[24] In the short term, however, the currency crisis led
the economic departments in Whitehall, and the Treasury in particular,
to become more forceful in demanding lower defence expenditure. The
Treasury was alarmed at the government's inability to curb public spending,
seeing it as undermining attempts to bring the balance of payments under
control.[25] In August, therefore, the Chancellor of the Exchequer, James
Callaghan, began to press for additional defence cuts: the defence budget
would have to be reduced to a new ceiling of £1,850 million by 1970–1,
from the earlier ceiling of £2,000 million by 1969–70. As this figure had

---

[19] For the July sterling crisis see Ben Pimlott, *Harold Wilson*, London 1992, 408–26, and
Kenneth Morgan, *Callaghan: a life*, Oxford 1997, 240–1.
[20] Britain, *PD HC*, 1966–7, dccxxxii.631–2; *Economist*, 23 July 1966.
[21] Dockrill, *Retreat*, 164.
[22] Britain, *PD, HC*, 1966–7, dccxxxiii.437; dccxxxiv.208.
[23] Pham, 'Suez', ch. iv.
[24] Pickering, *Withdrawal*, 152.
[25] Pham, 'Suez', ch. iv.

not yet been reached, the meeting of the new budget target meant cuts of £200–300 million by 1970–1.[26] Under pressure from the Treasury, senior ministers agreed in autumn 1966 to initiate a new Defence Review.[27] On 9 December the OPD discussed a joint memorandum by the Defence and Foreign Secretaries recommending that further studies be carried out on the premise of a 50 per cent force reduction in the Far East and a one-third cut-back in BAOR strength in Europe.[28] Both Healey and George Brown, Michael Stewart's successor at the Foreign Office, were seeking to implement the additional defence cuts demanded by the Treasury without relinquishing any Far Eastern commitments. Healey told the OPD that the government should 'exclude a total withdrawal' since 'such a withdrawal was not … politically practicable in the period in question'. The Defence Secretary was well aware of allied hostility to total withdrawal. The Brown-Healey memorandum, however, was received with scepticism. Callaghan and Richard Crossman, Lord President of the Council, questioned how the government could really achieve savings of £200–300 million without abandoning Far Eastern commitments. In the end, the OPD endorsed the memorandum, but also commissioned 'a full study of the political and military implications of a total withdrawal from the Far East'. Given the controversial nature of such a study, OPD ministers agreed to keep the progress of the new Defence Review secret;[29] Britain's allies were to be kept in the dark.

From January 1967 the Defence Review Working Party sought to find the necessary savings as indicated in the OPD terms of reference. It soon realised that the Far East was the only theatre where significant economies could be made.[30] Yet even a 50 per cent reduction in British forces in the Far East resulted in estimated savings of no more than £100–125 million.[31] Unless ministers were ready to contemplate a complete withdrawal from the Far East, savings would fall far short of the £200–300 million target set by the Treasury. Even then, the DRWP argued, savings were expected to increase only by £20 million in 1970–1, although they would be more substantial subsequently.[32]

While officials in the DRWP were secretly working on the review, pressure was mounting within the Labour Party for a radical overhaul of British policy east of Suez. In October 1966 the Labour Party Conference had endorsed a resolution calling for a complete withdrawal from the region by 1969–70.

---

[26] Dockrill, *Retreat*, 172.

[27] Pham, 'Suez', ch. iv; Dockrill, *Retreat*, 173–4.

[28] The Brown-Healey proposal also included force reductions in the Persian Gulf and cuts in supporting forces and facilities in Britain: CAB 148/25, OPD(66)48th, 9 Dec. 1966.

[29] Ibid.

[30] Dockrill, *Retreat*, 179–80. The DRWP was a subcommittee of the Defence and Overseas Policy Committee (Official).

[31] CAB 148/31, OPD(67)22, 20 Mar. 1967.

[32] CAB, 148/55, OPDO(DR)9th, 24 Feb. 1967.

The following February a new Defence White Paper met with considerable opposition from within the ranks of the Parliamentary Labour Party. Pending the completion of the secret Defence Review, the White Paper was 'essentially a progress report' on reductions implemented in 1966.[33] On 28 February, disgruntled that the White Paper contained no defence cuts, sixty-two Labour backbenchers revolted against their government's defence policy and abstained from the vote. In the end, the White Paper was approved in the Commons by a slim majority of thirty-nine votes. This incident 'was the largest demonstration of dissent since the government had taken office in 1964'.[34]

Under pressure from within their own party, and faced with the knowledge that the Defence Review was not finding the means for the necessary savings, ministers began to accept the inevitability of a withdrawal from east of Suez.[35] On 22 March ministers on the OPD examined the DRWP's interim report on the Defence Review. Drawing on its main conclusions, Healey argued that, if further savings of the order of £200–300 million were to be achieved, the government should contemplate a drastic contraction of commitments in the Far East. This would not only entail a 50 per cent force reduction by 1970–1 as originally planned, it would also involve, Healey explained, 'withdrawing our forces wholly from Singapore and Malaysia by 1975–6 and maintaining only a minimum military presence (consisting of naval and air forces) in the Far East based in Australia'. The OPD was in agreement. In summing up, however, Wilson introduced two *caveats*. First, his government would leave the door open to an 'earlier withdrawal if political events made this feasible'. Second, while seeking to retain a minimum military presence in Australia, the government would not be bound to such an undertaking. In other words, the retention of a military presence in Australia would not preclude 'the possibility of the Government deciding in June or July, after the initial series of consultations with our allies, that we should withdraw wholly from this area, while still honouring our obligation to assist Australia and New Zealand in the event of their being attacked'.[36]

The OPD conclusions were brought to the Cabinet for approval.[37] On 11 April the Commonwealth Secretary, Herbert Bowden, warned Cabinet against so sudden a reversal of policy. In a memorandum he argued that it would have a grave effect on Britain's Commonwealth partners in the Far East. Australia and New Zealand, for instance, would face 'major readjust-

---

[33] Healey quoted in CAB 128/42, CC(67)6th, 3 Feb. 1967.

[34] Harold Wilson, *The Labour Government, 1964–70: a personal record*, Harmondsworth 1974, 483.

[35] For the role of the various ministers in the formulation of Britain's defence policy in early 1967 see Dockrill, *Retreat*, 178–85; Pham, 'Suez', ch. v; and Jones, 'Decision delayed', 585–7.

[36] CAB 148/30, OPD(67)14th, 22 Mar. 1967.

[37] CAB 129/128, C(67)40, 31 Mar. 1967.

ments in the disposition and possibly the shape of their own forces'. As for Malaysia and Singapore, the total withdrawal of British forces from the region would not only entail a radical overhaul of their defences, but would also impose significant strains on their economies. Britain's withdrawal was expected to have a particularly serious impact on Singapore, the prosperity of which appeared to depend on the economic activity generated by the presence of large British military installations.[38] The Commonwealth Secretary advocated a more cautious course of action which would involve a reduction of British forces 'to about half their present level' by 1970, while leaving open a decision on the date of an eventual withdrawal.[39] However, with several ministers remonstrating that 'the cuts [agreed at OPD level] were not radical enough', Bowden's pleas fell on deaf ears.[40] Cabinet agreed to begin consultations with the allies on the basis of the OPD's conclusions. To this end, Brown would go to Washington for a SEATO meeting where he would break the news to the ANZUS countries. Healey would fly to Kuala Lumpur and Singapore for consultations with the local governments. Once these were concluded, Cabinet would take a final decision in June or July.[41]

Despite leaving the door open to the retention of a minimum military presence in Australia, the government's decisions of March–April 1967 effectively spelled the end of Britain's role east of Suez. Less than three years after taking office, the Wilson government had accomplished a significant reversal of policy. Cabinet's decision was influenced by various factors. The 1966 sterling crisis and the end of *Konfrontasi* clearly provided the economic and political context for further defence cuts in the Far East.[42] However, the defence cuts demanded by the Treasury soon proved unattainable without a more radical course of action. A 50 per cent reduction in the Far East force would not only fail to produce the necessary savings, but would also drastically impair the effectiveness of British forces there. In these circumstances, and under party pressure, Labour ministers opted for a radical contraction of south-east Asian commitments.[43] Another factor was Wilson's 'approach to Europe'.

---

[38] CAB 129/128, C(67)41, 31 Mar. 1967. Singapore's future was not, however, as grim as it looked. As Hack has noted, investment was pouring in from Japan and Hong Kong and the 'war boom' effect of American aid to South Vietnam was seeping through: *Defence and decolonisation*, 286.

[39] CAB 128/42, CC(67)19th, 11 Apr. 1967.

[40] Richard Crossman, *The diaries of a cabinet minister*, II: *Lord President of the Council and leader of the House of Commons, 1966–68*, London 1976, 308.

[41] CAB 128/42, CC(67)19th, 11 Apr. 1967.

[42] Darby, *British defence policy*, 313; Reynolds, *Britannia overruled*, 229–30.

[43] Pham, 'Suez', chs iv–v; Dockrill, *Retreat*, 178–90.

Australian policy and the British withdrawal

Predictably, Canberra's reaction to British plans was one of 'shock' and 'consternation'.[44] Australian distress was compounded by the fact that, as recently as February 1967, Bowden had reaffirmed Britain's intention to maintain a military presence in Malaysia and Singapore for some time to come.[45] In Washington, Hasluck conveyed Australia's deep disappointment to the British Foreign Secretary. He gave Brown a long list of reasons why Britain was wrong to contemplate total withdrawal.[46] He argued that withdrawal would not only have a negative impact on Anglo-Australian relations, it would also harm Britain's special ties with the United States, weaken its standing in the world, damage its trade with Asia and undermine regional security.[47] Brown found the Australian minister 'harder than any of the others' (i.e. Rusk and Holyoake) and gained the impression that Hasluck was seeking 'to organise them against us'.[48] He counselled the Australian government not to 'react too hastily or too violently'. If Canberra took a strong and uncompromising line, Brown warned, those elements in Cabinet calling for a complete withdrawal 'would triumph'.[49] On his return to London, he reported to the Cabinet that 'opposition to our plans in the area generally had stiffened following consultations between our three allies, particularly because of the attitude of the Australians'.[50]

The British High Commissioner in Canberra reported that Holt looked 'badly shaken' and 'profoundly upset'.[51] The Australian prime minster wrote to Wilson on 21 April that he was 'gravely troubled' by what Hasluck had told him. Holt believed that Britain was on the verge of 'making an error which history would condemn'. He urged Wilson 'to consider the course [to which] ... you appear to be committing yourself' and to make sure that 'whatever reduction you make in your military forces east of Suez, it should be neither intended by you, nor publicly presented, as a final withdrawal'.[52] Holt's message was delivered personally by High Commissioner Downer to Wilson's private secretary, Michael Palliser. He found Downer 'in a distinctly emotional condition'. The High Commissioner was critical of the British attitude since it seemed 'to represent an abandonment of the numerous and firm undertakings given in the past to the Australian government'. He warned that the decision to withdraw 'would produce a very strong reaction

---

44 Canberra to CO, telegram 635, 21 Apr. 1967, FCO 24/51.
45 Herbert Bowden and Australian Cabinet, memcon, 22 Feb. 1967, FCO 24/5.
46 Brown and Hasluck, memcon, 19 Apr. 1967, PREM 13/1455.
47 Hasluck to Holt, cablegram 1585, 21 Apr. 1966, NAA, A1838/80, 1966/7335 pt 2.
48 Washington to FO, telegram 1277, 19 Apr. 1967, and Washington to FO, telegram 1269, 19 Apr. 1967, FCO 24/51.
49 Hasluck to Holt, cablegram 1585, 21 Apr. 1966, NAA, A1838/80, 1966/7335 pt 2.
50 CAB 128/42, CC(67)23rd, 27 Apr. 1967.
51 Johnston to CO, telegram 636, 21 Apr. 1967, PREM 13/1384.
52 Holt to Wilson, 21 Apr. 1967, PREM 13/1455.

throughout Australia, particularly in view of its timing'. In fact, according to Downer,

> if it were publicly declared at a time when Australia and New Zealand were becoming ever more deeply involved in the Vietnam war and Britain for [its] part was apparently seeking not only to abandon [its] Far Eastern commitments but also to join the Common Market ... it would be catastrophic for Anglo-Australian relations and would make inevitable the break up of the Commonwealth itself.[53]

Indeed, the decision to withdraw, coupled with Britain's application to the EEC, dealt a severe blow to Anglo-Australian relations. Both were perceived in Canberra as a determined effort on the part of the Wilson government to reorient British policies towards Europe. Policy-makers in Canberra took the view that the British application had paved the way for the decision to pull out of the Far East. In their eyes, while not directly causing it, the EEC application certainly reinforced the decision of the British Cabinet to withdraw and was providing a rationale for sticking to it. From London, Tom Critchley, the Senior External Affairs Representative, commented that the EEC bid 'gives additional ammunition to those pressing for withdrawal'.[54]

In May 1967 the Holt government set out to devise a strategy aimed at reversing some aspects of the British decision to withdraw. To this end, Canberra was careful to avoid confrontation on the EEC issue and gave priority to what it regarded as the most pressing question – defence. Ministers thought it unwise to open up a 'second front' on the EEC issue as doing so could irritate British sensitivities in a manner which would be detrimental to 'the fundamental defence issue'.[55] Australian policy-makers were mindful of the difficult task confronting Australian diplomacy. 'The British are preoccupied with Europe and ... there is little concern about South-East Asia', the High Commission in London reported.[56] Canberra recognised that, regardless of London's claims to the contrary, 'present British proposals ... appear to be virtually decisions'. Australian policy-makers thought it 'necessary to present a well argued and persuasive case' if these proposals were to be reversed.[57]

In a working paper the DEA argued that, by simply urging the British to

---

[53] Palliser to Wilson, 21 Apr. 1967, ibid.

[54] Critchley to DEA, cablegram 5660, 9 May 1967, NAA, A1838/346, TS691/1/1 pt 1. It is noteworthy that until 1972, when its control passed to the Department of Foreign Affairs (formerly the Department of External Affairs), the London High Commission was under the PMD's political and administrative control. Between 1954 and 1969 the DEA maintained its own separate 'political channel' (also known as the External Affairs Office) within the High Commission. The officer in charge, the Senior External Affairs Representative, reported to the DEA.

[55] Peter Lawler to Holt, 27 Apr. 1967, NAA, A1209/43, 1967/7117 pt 2.

[56] Tom Critchley to DEA, cablegram 4804, 24 Apr. 1967, NAA, A1838/346, TS691/1/1 pt 1.

[57] FAD submission 283, 25 May 1967, NAA, A5619/1, C22 pt 1.

refrain from long-term decisions, Australia would 'leave the field to those who want to "pull out" from [sic] South East Asia'. Holt would need 'an alternative which offers the British a realistic and convincing role and which presents the British future in South East Asia in a politically attractive light within Britain'. But what alternative? Officials in the DEA thought that 'the future British role' could be 'presented as ... a modern and acceptable development from the imperial past, as a more limited and constructive role ... and a lesser burden and larger partnership with the Commonwealth countries'. In this, of course, there was an element of wishful thinking as Holt had already deployed similar arguments with no tangible result during his visit to London in July 1966. Yet External Affairs officials were aware that 'much more is needed than persuasion' and that the government also needed to 'press actual policies'. To this end they devised an action plan, the main points of which were: first, an insistence that the British 'drop their plans for total withdrawal by 1975'; second, an agreement on British 'reductions to [a] strength of 40,000 by 1970/71 and even below'; and third, an offer 'to maintain [Australia's] own contribution in full' and acceptance of 'additional burdens arising from the withdrawal of British support'. DEA officials argued that no one was asking Britain to maintain 'a vast and impressive military establishment' in south-east Asia – 'that belongs to history'. What Canberra was seeking was 'a British military presence sufficient to make it feasible for us to maintain our own forces in the theatre'. Australian policies and relationships in the region had in fact been developed on the basis of a British politico-military presence. This, however, was 'bound to change' and, as Australia was 'a growing Power', Canberra should strive to 'consolidate its position in other directions'. This would 'need time, and careful political handling'. Meanwhile, Australia's interest lay in ensuring that south-east Asia remained stable, which in turn required that a continuing, if much reduced, British presence be maintained in the area.[58]

Most of these arguments were included in a Defence Committee report submitted to the FAD on 25 May 1967. In particular, the committee advised ministers to urge Britain 'to retain the Commonwealth Brigade in Malaysia/Singapore as close as possible to its present form until 1970, and as long as possible thereafter' whilst also accepting 'in principle the need to retain indefinitely after 1970 British Armed forces'.[59] The DC had in fact ruled out the possibility that Australia 'could argue successfully against the British aim to reduce a further 50% by April 1970 or at the latest by April 1971'.[60] To induce the British to alter their proposals, the committee recommended that ministers present a well-argued and persuasive case to the British along

---

[58] Australian policy on British defence policy east of Suez, DEA working paper, 19 May 1967, NAA, A1838/346, TS3006/10/4/1 pt 3.
[59] FAD submission 283, 25 May 1967, NAA, A5619/1, C22 pt 1.
[60] Ibid. See also meeting of the Defence Committee, British defence policy east of Suez, 17 May 1967, NAA, A1838/346, TS3006/10/4/1 pt 3.

the lines seen in the DEA working paper. In spite of Treasury opposition, ministers should ensure that the British understood Australia's 'willingness to continue and possibly increase [its] own contribution' to Malaysia and Singapore.[61] However, it would not be possible for 'a country of Australia's size to underwrite alone the security of Malaysia/Singapore' – indeed Australia 'could not contemplate taking over the United Kingdom's treaty and defence responsibilities'.[62]

The FAD agreed that 'the central objective of Australian policy is to secure a continuing British commitment to the Malaysian region'. Consequently, in his forthcoming visit to London, the prime minister should seek 'to affect the British Government's mind on the long term position – that is, after 1970/71 – rather than allow the discussion to concentrate itself on the detail of the reduction of British forces in the short and medium terms'. To put this strategy into effect, the FAD suggested that Holt employ a variety of political, strategic and economic arguments to impress upon the British the importance of remaining in south-east Asia. He should stress 'the developing economic significance of Asia' for British interests; and he should invite the British to consider the consequences of withdrawal from the area for their world position as well as for their special relationship with the United States. He should also emphasise the fact that withdrawal would undermine the West's regional strategic interests. Finally, he should make it clear 'that any final decision by the British Government to withdraw from South-East Asia would have [such] fundamental and far reaching consequences for Australia's external position as to require the re-casting of Australian external policy in fundamental terms'. Contrary to the advice of the Defence Committee, the FAD avoided, for the time being, taking any decision on the continuance, or even increase, of Australia's military contribution to the defence of the Malaysian area. Instead, senior ministers felt that, should London decide to withdraw by the mid-1970s, the government should concentrate on a fall-back position designed 'to have all announcement of such a decision withheld'. The FAD concluded that, if the British did choose to withdraw, it would not necessarily be in Australia's best interests 'to have the British established in Australia'. Therefore, 'any commitment by Australia to make financial contributions towards the establishment of British bases in Australia should not be assumed'.[63]

Holt flew to London in mid-June with this brief. On his way he stopped in Washington for talks with the Johnson administration, and received fresh

---

[61] Ibid. For possible ways in which Australia could increase its contribution see FAD submission 283, 25 May 1967, NAA, A5619/1, C22 pt 1.

[62] Ibid. Britain's treaty responsibilities were those laid down in AMDA. See chapter 3 above.

[63] Cabinet decision 357 (FAD), 25 May 1967, NAA, A5840/XM1, vol. 2.

assurances as to the strength of American opposition to British plans.[64] Since April 1967 Canberra had relied on the administration to influence the British. In May the DEA had instructed Keith Waller, the Australian ambassador in Washington, to impress upon the Americans the importance of their role in seeking to secure a revision of British plans.[65] On this point, however, the Americans needed very little prodding. Since Brown's visit to Washington in late April, the Americans had wasted no time in conveying to London their displeasure at his plans. In talks with Wilson in Bonn on 28 April, President Johnson openly asked the British prime minister whether the British were 'going crazy' in their insistence on a withdrawal from south-east Asia at a time when Britain's ANZUS allies were fighting in Vietnam.[66] A few days later, the American ambassador to London, David Bruce, launched into an angry outburst over the issue, telling George Brown that

> the appearance of our being deserted ... in the midst of our Vietnamese involvement, by a Government assumed to be our most reliable ally, headed by a Prime Minister who had repeatedly declared himself an 'East of Suez Man' was unwise, provocative, and absolutely unacceptable.[67]

While more restrained, Dean Rusk was no less critical, complaining to Brown in mid-May that a British withdrawal would not only have 'devastating repercussions in all kinds of directions', but would also 'strike at the very basis of our whole post-war foreign policy'.[68] As the United States was increasingly drawn into a costly and unpopular commitment in Vietnam, the administration was willing neither to shoulder new military commitments in south-east Asia, nor to be seen domestically to be playing the role of the lone world policeman.

While relying primarily on American pressure, the Holt government had also sought to concert its actions with those Commonwealth allies – New Zealand, Singapore and Malaysia – who would be directly affected by British plans. In particular, Canberra had sought to stiffen Malaysian and Singaporean resolve to oppose Britain's withdrawal.[69] Australia had in fact regarded

---

[64] Washington to DEA, cablegram 2354, 2 June 1967, NAA, A1209/80, 1966/7335 pt 4A. See also McGeorge Bundy to Johnson, 1 June 1967, *FRUS, 1964–68*, xxvii, doc. 24. For earlier reassurances see Washington to DEA, cablegram 1804, 2 May 1967, NAA, A1838/346, TS691/1/1 pt 1.

[65] DEA to Keith Waller, cablegram 1371, 2 May 1967, NAA, A1838/346, TS691/1/1 pt 1.

[66] Palliser to MacLehose, 28 Apr. 1967, PREM 13/1455.

[67] Bruce quoted in Jonathan Coleman, 'The London ambassadorship of David K. E. Bruce during the Wilson-Johnson years, 1964–68', *Diplomacy and Statecraft* xv (2004), 344.

[68] Rusk to Brown, 12 May 1967, PREM 13/1455; Pham, 'Suez', ch. v; Tepper, 'The dollar, the pound', ch. v.

[69] See, for instance, Eastman to DEA, cablegram 1166, 3 May 1967, and Singapore to DEA, cablegram 808, 4 May 1967, NAA, A1838/346, TS691/1/1 pt 1.

the lack of a strong reaction in Singapore and Malaysia with concern. When Healey visited the two south-east Asian countries in late April, he was not subjected to the barrage of criticism that Brown had endured in Washington. The Singaporean authorities appeared less worried by the proposed troop reductions than by the announcement of withdrawal. They feared that if plans for withdrawal were made public, Singapore's viability as a city state could be seriously undermined. Across the Causeway, the Malaysian government appeared even less troubled, and expressed no opposition in principle to a British withdrawal in the mid-1970s. As long as London did not make 'too much noise about it' and stood by AMDA, Kuala Lumpur would not oppose Britain's timetable for disengagement.[70]

In London, Holt pleaded Australia's case along the lines agreed by ministers in Canberra. He emphasised the importance of a continued British presence to regional security, to western interests in the area and to London's global partnership with the United States. '[A] continuing British presence, however small', he declared, 'would have a disproportionate value in this context'. Not holding entirely to his predetermined brief, Holt queried whether the cost of a British presence could not be 'shared with some of the Commonwealth countries, including Australia'. He also hinted at the possibility that, once the Vietnam war was over, 'Australia and the others might be able to do considerably more themselves'. He stressed that withdrawal would have a 'shattering effect' on Britain's relations with Australia and the other Commonwealth allies, and also reminded the British of the various assurances that Britain had given to Australia since 1965.[71]

During his first meeting with Wilson, Holt also discussed Britain's plans to halve its forces in south-east Asia by 1970–1. In accordance with his brief, Holt did not question these plans, telling Wilson that he did not intend to 'twist the British arm', and that he 'sympathised with Britain's problem'.[72] Instead, he asked Wilson to maintain the British contingent in the Commonwealth Brigade up to 1970–1 'even if substantial modifications in supply or logistics might be required'.[73] He also urged Wilson to refrain from either taking or announcing a final decision to withdraw, while accepting the fact that British contingency planning might include withdrawal among various possibilities.[74] The Australians were assured that no final decision had yet

---

[70] Singapore to CO, telegram 196, 23 Apr. 1967, and telegram 200, 24 Apr. 1967, FCO 24/23; Kuala Lumpur to CO, telegram 411, 26 Apr. 1967, FCO 24/23, and Kuala Lumpur to CO, telegram 430, 1 May 1967, FCO 24/24. See also Pham, 'Suez', ch. vi.

[71] Wilson and Holt, memcon, 13 June 1967, PREM 13/1323.

[72] Ibid.

[73] Ibid. The Commonwealth Brigade included a battalion from Britain, Australia and New Zealand, with British supporting units. It was stationed at Terendak, Malaysia. In 1967 it comprised 1,100 Australian, 700 New Zealand and 2,400 British troops: Healey, Holt and Allen Fairhall, memcon, 14 Jan. 1967, ibid.

[74] Wilson and Holt, memcon, 13 June 1967; Healey, Holt and Fairhall, memcon, 14 June 1967, ibid.

been reached and that it was proposed to retain a military capability in the region beyond 1975, although the size and the location of it had not yet been decided.[75] The British remained unhelpful on the Commonwealth Brigade.[76] Nor did they appear more forthcoming on the possibility of avoiding withdrawal.

On the second day of talks, however, they appeared slightly more accommodating. According to the Australian High Commission, 'while yield[ing] no ground' with regard to the proposition that withdrawal be avoided, Healey 'was receptive to the argument that a decision for final withdrawal not be announced'.[77] He told Holt that, in his personal view, there had to be 'a way of presenting the British position without saying that we proposed to leave the bases in 1975'. He indicated that it would be helpful if he could say in Cabinet that the Australian prime minister agreed to a formula, which 'left open the possibility of leaving the bases earlier than 1975 as well as later'. Holt told Healey that if this could be done 'without giving the impression [that] the world East of Suez could go to hell, it would be highly desirable'.[78] In the end, the Australian party was reasonably hopeful.[79] The High Commission in London thought it 'more likely now that an announcement of a decision to withdraw in the mid-70s can be avoided'.[80] The Australian government remained moderately optimistic in the following weeks.[81] The Australian Cabinet noted that in relation to the 'avoidance of decision and announcement of withdrawal ... it appeared that the submission made by the Prime Minister (and other Heads of Government) might be successful ... [W]hat was likely to be announced was details of run down of forces up to 1970/71 with provision for a review of the situation at the end of that period'.[82]

Australian hopes were to be sorely disappointed. On 6 July the Wilson Cabinet decided not only to halve British forces in Malaysia and Singa-

---

[75] According to MOD plans, the British capability would consist of an amphibious force based on two commando battalions and 'six substantial naval vessels'. Singapore and Australia were considered as possible locations: London to DEA, cablegram 7501, 13 June 1967, and London to DEA, cablegram 7763, 16 June 1967, NAA, A1838/346, TS691/1 pt 2.

[76] Healey, Holt and Fairhall, memcon, 14 June 1967, PREM 13/1323.

[77] London to DEA, cablegram 7763, 16 June 1967, NAA, A1838/346, TS691/1 pt 2.

[78] Healey, Holt and Fairhall, memcon, 14 Jan. 1967, PREM 13/1323.

[79] Wilson and Holt, memcon, 15 June 1967, ibid.

[80] London to DEA, cablegram 7763, 16 June 1967, NAA, A1838/346, TS691/1 pt 2.

[81] So remained some allies. In late June, following his talks with the British, the prime minister of Singapore, Lee Kuan Yew, was reported as feeling 'reasonably confident that the British will make no announcement': London to DEA, cablegram 8258, 27 June 1967, ibid.

[82] Cabinet decision 403, 4 July 1967, NAA, A5840/XM1, vol. 2. As for the retention of effective ground forces in Malaysia and Singapore, however, the Cabinet noted that 'the British position was unchanged and that it would be moving in the 1970s to a situation in which naval and air forces only would be maintained for the area'.

pore by 1970–1, but also to announce its intention to withdraw altogether from the theatre (with the exception of Hong Kong) by the mid-1970s.[83] The precise timing of withdrawal – and this was the only concession to Australian demands – would 'depend on progress made in achieving a new basis for stability in South East Asia and in resolving other problems in the Far East'.[84] The British Cabinet also decided to provide a general military capability for use in the Far East once withdrawal had been fully accomplished. The question whether the naval and amphibious elements of this capability would be based in Australia, Singapore or Britain was left open.[85] These decisions would be made public in a *Supplementary statement on defence policy* on 18 July.[86] The die was cast. After three years in which it had sought to disentangle itself from onerous politico-military commitments in southeast Asia, the Wilson government was finally achieving its objective; the strong pressure applied by Britain's ANZUS and Commonwealth allies in late June and early July had failed to produce the desired results.[87] With the British Cabinet divided between those who demanded a faster withdrawal without a residual military capability in south-east Asia (Crossman), and those who favoured a more gradual pull-out with no public announcement (Healey and Bowden), ministers had settled for a compromise.[88]

Not surprisingly, the Holt government regarded this as bitterly disappointing. In a message to Wilson on 13 July, Holt regretted that Australian representations had 'made so little impact on the mind of your Cabinet'. He added:

> We see the United Kingdom as having taken historic decisions to reduce its world role and contract, to a significant degree, from the kind of international responsibility Britain has carried for many, many years ... Some of the basic assumptions on which the foreign policies of our two countries have been based – at least in relation to this area of the world – seem to us to have been destroyed, and we must re-think our whole situation.[89]

Despite its bitterness, the response of the Australian government remained restrained. In London Downer felt it to be so 'subdued' that he encouraged

---

83 CAB 128/42, CC(67)45th, 6 July 1967. In 1967 total personnel working in and for the British Services in Singapore and Malaysia numbered roughly 80,000. By 1970–1 it was expected to drop to a total of about 40,000. Between 1970 and 1971 and the mid-1970s the remaining British commitment in the region would largely consist of naval and air forces. In Hong Kong, Britain would maintain one garrison (about 9,000 men).
84 Ibid.; Cmnd. 3357, *Supplementary statement on defence policy, 1967*, London 1967.
85 CAB 128/42, CC(67)45th, 6 July 1967.
86 Cmnd. 3357, *Supplementary statement on defence policy, 1967*. In relation to the Middle East, the British government agreed to withdraw from the area by the mid–1970s, but avoided making public the exact date for withdrawal: Dockrill, *Retreat*, 154–5, 194–6.
87 For ANZUS and Commonwealth pressure see Pham, 'Suez', ch. vi.
88 For a detailed study of the Cabinet's decisions see ibid.
89 Holt to Wilson, cablegram 7227, 13 July 1967, NAA, A1838/346, TS3006/10/4/1 pt 4.

Holt to be 'more forthright' with the British. 'If we are too polite', the High Commissioner argued, 'then our British friends, with intellectual dishonesty, will twist our phrases publicly into signifying acquiescence, and declare that the Australians really do not mind very much ... Many prominent people here are now in a mood to use every weapon to justify their desertion of the Old Commonwealth both in the way of defence and of trade.'[90] Downer's arguments cut no ice in Canberra. Holt informed his High Commissioner on 20 July that 'the general disposition [in Australia was] to accept the British decisions without much demur, with recognition that only some dramatic development in the area is likely to have significant effect on them'.[91] Withdrawal was now an irreversible fact.

The Australian Cabinet took a realistic approach and endeavoured to salvage what it could from the situation. The view in Canberra was that, while on their way out, the British could still play a useful, if only residual, role in the security of the region. Therefore, rather than yielding to fruitless recriminations, it was decided on 18 July that 'as much as possible should be made of the assurances which the British messages and White Paper contain as to the careful timing of the withdrawal and as to the continuing part which Britain will have in the Far East'. Ministers had in fact noted that the British decision had left some 'room for flexibility in the timing of the eventual withdrawal'.[92] It was hoped that with careful political handling the withdrawal could be pushed into the late 1970s. It was also noted that London had not yet decided on the size and location of the British military capability for the area in the post-withdrawal period. A further – and more important – consideration in the minds of the Australian ministers was the need 'to avoid unnecessary scare or upset in Singapore and Malaysia'. Canberra was loath to create undue alarmism in the region by emphasising the negative consequences of withdrawal lest it undermined confidence in, and the stability of, Malaysia and Singapore.[93] It was for these reasons, as Holt explained to Downer, that Australia's response to the British decision had been 'more moderate in tone than our feelings warranted'. But Australian leaders had no doubt that it was time to 're-examine our foreign policy assumptions'.[94]

Rethinking Australian strategic policy

In the late summer of 1967 the Holt government began a gradual reappraisal of Australia's defence and foreign policies in south-east Asia; the

---

[90] Downer to Holt, 20 July 1967, NAA, A1209/80, 1966/7335 pt 6.
[91] Holt to Downer, 27 July 1967, ibid.
[92] Cabinet decision 473, 18 July 1967, NAA, A5840/XM1, vol. 2.
[93] Ibid; Holt to Downer, 27 July 1967, A1209/80, 1966/7335 pt 6.
[94] Ibid.

British decision to withdraw had raised a number of complex questions. The most important of these was whether Australia should maintain a military presence in the Malaysian region largely independent of Britain and enter into direct arrangements with the governments of Singapore and Malaysia for the stationing of Australian forces on their soil. Deploying troops in this area without a relevant British military presence presented significant military risks for Australia. The Defence Committee emphasised in a submission to Cabinet in late August that 'a continuing military presence could become a military commitment of unpredictable magnitude in the event of an insurgency situation developing in Malaysia or conflict with Indonesia'. As a result, Australia 'could become committed beyond [its] resources' and this could in turn 'inhibit [Australia's] capacity to undertake operations elsewhere'. On the other hand, policy-makers in Canberra accepted that a continuing military presence also had some positive aspects. It could for instance boost Australia's standing and influence in the region. It could also enhance confidence and stability in Malaysia and Singapore, promote the development of their military capabilities, and foster military co-operation between them. More crucially, a continuing military presence could assist in keeping the United States engaged in south-east Asia. Were Australia to disengage, Canberra would be sending the wrong signal to Washington at a time when American support was most needed following the British decision to pull out. An Australian withdrawal could also encourage the British to accelerate their pull-out from the region.[95]

Cabinet considered these issues on 25 August 1967. Without reaching a decision, ministers expressed a general disposition to continue a military presence in Malaysia and Singapore. They stressed the need for close consultations with Washington since American support was necessary for whatever strategy Australia adopted. In practice, the government needed to find out 'what the United States would do in support [if] Australia was to extend herself in Malaysia and Singapore'. As ministers pointed out, 'only if Australia is in the area with the assurance of United States' backing ... [will] her presence there ... have any military significance'. Ministers also stressed the importance of a 'continued British underwriting in the area'. 'There was a question of what Australia can do and what she can get the British to do in helping to build up local forces in Malaysia and Singapore.' Australia should seek to 'influence the British as to the manner of their withdrawal from the area'. Ministers were aware that 'the British may be sliding away from their commitments under their new policy towards South East Asia'. Australia, therefore, 'would only be seeking to hold the British to what they had already promised, and not asking them to do more'.[96]

As the Cabinet meeting of 25 August revealed, policy-makers in Canberra

---

[95] Cabinet submission 443, Aug. 1967, NAA, A4940/1, C4626.
[96] Cabinet decision 656 (FAD), 25 Aug. 1967, NAA, A5840/XM1, vol. 3.

had more questions than answers on how to deal with the vacuum in the region that the British departure would create.[97] They were confronted with many uncertainties regarding the progress of the Vietnam war, the unknown impact of British withdrawal on regional security and the unclear course of Indonesian and Chinese policies. Consequently, they relied on traditional and well-tested methods: the continuation, for the moment, of Australia's forward defence strategy, and the close alliance with the United States, both of which would lead to an increased Australian engagement with its neighbouring region.

The course Canberra was now taking began to manifest itself in the late summer of 1967 with Australia's decision to increase its commitment to the Vietnam war. Under strong pressure from Washington to send more troops, Holt and his ministers agreed in principle on 6 September 1967 to commit a third battalion group. They also approved the deployment of a tank squadron, a joint RAAF-RAN contribution of four helicopters, an additional engineering construction capability and about 125 additional personnel for headquarters and other units.[98] This was not an easy decision given Australia's overstretched military capabilities and the trauma of the recent British announcement. Ministers felt that the United States 'should be given to understand that the battalion represents a special contribution by Australia made notwithstanding major difficulties, and also represents the practical sheer limit of contribution'. At the same time, they believed that 'Australia should take the opportunity to strengthen still more its defence alliance with the United States as and when it can', and that 'a contribution now of a significant new ground force … would have this effect'.[99] As McEwen explained to Holyoake a month later, 'Britain would soon be out of South-East Asia and we would be dependent on the United States for our security. Our attitude should be to bind ourselves to the United States and to induce the United States to accept a security responsibility towards us'.[100]

American acceptance of 'a security responsibility' towards Australia in Malaysia and Singapore was the Holt government's priority in the autumn of 1967. In mid-October Hasluck flew to Washington to raise the question of a possible ANZUS guarantee to cover Australian troops in the Malaysian area. Canberra was eager to establish whether Australia could invoke American military support under the ANZUS Treaty, should its troops in the region incur the risk of hostilities.[101] Although Hasluck pointed out that Australia was seeking 'an understanding rather than commitments' from the

---

97   Edwards, *Nation at war*, 149.
98   Ibid. 153; Cabinet decision 563 (FAD), 6 Sept. 1967, NAA, A5840/XM1, vol. 2.
99   Cabinet decision 563 (FAD), 6 Sept. 1967, NAA, A5840/XM1, vol. 2.
100 Cabinet decision 659 (FAD), 3 Oct. 1967, ibid.
101 Hasluck to DEA, cablegram UN1336, 11 Oct. 1967, and Hasluck to DEA, cablegram 4241, 9 Oct. 1967, NAA, A1209/80, 1966/7335 pt 8.

Table 5
Australian military presence in Singapore and Malaysia, 1967

Royal Australian Navy (based in Singapore)	Royal Australian Regiment (based at Terendak, Malaysia)	Royal Australian Air Force (based at Butterworth, Malaysia)
2 destroyers or frigates	1 infantry battalion	1 Mirage squadron
1 aircraft carrier (on annual visit of 6–8 weeks)	1 field battery	1 Sabre fighter squadron (to be replaced by a second Mirage squadron)
	1 field engineer troop	
	Supporting signal and administrative element	HQ and supporting units

Source: DOD brief, 25 May 1967, NAA, A1209/84, 1967/7334, attachment 2.

United States, the American response was non-committal.[102] The Johnson administration advised the Australian embassy that 'it would be months rather than weeks' before it could reply to Australian queries.[103] Owing to their deepening involvement in Vietnam, the Americans were clearly averse to taking on new commitments in south-east Asia. While favouring a continued Australian presence, Washington was, for the time being, more than happy to let the Commonwealth countries concerned work out new defence arrangements for the Malaysian area.[104]

The disappointing American response notwithstanding, Australian ministers reaffirmed on 11 December their disposition to maintain a military presence at current operational levels in Malaysia and Singapore (*see* table 5). This, they emphasised, was only a limited and provisional step and did not amount to a firm intention to continue to maintain an Australian military presence. They stressed that Australia was only engaged in a 'holding operation', and did not intend to replace the British in the area. The government was in fact awaiting an American 'response to the questions which have been put to them', and the 'clarification of British intentions' before making any binding commitment. In the longer term, ministers emphasised, Australia's attitude could not be determined until the outcome of the

---

102 Hasluck to DEA, cablegram 4240, 9 Oct. 1967, ibid; Robert McNamara and Hasluck, memcon, 10 Oct. 1967, doc. 30, and Dean Rusk and Hasluck, memcon, 9 Oct. 1967, *FRUS, 1964–68*, xxvii, doc. 29.

103 Washington to James Plimsoll, cablegram 4328, 14 Oct. 1967, NAA, A1209/80, 1966/7335 pt 8.

104 This was the substance of the US response when it came in January. In relation to the ANZUS guarantee Washington remained non-committal: Washington to DEA, cablegram 125, 9 Jan. 1968, NAA, A1838/346, TS3006/10/4/1 pt 6.

Vietnam conflict, and more generally future security arrangements in south-east Asia, were known.[105] Yet, it was clear that, 'if in the long term United States support on the mainland itself is not kept up, it may well be that Australia should also withdraw'.[106] Ministers also reiterated their support for a Malaysian-sponsored five-power conference with Britain, New Zealand, Malaysia and Singapore.[107] In their view, the chief value of this initiative lay in 'ascertaining from the British what their future role will be and giving such substance as is possible to their statements about continuing obligations towards, and economic support for, the security of the region'. The initiative was also aimed at 'bringing Malaysia/Singapore together to co-operate more effectively in the common defence'.[108]

By early December the Holt government had begun to set out guiding principles for Australia's future strategic engagement in south-east Asia. Albeit cautiously, it had taken steps to deepen Australia's involvement in the region. This was done through a growing reliance on the United States, through increased co-operation with Malaysia and Singapore, and in accordance with plans for a continuing, if only residual, defence partnership with Britain, although it was realised that little could be expected from London. As ministers put it, 'there can be no longer faith that the British attitude can be stiffened to anything beyond this [i.e. a residual military capability for use in the area] – or even stopped from weakening further'.[109] Yet, as Bunting advised Holt, the government would 'do better to treat them [the British] on the basis of a continuing interest in the area rather than to drop them out of the picture'.[110] With these convictions in mind, Australian policy-makers were showing not only a greater inclination to engage with the region, but also an increased awareness that a deeper Australian involvement was needed if Canberra wished to achieve its aim of a stable south-east Asia.

The sterling crisis and the acceleration of the withdrawal

Australian hopes for a gradual rundown of British forces in south-east Asia were soon disappointed. In the summer of 1967 the economic situation in Britain again took a turn for the worse. In late October speculation against the pound intensified. Despite efforts to prop up the ailing currency, pressure did not abate. On 18 November the Wilson government, resigned to

---

[105] Cabinet decision 771 (FAD), 11 Dec. 1967, NAA, A5840/XM1, vol. 3.
[106] Cabinet decision 658 (FAD), 28 Aug. 1967, ibid.
[107] Cabinet decision 771 (FAD), 11 Dec. 1967, ibid. Ministers had already expressed their support for five-power talks in late August and September: Cabinet decision 656 (FAD), 25 Aug. 1967, and Cabinet decision 658 (FAD), 28 Sept. 1967, ibid.
[108] Ibid.
[109] Ibid.
[110] Bunting to Holt, 13 Oct. 1967, NAA, A1209/80, 1966/7335 pt 8.

the inevitable, announced a devaluation of the pound. This inevitably led to a new round of cuts in public expenditure. The change in the pound's parity from US$2.80 to US$2.40 meant that, all things being equal, defence costs would at once increase by £50 million per year.[111] On 20 November, Callaghan announced a new deflationary package, which included cuts of more than £400 million in the expected rate of growth in public expenditure. Defence, too, would suffer cuts. As Callaghan told the Commons, these would amount to more than £100 million in 1968–9. The Chancellor, however, remained confident that cuts could be made without significant changes to existing policy. [112] A week later Healey categorically ruled out any reversal of the July decisions on defence policy.[113]

Despite devaluation, the economic situation scarcely improved. Financial markets experienced continued turmoil.[114] The pound remained weak. A second devaluation was considered likely. Against this backdrop, on 18 December, Wilson announced his government's decision to initiate a stringent review of all areas of governmental spending. The new Chancellor of the Exchequer, Roy Jenkins, began to look in earnest at areas where savings could be made.[115] He was highly critical of the east of Suez role and thought that defence should not be spared, calling for a 'sharp' acceleration of the withdrawal from the Far East, to be achieved by 1970–1.[116] Jenkins's radical plans were resisted by Healey, Brown and George Thomson, the new Commonwealth Secretary, and their respective departments.[117] While deeming further defence cuts inevitable, the overseas and defence departments were not prepared to go all the way with Jenkins's calls for a much faster disengagement, seeking instead to delay the withdrawal until March 1972.[118] Yet, for all their efforts, Jenkins carried the day, thanks to Wilson's

---

[111] Pickering, *Withdrawal*, 164.

[112] Britain, *PD*, HC, 1967–8, dccliv.937.

[113] Ibid. dcclv.59.

[114] Morgan, *Callaghan*, 275.

[115] Roy Jenkins became Chancellor of the Exchequer on 29 November 1967. For Jenkins's role in demanding further defence cuts see Jeffrey Pickering, 'Politics and "black Tuesday": shifting power in the Cabinet and the decision to withdraw from east of Suez, November 1967–January 1968', *TCBH* xiii (2002), 154–7, 158–64, 169–70. See also Pham, 'Suez', ch. vii.

[116] Roy Jenkins and William Armstrong, memcon, 7 Dec. 1967, T 255/3066; Roy Jenkins, *A life at the centre*, London 1991, 225; I. P. Bancroft to Robin Butler, 23 Dec. 1967, T 225/3066; CAB 129/135, (68)5, 3 Jan. 1968.

[117] For the role played by Healey, George Thomson and George Brown in opposing further cuts see Dockrill, *Retreat*, 201, and Pham, 'Suez', ch. vii. For a differing view see Pickering, 'Politics and "black Tuesday"', 170, and Jones, 'Decision delayed', 594.

[118] Jenkins, Brown, Thomson and Healey, memcon, 20 Dec. 1967, PREM 13/1999; Trend, Armstrong, Paul Gore-Booth, James Dunnett and Saville Garner, memcon, 23 Dec. 1967, T 225/3066; Garner to Thomson, 22 Jan. 1967, FCO 46/43; CAB 129/135, C(68)7, C(68)11, 3 Jan. 1968.

support and his followers in Cabinet.[119] On 4 January 1968 the British Cabinet agreed that withdrawal from the Far East (with the exception of Hong Kong) should be completed by 31 March 1971. It also agreed that a special capability for use in the Far East should not be maintained. However, if circumstances demanded it, 'the general capability which [Britain] retained in Europe would be available to be deployed overseas'.[120]

It fell upon Thomson to break the news to the governments of Australia, New Zealand, Malaysia and Singapore. Brown was despatched to Washington. To avoid the charge of presenting Britain's allies with a *fait accompli* – as it most certainly was – Thomson and Brown informed them that, while firm, the Cabinet decision was not yet final. As expected, Britain's allies felt let down. While expressing genuine concern at the British Cabinet's decision, the governments of Malaysia and New Zealand responded with considerable restraint.[121] The United States, Singapore and Australia, by contrast, were less level-headed. In Washington Dean Rusk told Brown that 'the acrid aroma of a fait accompli' had hit the administration 'deeply and hard'. As a result, American confidence in the British government 'had been terribly shaken'. He complained that the British decision would have a negative impact on Asian security and Anglo-American relations. He urged the British to 'act like Britain'.[122] Learning from Rusk of the revised British plans, President Johnson made a last-ditch appeal to Wilson for 'a prolongation of [Britain's] presence in the Far East and the Gulf'.[123] In Singapore Prime Minister Lee Kuan Yew resented London's unilateral decisions, arguing that the announcement of a speedier British military rundown would 'destroy Singapore's future'. He threatened to withdraw Singapore's sterling holdings.[124] In Canberra, John Gorton, the newly-appointed Australian prime minister following Harold Holt's sudden death in December 1967, told Thomson that the British proposals 'filled him and his colleagues with anxiety and dismay'. He regretted that 'such large decisions should be made for the sake of comparatively small savings in such a sensitive part of the world'. He also expressed concern that Britain's withdrawal would 'be creating a partial military vacuum in the Far East in an area where the United States had hitherto assumed no responsibility'.[125] Although Australian ministers showed some sympathy for the difficult task that Thomson had been asked to perform in

---

[119] Pickering, *Withdrawal*, 171. For Wilson's support see Palliser, note for the record, 25 Dec. 1967, PREM 13/1999.
[120] CAB 128/43, CC(68)1st, 4 Jan. 1968.
[121] Thomson to Wilson, telegram 21, 7 Jan. 1968; telegram 22, 8 Jan. 1968; telegram 78, 11 Jan. 1968, PREM 13/2081.
[122] CAB 128/43, CC(66)6th, 12 Jan. 1968; Brown to FO, telegram 54, 11 Jan. 1968, PREM 13/1999; British budget and defence cuts, memcon, 11 Jan. 1968, *FRUS* xii, doc. 288.
[123] Johnson to Wilson, 11 Jan. 1968, *FRUS* xii, doc. 289.
[124] Thomson to Wilson, telegram 26, 8 Jan. 1968, PREM 13/2081.
[125] Thomson to Wilson, telegram 92, 12 Jan. 1968, ibid.

Canberra, his talks with the FAD were very difficult at times.[126] Hasluck argued that Wilson's 'new policy would reduce Britain to a status little less then Italy and a little more than Sweden'. Treasurer William McMahon told Thomson that he could not accept a complete withdrawal, nor did he think it could be justified. He believed that Britain's economic prospects were better than the British made out. McEwen criticised Britain 'for confronting Australia with the prospect of either standing alone with Malaysia in future or facing up to the consequences of relations with Asian states or of declining to do so'. He bitterly observed that while in the past Australian troops had arrived in Belgium, Gallipoli and Greece without question, Britain would not even give Australia verbal support in Vietnam.[127]

The gap between Australian and British interests could not have been greater. Talks ended without an agreed *communiqué*; by refusing to issue one the Gorton government publicly indicated that the British proposals were not acceptable to Australia. Instead Gorton left an *aide-mémoire* with Thomson, which set out his reasons for opposing the British decision to bring forward withdrawal and called on Wilson to reconsider. In particular, Canberra asked that 'the time now set for the major withdrawal of British forces in Malaysia and Singapore be extended as long as possible and that thereafter some British forces should still remain available in the area to provide balanced forces in concert with those contributed by other partner governments'. It also urged the British to make clear, in any public announcement of policy, 'Britain's continued interest in the maintenance of security in the South-East Asia areas and its intention to continue to play such part in this as it can'.[128]

American and Commonwealth representations brought only minimal results. A last-ditch visit by Lee Kuan Yew to London on 14 January 1968 resulted in 'some successful lobbying'.[129] On 15 January, the British Cabinet agreed to postpone the date of the final withdrawal by nine months – from March to December 1971. This represented a hard-fought compromise between those ministers (including Thomson, Healey and Brown) who wanted to delay the final date of Britain's withdrawal to 31 March 1972 and those (Wilson himself, Jenkins and Crossman) who were determined to stick to 31 March 1971.[130] In his diaries Crossman recorded that during the meeting 'there was a tremendous effort to get the Cabinet to reverse the decision on east of Suez withdrawal that we had taken by such a large majority only ten days ago'.[131] On 16 January Wilson announced in the

---

[126] Johnston to Thomson, 16 Jan. 1968, FCO 24/95.
[127] Thomson to Wilson, telegram 92, 12 Jan. 1968, PREM 13/2081.
[128] *Aide-mémoire*: talks with Thomson, 12 Jan. 1968, FCO 24/95.
[129] Jenkins, *Life*, 228. See also Pham, 'Suez', ch. vii.
[130] CAB 128/43, CC(68)7th, 15 Jan. 1968; Jenkins, *Life*, 228; Crossman, *Diaries*, ii. 658.
[131] Crossman, *Diaries*, ii. 650.

Commons that the final date for Britain's withdrawal from east of Suez was irrevocably set for December 1971.[132]

Historians have generally regarded the British Cabinet's decisions of July 1967 and January 1968 as a significant turning point in twentieth-century British history.[133] Robert Holland, for instance, has reflected that the January decision 'fits the bill better than most' as 'a firm date to mark the end of the British empire' while Kenneth Morgan has argued that the withdrawal 'stripped away' Britain's 'last pretence' to being a world power.[134] British policy-makers at the time drew similar conclusions, variously describing the withdrawal as 'a watershed in our ability to influence world affairs', 'the abandonment of our claim to be a world power' or 'an end of an era'.[135] And, indeed, it was an end of an era, for by shedding its military commitments east of Suez, London was not only forsaking the last vestiges of its imperial past, but was also significantly reducing its capacity to shape events and defend its interests outside Europe. Consequently, as it was winding down its imperial and global commitments, London was also recasting its international role as that of an influential, yet essentially regional, power. As Healey acknowledged in a *Sunday Times* interview, the withdrawal also marked 'a decision to make Europe the focus in the future of our foreign policy and consequently our defence policy'.[136]

For Australia, too, withdrawal represented an important turning point in its recent history. With the British military rundown to be completed by the end of 1971, Australia was about to be confronted with 'the virtual disappearance east of Suez of British military power and the capacity to deploy it'.[137] As a result, one of the cornerstones of Australia's post-war defence policy – reliance on a British politico-military presence in southeast Asia – had collapsed and was destined to disappear. It is, therefore, no surprise that Wilson's decision to withdraw was highly controversial in Canberra and brought about a serious conflict of interests between Britain and Australia. Inevitably, the ensuing rift put relations between London and Canberra under considerable strain. The British decision to withdraw, in fact, coincided not only with a new British bid for EEC membership,

132 Britain, *PD*, HC, 1967–68, dcclvi.1579–85. All British forces were then to be withdrawn simultaneously from the Middle and Far East.
133 Dockrill, *Retreat*, 209; Pickering, 'Politics and "black Tuesday"', 145; Jones, 'Decision delayed', 472–3.
134 Holland, *Pursuit of greatness*, 9; Kenneth Morgan, *The people's peace: British history, 1945–89*, London 1990, 283.
135 Patrick Dean quoted in Dean to Brown, telegram 185, 14 Jan. 1968, PREM 13/1999; Paul Gore-Booth quoted in Gore-Booth to Brown, 18 Jan. 1968, FCO 46/42; George Thomson quoted in Johnston to Thomson, 16 Jan. 1968, FCO 24/95.
136 Healey quoted in London to DEA, cablegram 291, 8 Jan. 1968, NAA, A1838/346, TS3006/10/4/1 pt 5.
137 Tange quoted in E. M. Andrews, *The Department of Defence: the Australian centenary history of defence*, v, Melbourne 2001, 148.

but also with an escalation in the Vietnam war and increased Australian involvement in that conflict. Withdrawal was seen in Canberra as seriously undermining Australia's forward defence strategy and the West's efforts to contain Communism in Asia. Australian policy-makers were concerned that it would leave a dangerous politico-military vacuum at a time of heightened Cold War tensions in Asia. In order to avert a British disengagement, both Menzies and Holt put the Wilson government under intense pressure, yet, to their disappointment, Australian lobbying bore no fruit. Nor was the American administration any more successful, despite Washington's greater sway in London. In the end the Australian government resigned itself to the inevitable and timidly began to reassess its defence policy in south-east Asia. With regard to the Malaysian region, it indicated its willingness to maintain a military contribution at present operational levels, at least for the time being. In so doing, Canberra showed that it was open to the possibility of playing a more prominent role in the region and willing to seek closer engagement with its Asian neighbours.

6

The 'Approach to Europe', October 1964–May 1967

'Even among the anti-Marketeers, the idea of the Commonwealth as an alternative to British entry into Europe seems to have few supporters, and the consequences of British membership for the Commonwealth is not now regarded as an important issue': Tom Critchley, 4 May 1967.[1]

Amidst growing uncertainty surrounding Britain's defence role east of Suez, the Wilson government began to a reconsider its policy towards Community membership.

Despite his initial desire to bolster the Commonwealth connection, Wilson grew increasingly disillusioned with the state of Commonwealth affairs and moved towards a renewed attempt to join the Community. At first with circumspection, but later with steadfastness, Wilson steered a divided Cabinet towards a second bid for EEC membership. In the event, his bid foundered due to French opposition, yet his decision to seek entry signalled a marked shift towards Europe at the expense of the Commonwealth. In contrast to the aftermath of the 1963 veto, the British application remained on the table after de Gaulle's second veto in 1967 and was revived by Heath's Conservative government in 1970.

The Australian government became gradually aware during 1966 of Wilson's increasing readiness to consider a new British bid to join the EEC. This could not and did not please Canberra, of course, especially as the British application was thought likely to have negative repercussions on Britain's role east of Suez. Yet, for a number of reasons, the Holt government's response was non-committal. A constant factor throughout the 1966–7 period was continuing French opposition to Britain's entry which made the outcome of Wilson's bid uncertain. Another factor was the Australian government's concern to avoid any action that could be construed as an attempt to obstruct Britain's application, lest it lead London to claim trade compensation from Australia in the case of a failed application. A third factor was the government's desire to prevent the Australian public gaining a true picture of the gloomy outlook for Australian farm exports to Britain, should the application be successful. Holt was also concerned that

---

1 Critchley to Plimsoll, 4 May 1967, NAA, A1838/275, 727/4 pt 37.

the timing of the application coincided with the British defence review, worrying that Wilson's 'approach to Europe' would further weaken Britain's resolve to remain east of Suez. His ministers even canvassed the possibility of implementing a 'soft' strategy, giving Britain some trade benefits in the hope that these might help strengthen Wilson's resolve to maintain a military presence east of Suez. Holt thus carefully avoided confrontation on the EEC question as he felt that this could drive a wedge between Australia and Britain at a time when British goodwill was still needed. Overall, Britain's second application sent out a clear and powerful message that, as Britain reoriented its policies towards Europe, it regarded Australia's concerns and interests as expendable.

Towards a new British application

The French veto of January 1963, which brought to a dramatic end Britain's first application to join the EEC, threw the Macmillan government's policy on closer engagement with Europe into disarray and made British entry impossible in the short term. Confronting this harsh reality, the Conservative leader, Alec Douglas-Home – who replaced Macmillan at Downing Street in October 1963 – quietly abandoned any plans for closer political and economic co-operation with the Community. As he explained to the German Chancellor, Ludwig Erhard, in January 1964, 'the present moment was not opportune for the United Kingdom government to reach a decision on the extent to which this country might participate in any further European move towards political integration'.[2] If anything, the Douglas-Home government wished to see Britain's ties with the Commonwealth strengthened.[3] Ultimately, however, Douglas-Home did not remain in power long enough to make any lasting impact. In October 1964 his government was defeated by Wilson's Labour Party in a close-run general election.

Wilson's accession to power did not lead to an immediate change of strategy in Britain's approach to Europe.[4] The Labour premier was a 'Commonwealth man' and, while in opposition, had been said to be against EEC membership.[5] To be sure, his party remained largely opposed to entry and upon taking office Wilson showed no interest in closer relations with the EEC.[6] As he admitted to Hasluck in November 1964, he did not see 'much pros-

[2] CAB 128/38, CM(64)5th, 17 Jan. 1964.
[3] CAB 128/38, CM(64)38th, 16 July 1964.
[4] For Wilson's early policy towards the EEC see Helen Parr, *Britain's policy towards the European Community: Harold Wilson and Britain's world role, 1964–1967*, Oxford 2006, ch. i.
[5] Idem, 'A question of leadership: July 1966 and Harold Wilson's European decision', *Contemporary British History* xix (2005), 437–58.
[6] Roy Denman, *Missed chances: Britain and Europe in the twentieth century*, London 1996, 227.

pect in the European Economic Community which had too many internal problems' and thought it 'impossible for Britain to become committed to the agricultural policies of the Six'.[7] Accordingly, in April 1965, he told the House of Commons that a new British application was out of the question 'in the immediately foreseeable future'.[8] Instead, he was eager to breathe new life into the Commonwealth economic relationship, seeking to expand Commonwealth trade through a number of initiatives. These included an increase in Commonwealth preferences, the establishment of a Commonwealth free trade area (or bilateral free trade areas between Britain and individual Commonwealth members), the proposal that Commonwealth countries join EFTA and a scheme under which Commonwealth countries would accord preferential treatment to British capital goods in return for British undertakings to purchase their farm commodities in bulk.[9] Although officials and senior ministers eventually persuaded him to drop some of his more ambitious ideas – namely the free trade area and the EFTA initiatives – on the grounds that they would find no support within the Commonwealth countries and might not accord with Britain's economic interests, Wilson none the less remained determined to broach Commonwealth trade expansion at the Prime Ministers' Conference in London in June 1965.[10] In June 1965 he also criticised opposition leader Douglas-Home for being 'prepared to sacrifice the Commonwealth for going in'. In claiming that his government would not do that, he exhorted Douglas-Home to open his eyes to the fact that 'the situation on agricultural policy in the Common Market would mean a levy of about 80 per cent on every ton of wheat imported from Canada or Australia'.[11]

Yet, despite Wilson's interest in reviving the Commonwealth connection, there were signs throughout 1965 that the Labour government's stance on the EEC question was perhaps not as firm as it appeared to be.[12] In early March the British Foreign Secretary, Michael Stewart, told Britain's partners in the Western European Union that the British government would

---

7 London to DEA, cablegram 7629, 10 Nov. 1964, NAA, A1838/2, 67/1/3 pt 3.
8 Britain, *PD*, HC, 1964–6, dccxi.623.
9 DO 215/135, CCP (65)5th, 13 Mar. 1965; M. Reid to Nicoll, 2 Mar. 1965, PREM 13/182; Jim Tomlinson, 'The decline of the Empire and the economic "decline" of Britain', *TCBH* xiv (2003), 209–11.
10 Issues such as higher Commonwealth preferences, Commonwealth economic planning and a stronger commitment by Commonwealth governments to buy Commonwealth manufactured goods remained on Wilson's agenda for the Commonwealth conference in London: Douglas Jay to Wilson, 3 June 1965, DO 215/138, and DO 215/138, MISC (56)3rd, 14 June 1965. For official and ministerial disagreements with some of Wilson's ideas see CAB 148/21, OPD(65)72, 7 Apr. 1965; CAB 148/41 OPD(O) (65)9th, 9 Apr. 1965; Commonwealth trade, note for record, 28 Apr. 1965, DO 215/135, and Brown to Wilson, 11 June 1965, James Callaghan to Wilson, 14 June 1964, Bottomley to Wilson, 11 June 1965, and Stewart to Wilson, 11 June 1965, DO, 215/138.
11 London to DEA, cablegram 4650, 4 June 1965, NAA, A1838/349, 67/1/1 pt 7.
12 Parr, *Britain's policy*, ch. i.

eventually wish to join the EEC.[13] A few weeks later, Wilson referred to plans for 'bridging the gap' between the EEC and EFTA.[14] According to sources within the Commonwealth Relations Office, 'the [British] Government could not appear to ignore opposition statements of the desirability of Britain's entry into Europe, nor could they ignore the signs that public opinion was beginning to believe that this was inevitable'.[15]

In Australia, the Menzies government maintained a watchful eye on Wilson's European policy. Advice sent from Australian posts in Western Europe had indicated that, while ruling out any move towards the EEC for the present, the Labour government could soon review its policy.[16] In June 1965 Menzies remarked privately that, in the short term, the Common Market was 'a good subject to keep off since it is impossible to know in which direction the United Kingdom will have to move in due course'. In his view, Australia should refrain from 'taking positions' to avoid the risk of finding itself 'out on the limb'.[17]

Australian caution seemed justified as there were signs towards the end of 1965 that the Wilson government was slowly warming to the idea of a renewed application to the EEC. By November, Wilson's efforts to expand Commonwealth trade had borne no fruit and his proposals on closer Commonwealth economic cooperation had found little support at the Commonwealth Prime Ministers' Conference in June 1965. Neither the developing members of the Commonwealth nor the old dominions appeared keen on tighter economic links with Britain.[18] Disheartened by this response as well as by the acrimonious intra-Commonwealth divisions over Rhodesia, Wilson began to consider the possibility of launching a new EEC bid.[19] In January 1966 he approved secret studies of membership.[20] In the lead-up to the 31 March general election, he declared in Bristol that 'given the right conditions it

---

[13] Brussels to Arthur Tange, 18 Mar. 1965, NAA, A1838/349, 67/1/1 pt 7.

[14] Message from Prime Minister Wilson to President Johnson, 11 Mar. 1965, *FRUS, 1964–68*, XIII: *Western European region*, Washington 1995, doc. 76; London to DEA, cablegram 3653, 7 Apr. 1965, NAA, A1838/275, 727/4 pt 36. For Wilson's 'bridge-building' plan see Parr, *Britain's policy*, 26–9.

[15] Godfrey Shannon quoted in London to DEA, cablegram 3653, 7 Apr. 1965, NAA, A1838/275, 727/4 pt 36.

[16] London to DEA, savingram 46, 20 Oct. 1964, NAA, A1838/349, 67/1/1 pt 7; James Cumes to Tange, 16 Feb. 1965, NAA, A1838/275, 727/4 pt 36.

[17] Bunting to Downer, 13 May 1965, NAA, A463/50, 1965/2040.

[18] Singleton and Robertson, *Britain and Australasia*, 196; Ashton and Louis, *East of Suez*, pp. cxii–cxiii.

[19] For Commonwealth divisions over Rhodesia see Philip Alexander, 'From imperial power to regional powers: Commonwealth crises and the second application', in Oliver Daddow (ed.), *Harold Wilson and European integration: Britain's second application to join the EEC*, London 2002, 200–2. For the unfolding of the Rhodesian problem see Ashton and Louis, *East of Suez*, pp. lxxii–lxxxi.

[20] Parr, 'Question of leadership', 445.

would be possible and right to join [the] EEC'.[21] After the election, he established Cabinet committees to study the implications of European membership. As Helen Parr has argued, these initiatives were a turning point on Wilson's path towards EEC membership.[22]

In a recent doctoral thesis Philip Alexander has laid significant emphasis on the role played by the seemingly intractable Rhodesian problem in persuading Wilson to reconsider his pro-Commonwealth stance in favour of a more positive attitude towards EEC membership.[23] Although making too much of the link between the Rhodesian and the EEC issues, he convincingly demonstrates the growing sense of disillusionment that Wilson felt towards the Commonwealth in the years 1965–6 – a feeling that the Australian and other prominent Commonwealth governments were unable or unwilling to assuage. In the case of Australia, Menzies's lukewarm response to Wilson's plans to revive Commonwealth trade, and his refusal to heed British requests for an Australian peacekeeping force to be deployed on the Zambian-Rhodesian border to protect the Kariba hydro-electric dam complex, did not go unnoticed in London.[24] Without triggering a full-blown rift between London and Canberra, the latter's unforthcoming attitude deepened Wilson's disenchantment with the Commonwealth, creating the climate in which the Labour leader could complain to his Cabinet colleagues in April 1967 that Australia had made little effort to look beyond its narrow national interests.[25]

The Australian response

Wilson's renewed interest in closer ties with the Six did not jolt all sections of the Australian government into action. The attitude of the Department of Trade and Industry was indicative of the majority view. While recognising that the Common Market issue in Britain 'has become a more live one than it has been for some time', the DTI was in no hurry to discuss contingency planning as demanded by the DEA.[26] External Affairs, on the other hand, was particularly active in advocating the establishment of an interdepart-

---

21 Wilson, *Labour government*, 283.
22 Parr, 'Question of leadership', 445.
23 Philip Alexander, 'The Commonwealth and European integration: competing commitments for Britain, 1956–1967', unpubl. PhD diss. Cambridge 2002, 261–3.
24 For Canberra's unenthusiastic reaction to Wilson's economic ideas see Singleton and Robertson, *Britain and Australasia*, 196. For the Australian refusal to send troops to Southern Africa see Canberra to CRO, telegram 1503, 9 Dec. 1965, and CRO to Canberra, telegram 3142, 7 Dec. 1965, DO 207/122; and Ashton and Louis, *East of Suez*, 215. For a brief account of Australian policy in relation to the Rhodesian question see Goldsworthy, *Losing the blanket*, 91–2.
25 CAB 128/42, CC(67)26th, 30 Apr. 1967.
26 Alan Currie to Renouf, 22 Mar. 1966, NAA, A1838/275, 727/4/1 pt 5.

mental committee with the view to reassessing Australia's negotiating position. As Alan Renouf, First Assistant Secretary (DEA), pointed out, 'events would move quite quickly once the British Government took the plunge'.[27] In his view, 'Australia might be placed in a position of some embarrassment if the Government had not determined well in advance what our attitude should be to the negotiations and their outcome'.[28]

The DTI, however, considered the prospect of a British application with less urgency, an attitude important in understanding Australia's approach to the Common Market issue. Its minister, John McEwen, had always tended to regard the problem of British entry as falling within his exclusive sphere of competence. In this respect, Menzies had been the only personality in the Cabinet capable of restraining him, as indeed he did in 1962, over Britain's previous negotiations with the EEC.[29] But the Liberal leader had retired in January 1966 and with him gone, responsibility for Australia's policy on the EEC question rested primarily with McEwen and his department. The new prime minister, Harold Holt, who was still establishing himself in office, had not yet acquired the authority in Cabinet that had been Menzies's. On the EEC question he let McEwen take the lead. It was thus a further year before any consideration was given to the formation of an interdepartmental committee as requested by the DEA, with a preparatory meeting taking place first in June 1967.[30]

The prevailing mood in Canberra was in stark contrast to the growing concern felt by a number of Australian missions overseas. In London, Downer regarded the prospect of a British bid with great foreboding.[31] In Brussels Ambassador Ralph Harry repeatedly complained to Canberra about the lack of guidance.[32] He felt that Australian silence could be interpreted as indicating that no major Australian interest was at stake should Britain apply to the EEC. Harry even sought permission to fly to London to confer with McEwen when the latter passed through the British capital in June.[33]

Lack of guidance was due in part to the fact that in the first half of 1966 a British bid was still regarded as hypothetical in Canberra. Cabinet discussed the issue briefly on 17 May and concluded that no diplomatic *démarche* was required at this stage: there was 'nothing said to date by the British Govern-

[27] Renouf to Alan Westerman and Currie, 1 Apr. 1966, ibid.
[28] Renouf to Westerman, 4 Feb. 1966, NAA, A1838/275, 727/4 pt 36.
[29] Ward, *British embrace*, 173–6.
[30] Interdepartmental meeting on UK/EEC, 7 June 1967, NAA, A1838/275, 727/4/2 pt 7.
[31] Downer to Royal Commonwealth Society, 11 Mar. 1965, NAA, A464/50, 1965/2040.
[32] Alexander Campbell to Currie, 31 May 1966, NAA, AA4092/T1, 79; Brussels to DEA, cablegram 80, 17 Mar. 1966, NAA, A1838/275, 727/4/1 pt 4.
[33] Harry to DEA, 1 June 1966, and Renouf to Hasluck, 2 June 1966, NAA, A1838/275, 727/4/1 pt 5.

ment' to which it could react.[34] In finally sending some belated guidance to Harry in June, McEwen advised that 'ministers in Australia had deliberately decided not to attempt to reach an overall policy regarding British entry, but to take decisions as circumstances developed'. He also informed the ambassador that 'Australian representatives would have to live with not having a policy for the time being' and expressed concern over the strong statements against British entry made by Downer in London.[35]

However, the as yet uncertain nature of British policy towards the EEC was not the only reason for Canberra's muted attitude. There was an ulterior motive, based on the belief that 'since the question of British entry and trade might be mixed up with defence and other considerations, it was terribly important that Australian representatives should not make statements predicting Australian future policy'. McEwen said that

> the attitude of the Australian Government in the event of a British application for entry or opening of negotiations could be very different from the attitude adopted in 1962/63. There [is] not merely a possibility that Australia might go 'soft' but that Australia might be prepared to give Britain some trade benefits even if these were not required. Because of the desirability of ensuring a continued British presence east of Suez, it might be necessary to help meet the cost of British defence policy.[36]

This marked a considerable change of emphasis in the Australian view since the first and second applications. In the period between the two applications Canberra began to attach greater importance to a continuing British role east of Suez than to trade issues. It was hardly surprising, therefore, that Australia's response, now, to a new British application would be influenced by strategic considerations.

The depth of Holt's concern over the uncertainty surrounding Britain's military presence in south-east Asia was apparent when he met Wilson in London in July 1966. Discussions between the two leaders centred on British plans to reduce military forces east of Suez, and only cursory attention was given to the Common Market issue. Holt raised the matter briefly on 11 July, asking Wilson his views 'on the prospects and the timing of Britain's entry into the EEC'.[37] In reply, Wilson said that Britain would go in – and indeed was 'keen to go in' – if it could do so on the right terms.[38] However, in order not to alarm his Australian visitor, Wilson immediately drew Holt's attention to the difficulties facing a British application.[39] George Thomson, Chancellor of the Duchy of Lancaster, who had been given special respon-

34 Cabinet decision 260, 5 May 1966, NAA, A5839/XM1, vol. 1.
35 Record of conversation with Campbell, 8 June 1966, NAA, A1838/346, 727/4.
36 Ibid.
37 CAB 133/329, AMV(66)3rd, 11 July 1966.
38 Holt to McEwen, cablegram 6856, 11 July 1966, NAA, A1838/1, 792/1 pt 4.
39 CAB 133/329, AMV(66)3rd, 11 July 1966.

sibility for European affairs in the new Labour administration and was also present at the meeting, reassured Holt that 'British entry was still a long way ahead', emphasising the importance of the French attitude in any eventual British move.[40] The French, of course, were hardly forthcoming.[41]

Towards a new bid

Despite continuing uncertainty about French intentions, during the summer of 1966 London began to sound out the EEC countries about British entry.[42] By mid-1966 Wilson had concluded that integration with Europe offered better long-term prospects for British trade than closer economic relations with the Commonwealth. There was a feeling among ministers that Britain could no longer afford to drift on the EEC question. According to Arthur Snelling, Deputy Under-Secretary of State at the Commonwealth Office, ministers held the view that 'if nothing is done now the domestic arrangements within the Six would be hardening and the problem of entry would become more difficult'.[43] Of particular concern to the British was the completion of the Community's farm regime, scheduled for 1969. The sterling crisis of July 1966 may also have been instrumental in persuading Wilson to seize the initiative on Europe. In fact, Helen Parr, Ben Pimlott and Peter Hennessy have all argued that the Common Market option looked like a good opportunity for Wilson to revive his government's dwindling fortunes after July's financial crisis.[44] Parr has further observed that 'compulsion for Wilson to show his hand in favour of Europe also derived from external sources, as the Americans reiterated a wish to see Britain join the EEC'.[45] In July the State Department had concluded that unequivocal British interest in joining the Community would strengthen the Five in their dealings with Gaullist France and indirectly help to hold NATO together, following de Gaulle's decision to abandon NATO's integrated military structure in March 1966.[46] In August, therefore, Wilson reshuffled his Cabinet and moved the

---

[40] Holt to McEwen, cablegram 6856, 11 July 1966, NAA, A1838/1, 792/1 pt 4. The British record instead quotes Thomson as simply saying that 'he did not expect any dramatic moves soon': CAB 133/329, AMV(66)3rd, 11 July 1966.

[41] Ibid. See also Holt to McEwen, cablegram 6856, 11 July 1966, NAA, A1838/1, 792/1 pt 4.

[42] CAB 129/127, C(66)149, 7 Nov. 1966. See also Parr, British policy, ch. iii.

[43] Arthur Snelling, quoted in Commonwealth Liaison Committee meeting on Britain and the Common Market, 4 Jan. 1967, NAA, A1838/275, 727/4/1 pt 6.

[44] Helen Parr, 'Harold Wilson, Whitehall and British policy towards the European Community, 1964–1967', unpubl. PhD diss. London 2002, ch. iii; Pimlott, Wilson, 435; Peter Hennessy, The prime minister: the office and its holders since 1945, London 2000, 311.

[45] Parr, Britain's policy, 86–7.

[46] Anthony Solomon and Walter Stoessel to Ball, 19 July 1966, FRUS, 1964–68, xiii, doc. 188; James Ellison, 'Dealing with de Gaulle: Anglo-American relations, NATO and

Europeanist George Brown from the Department of Economic Affairs to the Foreign Office. As Wilson himself recalls in his memoirs, 'we seemed to be drawing nearer to the point where we would have to take a decision about Europe, and George Brown seemed to me the appropriate leader for the task which might lie ahead'.[47]

Although his Cabinet was divided between those favouring and those opposing entry, Wilson was clearly gearing up for a decision on Britain's future relationship with Europe.[48] The acrimonious debate over Rhodesia at the London Commonwealth Prime Ministers' Conference in September 1966 had raised further doubts about the Commonwealth's effectiveness as a conduit for British influence in the world and, in so doing, it had strengthened Wilson's resolve to consider EEC membership.[49] Thus, once a number of studies on the EEC had been carried out in Whitehall, Wilson felt that the time had come for a Cabinet debate and a decision.[50] He convened a full-day Cabinet meeting at Chequers on 22 October to allow for a thorough discussion on whether he and Brown should undertake a tour of the EEC capitals. The aim was to conduct a series of high-level probes which would enable the British government to obtain a clearer indication of the EEC countries' views on British entry.[51] As George Brown and Michael Stewart, now First Secretary of State and Secretary of State for Economic Affairs, explained to a further meeting of Cabinet on 1 November, such action was necessary because 'the exploratory discussions which they and the Duchy of Lancaster had been conducting with European countries during 1966 had been taken as far as the current authority allowed'.[52] Further talks were therefore needed 'to ascertain with the necessary authority and precision, what kind of terms we might hope to get in a negotiation for membership'.[53]

At Chequers, Brown and Stewart tabled a paper setting down the political and economic arguments for Britain's entry into the EEC. The two ministers argued that Britain would see its influence in world affairs dramatically reduced unless it joined the Community. Continuing reliance on EFTA and

---

the second application', in Daddow, *Harold Wilson*, 172–3. The Five were West Germany, Italy, The Netherlands, Belgium and Luxembourg.

47 Wilson, *Labour government*, 352. However, according to Pimlott, Brown's appointment to the post of foreign secretary seems to have been dictated by Wilson's desire to neutralise the influence of Callaghan within the Cabinet: *Wilson*, 435–6. According to Parr, while Wilson's decision 'indicated his willingness to endorse a shift in European policy', 'managing his ministers' remained his 'priority in the paranoia generated by the July crisis': 'Wilson and British policy', ch. iii.

48 Pimlott, *Wilson*, 434–5. For divisions inside the Wilson Cabinet see also Douglas Jay, *Change and fortune: a political record*, London 1980, 365–6.

49 On this point see Alexander, 'From imperial power to regional powers', 201–2.

50 For these studies see file CAB 134/2705. See also Wilson, *Labour government*, 352, and Young, *Britain and European unity*, 94.

51 CAB 128/41, CC(66)53rd, 1 Nov. 1966.

52 Ibid.

53 Ibid.

the Commonwealth as an alternative to EEC entry would offer no great comfort as both groupings were likely to seek closer links with a flourishing European economic bloc. Brown and Stewart warned their colleagues that remaining outside the EEC made little economic sense as Britain would find it difficult to thrive economically without greater integration with the continent's most dynamic economies. In the short term, Brown and Stewart concluded, the government should impress on the Six London's continuing interest in EEC membership.[54] Not all ministers agreed. Supported by Anthony Wedgwood Benn (Technology), Barbara Castle (Transport) and Richard Marsh (Power), Richard Crossman rejected Brown and Stewart's political argument for entry, claiming that Britain did not have to join the EEC to remain a great power. Disagreements were also recorded on the economic merits of entry.[55]

The Chequers meeting did not reach a decision, but, on 9 November, the Cabinet gave the 'green light' to the proposed tour of the EEC capitals.[56] On 10 November Wilson informed the Commons that he and Brown would conduct high-level consultations with the Six in order to establish 'whether conditions exist – or do not exist – for fruitful negotiations, and the basis on which such negotiations could take place'.[57] He left the House in no doubt that his government was approaching discussions with the Six with the clear determination to enter the EEC.[58] He then reaffirmed his pledge that Britain would join if, and only if, essential British and Commonwealth interests were safeguarded.[59]

In Australia the government's reaction was muted. Australian posts in western Europe, however, monitored Wilson's moves closely. On 28 November the Senior Trade Officer in London reported that 'a continuing acceleration to the momentum of Britain's tentative moves towards a renewal of [its] application to join the E.E.C. has been imparted over the last month'. He pointed out that 'most top civil servants are now urging entry, as they cannot see any other viable position for Britain at the end of the century … There is open support from a large majority in the Commons'. He therefore advised the DEA that 'time is growing short for a credible British attempt, as the Community will crystalise [sic] most of its arrangements in the next year or two. Opinion throughout the country appears to be moving in favour of British membership'.[60]

Once he had gained the Cabinet's approval, Wilson moved swiftly. A timetable for the tour of the EEC capitals was soon devised, and it was agreed

---

54 CAB 134/2705, E(66)11, 19 Nov. 1966.
55 Parr, *Britain's policy*, 90.
56 CAB 128/41, CC(66)55th, 9 Nov. 1966.
57 Britain, *PD*, HC, 1966–67, dccxxxv.1539–40.
58 Ibid. dccxxxv.1540.
59 Ibid.
60 P. J. Lloyd to DEA, 28 Nov. 1966, NAA, A1838/2, 727/4/1/3 pt 3.

that consultations with Commonwealth governments should take place after the probe and before the announcement of any decision to proceed with negotiations.[61] The British government desired to leave itself with as much room for manoeuvre as possible in these consultations.[62] A Commonwealth Prime Ministers' Conference was to be avoided but, for the time being, Commonwealth governments would be kept informed and given a short account of each visit.[63]

On the eve of the visit of Wilson and Brown to Rome, the Commonwealth Office instructed the British High Commissions to remind Commonwealth governments that Britain would 'have fully in mind' the interests of Commonwealth countries.[64] Was the Holt government to be reassured by this British declaration of intent? Hardly. Throughout 1966 Australian officials had remarked more than once that the implications for Australia of British membership did not loom large in British thinking.[65] At the end of December, Critchley warned the DEA that 'the British Government is committed to entering the EEC if at all possible and that it has made up its mind to try every possible approach'. He emphasised 'the firm and sometimes emotional belief on the part of many people, including a great number of M.P.s, that Britain's destiny is now linked with Europe. Admittedly long-term considerations are involved in this belief, but it is a mood rather than a reasoned analysis'. Critchley pointed out that 'Commonwealth interests and more specifically Australian interests are therefore unlikely to be allowed to stand in the way of British entry. Australia can expect sympathetic consideration but no more'.[66]

Australian defence concerns

Other than the loss of Australian trade preferences in the British market the Australian government, of course, faced a range of pressing political and strategic considerations with regard to a renewed British bid to join the EEC. Critchley further noted in the same December despatch that

> Britain's entry into the EEC can ... be expected to reinforce current pressures for Britain to abandon its defence role east of Suez. This could be expected

---

[61] Consultations with other Commonwealth countries, 30 Nov. 1966, FCO 62/16, Eur(0) (66)11 (Final).
[62] Ibid.
[63] Snelling to Garner, 5 Jan. 1967, FCO 62/16.
[64] CO to Canberra, telegram Y circular 2, 12 Jan. 1967, ibid; Consultations with other Commonwealth countries, 28 Mar. 1967, FCO 62/16, Eur(0) (67)40.
[65] See, for example, Renouf to the acting minister, 24 Mar. 1966, and R. F. Osborn to Plimsoll, 31 Jan. 1966, NAA, A1838/275, 727/4 pt 36. See also Lloyd to DEA, 28 Nov. 1966, NAA, A1838/2, 727/4/1/3 pt 3.
[66] Critchley to DEA, savingram 1, 22 Dec. 1966, NAA, A1838/275, 727/4/2 pt 6.

to follow from the growing British sentiment for Europe, from European pressures and by no means least the short-term balance of payments problems that entry into Europe will involve.[67]

Critchley's words accurately summed up the growing sense of unease prevailing in Australian official circles with regard to the strategic implications of what became known as Wilson's 'approach to Europe'. The serious sterling crisis in July, and the conclusion of the Indonesian-Malaysian *Konfrontasi* in August, had raised additional concerns about Wilson's resolve to maintain a meaningful British defence presence east of Suez. From an Australian viewpoint, Wilson's 'approach to Europe' was clearly a disturbing and potentially damaging complication. As early as 1961 the DEA had advised the Menzies Cabinet that Britain's entry into the EEC 'would be likely to accelerate the shedding of United Kingdom commitments east of Suez'.[68] In the five years since, Canberra had remained concerned that British entry might result in 'a diminution in British concern and interest in maintaining an effective political and strategic role east of Suez where [Australia's] main concern lies'.[69] Thus, the crucial problem in late 1966 was that Wilson's approach to Europe would spell the end for Britain's already wavering determination to remain in the south-east Asian region. This time – unlike in 1961 when the prospect of a British departure still appeared to be relatively remote – the danger of a withdrawal was real.

From the British records it is not possible to establish a clear and direct correlation between Wilson's 'approach to Europe' and his east of Suez policy. The documents pertaining to the defence review that took place between December 1966 and April 1967, and that led to the decision to withdraw from Malaysia and Singapore, make virtually no reference to the Common Market. Nor do the documents relating to the 'approach to Europe' shed any light on linkages between the two issues. This is hardly surprising given the highly compartmentalised nature of the policy-making process through which the Labour government reached two of the most controversial decisions in post-Second World War British history. The resulting lack of coordination within Whitehall – in some measure attributable to the workings of the bureaucratic machinery itself – reflected primarily Wilson's desire to keep two politically divisive questions distinct. The Labour leader was concerned that domestic opposition to the EEC bid would grow stronger were these two issues to be seen as part of a coordinated attempt to undertake a major shift in Britain's foreign and defence policies.[70]

---

[67] Ibid.
[68] Cabinet submission 1183, 26 June 1961, NAA, A1838/269, TS899/1/4 pt 2.
[69] British entry into the EEC, n.d., NAA, A1838/275, 727/4/2 pt 7; L. D. Thomson to Keith Shann, 11 Jan. 1967, A1838/275, 727/4/2 pt 6.
[70] Parr, *Britain's policy*, 141. See also idem, 'Going native: the Foreign Office and Harold Wilson's policy towards the EEC, 1964–67', in Daddow, *Harold Wilson*, 88.

Yet, connections, if not a direct correlation, between these issues did exist. Some ministers certainly made a connection in the Cabinet debate on the EEC question on 30 April when it was argued that 'if we were to join the Community ... we could hope to gain a new role of political leadership which would provide the political stimulus formerly given by our imperial role'. Wilson himself, in drawing the day-long debate to a close, highlighted the importance of EEC membership as a means of increasing British clout in Europe, of providing an alternative to the increasingly unwieldy Commonwealth as a conduit of British influence in the wider world and of securing a certain degree of autonomy from American policies east of Suez.[71] While intriguing, these did not appear to be the only significant points of contact between the Common Market and east of Suez questions. In early May 1967, following the decision both to join the EEC and to withdraw from east of Suez, Callaghan reminded High Commissioner Downer that the British

> must cut their coat according to their cloth. The price of entry to the E.E.C. for the first few years would be great. It could amount to as much as pounds 300 million or even pounds 400 million. Obviously the advantages lay in the long term; there is none in the short term. So the initial period would be difficult and costly. This meant ... that [the British] must prune severely the defence bill. It was just impossible for Britain to remain in Malaysia. He hoped he could save pounds 100 million a year in that direction alone. The Government, in order to pay the price of entering the Common Market, must economise on defence.[72]

A few days later, Healey told the US Secretary of Defense, Robert McNamara, that 'the decision [to withdraw] was being made partly for budgetary reasons, but he [Healey] also acknowledged that it was related to the British desire for association with Europe'. He 'indicated that, in the British view, it would be psychologically incompatible with their proposed role in Europe for them to maintain commitments on the mainland of Asia'.[73] Australian concerns were hardly misplaced, therefore, despite the lack of an unequivocal correlation between the Common Market and the east of Suez questions.

---

[71] CAB 128/42, CC(67)26th, 30 Apr. 1967; Parr, *Britain's policy*, 141, and 'Going native', 87.
[72] Downer to Holt, cablegram 5326, 3 May 1967, NAA, A1209/80, 1966/7335 pt 3; London to DEA, cablegram 5322, 3 May 1967, A1838/346, TS691/1/1 pt 1.
[73] Washington to DEA, cablegram 1995, 11 May 1967, NAA, A1209/80, 1966/7335 pt 3.

Probing visits to the EEC capitals

Publicly, the British government had so far avoided defining in clear terms what it meant by the Commonwealth's 'essential interests'. Likewise, it had refrained from indicating how it proposed to defend them. The reasons were obvious. First, there was no point in upsetting Commonwealth countries before negotiations had even begun. Revealing its intentions would certainly attract strong criticism from the Commonwealth which in turn could provide the French government with ammunition with which to oppose British entry. Second, and perhaps even more important, it would be unwise for the British government to spell out its negotiating aims before any probe had taken place: the Wilson and Brown tour of the EEC capitals was meant to ascertain whether the conditions for meaningful negotiations with the Six existed. If the British wished their bid to succeed, it was important to avoid presenting the Six with a list of detailed requests. Privately, however, the British government was more specific. On 9 November, Brown told his Cabinet colleagues that 'we might hope, and should need, to negotiate not merely transitional arrangements ... but also certain permanent adaptations of the present arrangements in the Community. The position of New Zealand, for example, would be a point of fundamental importance to us'.[74] In the same Cabinet meeting, Herbert Bowden, the Commonwealth Secretary, added that 'it would ... also be desirable to inform the governments of the Six in general terms that we should need to know whether terms at least as good as those negotiated by the previous administration in 1962 could be assumed for Commonwealth countries in Asia, Africa and the Caribbean, as well as special safeguards for New Zealand'. At no stage was mention made of Australia. The implication was clear: the most Australia could hope for was a lengthy transitional period.

In the opening meeting with the Italian government on 16 January, Wilson told the Italians that 'we have come to the discussions with the clear intention of entering into the Community: and we have decided to go right to the very end'.[75] Wilson emphasised that Britain 'had embarked on a great effort and would not like to see the great issues bogged down in discussions of questions such as kangaroo meat'.[76] Kangaroo meat had become a byword for Australia's stubborn defence of its own interests during the 1961–3 negotiations. Brown told the Italians that 'in relation to the Commonwealth trade it was well known that there were problems affecting Australia and Canada, but the really difficult case was that of New Zealand'. He added that 'New Zealand was an area in which he doubted whether a transitional period would suffice as final answer to our problems'. On the following day Brown stressed the need for special arrangements for New

[74] CAB 128/41, CC(66)55th, 9 Nov. 1966.
[75] Rome to DEA, cablegram 76, 17 Jan. 1967, NAA, A1838/275, 727/4/1 pt 6.
[76] CAB 129/128, C(67)33, 16 Mar. 1967.

Zealand as opposed to transitional arrangements for other Commonwealth countries. In the following weeks Wilson and Brown presented the same arguments during their visits to the remaining capitals of the EEC.[77]

These tactics did not escape the Australians' notice. In cabling Canberra in February 1967, the External Affairs branch in London reported that 'if Britain sees an opportunity for a successful application ... she may be expected to seize it quickly, with a minimum of discussion on broad principles only, and with little disposition to engage in protracted negotiations on matters of detail which might be of primary interest to Australia'.[78] Advice tendered by other Australian missions in western Europe followed similar lines.[79] Yet the news coming from Europe was not as discouraging as it seemed. In particular, the Australians could take some comfort from the fact that the French attitude towards Britain remained extremely unhelpful, if not downright negative. Despatches from the Australian embassy in Paris were pessimistic about British chances of overcoming French hostility. As the ambassador, Ronald Walker, noted in February 1967, 'the strong impression here is that [the French] are opposed to [British entry]'.[80]

In Canberra, the Holt government recognised the difficulties that Britain was encountering over its European bid. It doubted that, even if it decided to apply, Britain would be able to join in the light of persistent French hostility. The overall Australian view, therefore, was that the best course of action was to adopt a 'wait and see' approach. As Bunting noted in February 1967, 'there is not a great deal of anxiety here over Britain's prospects though we are keeping a close watch on developments'.[81] Yet not all Australian officials were in agreement with the government's 'wait and see' policy, particularly those not in Canberra. In mid-February Harry sent a despatch to the DEA once again complaining about a lack of guidance. According to him, the government's 'public attitude towards the "Wilson Round" has not indicated much Australian interest'. In his view, guidance 'would seem desirable, if we wish to make any attempt to influence the outcome', and to dispel the impression that Australian trade had been so diversified that 'Australian exports to Great Britain would not constitute a major problem in any negotiations'. Harry warned the DEA that '[Australia's] silence could in certain circumstances be construed as an act of policy'.[82]

Harry's despatch was not particularly well received in Canberra. Alexander Campbell, Deputy Secretary at the DTI, remarked rather harshly that 'until

[77] Ibid.
[78] London to DEA, savingram 4, 1 Feb. 1967, NAA, A1209/43, 1967/7117 pt 1.
[79] See, for instance, The Hague to DEA, cablegram 104, 28 Feb. 1967, NAA, A1838/275, 727/4/1 pt 7; Harry to DEA, savingram 3, 10 Feb. 1967, A1838/275, 727/4/2 pt 6.
[80] Walker to DEA, despatch 1, 28 Feb. 1967, NAA, A1838/2, 727/4/1 annex; Walker to DEA, savingram 5, 14 Feb. 1967, A1209/43, 1967/7117 pt 1.
[81] John Bunting to J. L. Knott, 10 Feb. 1967, NAA, A1209/43, 1967/7117 pt 1.
[82] Harry to DEA, savingram 3, 10 Feb. 1967, NAA, A1838/275, 727/4/2 pt 6.

told otherwise [Harry] should stick to the guidance notes' he had already been given.[83] On 29 March the DEA belatedly sent guidance. In noting that the '"Wilson round" has aroused great public interest in Britain and the Six', the DEA conceded that 'it is not unnatural to feel that Australia should adopt a comparably outspoken attitude'. Yet, it hastened to point out that 'doing so would be profitable only if it were consistent with the tactical requirements of policies adopted by the Australian Government'. External Affairs stressed that 'departments do not … consider the UK-EEC position in isolation. It is necessary to strike a delicate balance between Government policy in this field, in the Kennedy Round, in other international fields and in relation to the totality of Australian trade, economic and political aims and objectives.' External Affairs therefore urged Australian posts in Europe to keep strictly to the government's basic line on the question of British entry and summarised Australia's position in three main points: first, 'the decision to enter the EEC is one for Britain alone to take'; second, 'the adoption by Britain of the Common External Tariff and the CAP as has evolved so far, could cause serious damage to Australian industries'; and third, 'if Britain decided to negotiate we hope she will press for terms and conditions to protect vital Australian trade interests'.[84]

Harry had been forewarned of the kind of response he could expect from Canberra. In a message dated 23 March, Keith Shann, First Assistant Secretary at the DEA, advised him that 'Trade and Treasury, at present, seem inclined to a policy of "layin' low and sayin' nuffin" or at least as little as possible'. Shann pointed out that 'one of the Government's major concerns is not to be laid open to moral pressure from Britain for some forms of compensation e.g. in the trade field in the event of a second failure to vault the ramparts, should anything we do have presented a major stumbling block in the way'.[85] Of course, there were also other reasons for 'layin' low and sayin' nuffin'. Until 'essential Commonwealth interests' were spelled out, there was no need for Australia to voice disapproval, especially as the British prospects for entry remained uncertain. Furthermore, with the Kennedy Round of the General Agreement on Tariffs and Trade negotiations reaching their final stage in the spring of 1967, the Holt government was keen to negotiate the best possible outcome for Australian export markets, and British co-operation was thought to be important in achieving this aim. The Australian view was that a good deal on a number of farm commodities would soften the impact of a possible British entry. Thus, the Kennedy Round was seen in Canberra as a useful, albeit partial, remedy for the loss of British markets.[86] Finally, but no less important, the question of a possible British withdrawal from east of

[83] J. P. Pomeroy to Thomson, 23 Feb. 1967, ibid.
[84] DEA to Brussels, cablegram 93, 29 Mar. 1967, ibid.
[85] Shann to Harry, 23 Mar. 1967, ibid.
[86] See, for instance, McEwen to Holt, cablegram 4808, 25 Apr. 1967, NAA, A1209/43, 1967/7117 pt 2.

Suez with its strategic implications for Australia was a major concern, and consequently another reason for not disturbing Anglo-Australian relations unduly at this point.

From the probe to the launch of a new bid

Wilson and Brown's European tour proved less successful than expected. In Paris, in spite of de Gaulle's recognition of Britain's willingness to 'moor itself alongside the Continent', the talks had been less than reassuring.[87] De Gaulle had reminded the British that 'the participation of Britain in the Community presented great problems, given the differences of its economic interests, its monetary arrangements, its contacts with the outside world'.[88] Somewhat ominously, he had hinted at the possibility of 'association'. There was nothing in his attitude to indicate that he would refrain from vetoing a British bid again. Yet, Wilson seemed to believe that a rebuff would be a difficult course of action for the French to take.[89] In Bonn, consultations with the Kiesinger government were also disappointing. The German Chancellor not only warned the British of the strong French resistance to British entry that he had detected in his recent discussions with de Gaulle, but he also signalled Bonn's unwillingness to 'get deeply involved in controversial matters' with the French.[90] The implications were clear: West Germany supported British entry, but not at any cost, and certainly not at the cost of jeopardising Franco-German relations. None the less, having completed the probe of the EEC capitals, in early March Wilson mounted a new bid for membership despite the mixed outcome of his European tour and some domestic resistance to EEC entry.[91] Both the Cabinet and the Labour Party were still seriously divided on the approach to Europe.[92]

In this context, it is noteworthy that three ministers encouraged Australia to take a vocal stance. In mid-February, the Minister of Agriculture, Fred Peart, asked A. P. Fleming, the Australian Special Commercial Adviser in London, why Australia was 'so quiet about the possibility of the United Kingdom entering the Common Market'. A few days later Peart told another Australian representative that 'it is time that you (meaning Australia) took action'.[93] In late April 1967, following his talks with Peart, Bowden and Jay, McEwen reported to Holt that the British ministers put to him quite strongly the view that Australia should publicly denounce the negative

87 CAB 129/128, C(67)33, 16 Mar. 1967.
88 Ibid.
89 Parr, Britain's policy, 106–8. See also CAB 128/42, CC(67)14th, 21 Mar. 1967.
90 CAB 129/128, C(67)33, 16 Mar. 1967.
91 Parr, Britain's policy, ch. v.
92 See Pimlott, Wilson, 440, and Anne Deighton, 'The Labour Party, public opinion and the "second try" in 1967', in Daddow, Harold Wilson, 42–3.
93 NAA, A1209/43, 1967/7117 pt 2, UK-EEC, 24 Feb. 1967.

effects of British entry on both Australian and British interests. According to McEwen, 'they deplored that without this it would be accepted that for Australia [Britain's] possible entry posed no problems'. Clearly, as McEwen remarked, some British ministers 'were looking for ammunition' to sway a divided Cabinet against a new application to the EEC.[94] Australia, however, was not prepared to provide it.

Between mid-March and 2 May 1967, when the formal decision to apply to the EEC was finally taken, the Cabinet was convened several times to examine the 'approach to Europe'.[95] Step by step, Wilson adroitly managed to steer his ministers in the direction he favoured. Those who opposed a British application comforted themselves with the thought that de Gaulle would veto it yet again. On 2 May Wilson announced in the Commons that Britain would again bid for membership under article 237 of the Treaty of Rome.[96] On the Commonwealth question he informed the House that

> [t]here are also highly important Commonwealth interests, mainly in the field of agriculture, for which it is our duty to seek safeguards in the negotiations. These include, in particular, the special problems of New Zealand and of Commonwealth sugar producing countries, whose needs are at present safeguarded by the Commonwealth Sugar Agreement. We have, as the House knows, been in touch with all our Commonwealth countries, and will make special arrangements to keep in close consultation with them, as with our E.F.T.A. partners throughout the negotiations.[97]

On 10 May the House of Commons endorsed the new bid.[98] On 11 May the application was deposited in Brussels. Britain was again knocking at the door of the Six.

Australian and Commonwealth problems

How was the British government planning to safeguard what Wilson called 'highly important Commonwealth interests'? As far as Australia was concerned, the British Cabinet discussions, which took place in the days immediately preceding the decision to apply, gave a clear indication of British thinking. And, for Australia, they were far from reassuring. On 27 April the Cabinet had considered two memoranda by the Commonwealth Secretary, one on the value of the Commonwealth,[99] the other on Commonwealth

---

[94] McEwen to Holt, cablegram 4808, 25 Apr. 1967, ibid.

[95] For the Cabinet's decision to apply see Parr, *Britain's policy*, ch. v.

[96] In 1961 the Macmillan government had also applied under article 237. Unlike Wilson, however, Macmillan had stressed the purely conditional nature of the British application. See Britain, *PD*, HC, 1960–1, dcxlv.930.

[97] Cmnd. 3264, *Membership of the European Communities*, London 1967, 4.

[98] Wilson, *Labour government*, 499.

[99] CAB 129/129, C(67)59, 24 Apr. 1967.

interests in Britain's negotiations for entry.[100] In presenting the first memorandum, Bowden highlighted that 'there had been major changes in recent years, and we should make it clear that we were not prepared to sustain the Commonwealth whatever the cost to us might be'.[101] In the second memorandum he explained that Australia was likely to ask Britain to secure permanent arrangements, 'except to the extent that prices and access to the enlarged Community for cereals, meat, dairy produce and sugar are assured by international commodity agreements'.[102] He told the Cabinet, however, that 'it would not, in practice, be possible to obtain all [Commonwealth] desiderata'.[103] The memorandum stated that, with regard to the Australians, 'we should probably be unable to secure any permanent derogations for them and the outcome would probably be transitional periods for the gradual application of the levy and/or the common external tariff, with perhaps some reduced duty quota on a few industrial raw materials'.[104] Although Bowden reminded his colleagues of the 'importance of sustaining as far as possible the interests of Australia', in the ensuing discussion he observed that

> in considering the interests of Australia and Canada, it was pertinent to bear in mind that not only had they a higher level of income per head than the United Kingdom, or any member of the EEC, but also that in recent years they had been guided solely by their own interests in reducing or eliminating preferences which they accorded [Britain], in pursuing a policy of rapid industrialisation and, e.g., in buying foreign aircraft when we might reasonably have looked to them to pay more regard to United Kingdom interests.[105]

A similar point was made by Wilson three days later during a Cabinet meeting at Chequers. He told his ministers that

> relations with the Commonwealth in recent years in economic matters had been disappointing. There had been little attempt on the part of other Commonwealth countries to look other than to their narrow national interest. In spite of the initiatives we had taken at the Meeting of Commonwealth Prime Ministers in 1965 there had been a complete failure to take concerted Commonwealth action, even in respect of Government purchases. Australia and New Zealand preferred to purchase American aircraft of types not superior to our own. ... In the Far East the policies of Australia and New Zealand were increasingly diverging from our own, with a very strong emphasis on their narrow area of interest in South-East Asia.[106]

---

100 CAB 129/129, C(67)63, 25 Apr. 1967.
101 CAB 128/42, CC(67)23rd, 27 Apr. 1967.
102 CAB 129/129, C(67)63, 25 Apr. 1967.
103 CAB 128/42, CC(67)23rd, 27 Apr. 1967.
104 CAB 129/129, C(67)63, 25 Apr. 1967.
105 CAB 128/42, CC(67)23rd, 27 Apr. 1967.
106 CAB 128/42, CC(67)26th, 30 Apr. 1967. Wilson was referring to the Menzies government's decision in 1963 to replace the RAAF's ageing Canberras fleet with a new generation of fighter bombers. In spite of Macmillan's pressure on Menzies, Australia

If these remarks betrayed disillusionment towards old Commonwealth partners, they also indicated Wilson's eagerness to avoid making the problem of Commonwealth safeguards a central issue in Britain's bid for entry. Yet it was not without irony that Wilson was reproaching Canberra and Wellington for putting narrow national interests before Commonwealth loyalties. His government stood equally exposed to the same accusation as it sought entry into the EEC regardless of the costs that such a move imposed on Britain's Commonwealth allies.

Unlike New Zealand, Australia was not to be considered a special case. Australia was less dependent on trade with Britain than New Zealand. It was also experiencing an extended period of sustained economic expansion,[107] and was gradually beginning to enjoy the benefits of a surging global demand for minerals.[108] Australia was also increasingly diversifying its pattern of trade from Europe towards the Asia-Pacific region (*see* figures 1, 2). Australian concerns over British accession to the EEC were therefore not likely to find much sympathy in Whitehall. From London's perspective, the Australian case, while deserving of attention, need not be the subject of too much concern. However, the question arose of how to inform the Australians, or how to prevent them – if they felt indignant at perceived British abandonment – from causing domestic political problems by encouraging those sections of the British public that were still sympathetic to the Commonwealth, to lobby for the protection of Australian interests.

Australia and the British decision to apply

For the time being British concerns over a possible Australian backlash with regard to the new bid were to remain unrealised. In Canberra reports that the British Cabinet was about to make a decision on the EEC application were overshadowed by the sudden announcement in late April of the British intention to withdraw completely from Malaysia and Singapore by the mid-1970s. The British decision was distressing news for the Holt government. In response, Canberra launched an intense diplomatic campaign to persuade the British not to take such a drastic course of action, but refrained from

preferred American F-111As to British TSR2 fighter bombers. This point is discussed in Goldsworthy, *Losing the blanket*, 141. As Menzies explained to Douglas-Home, Australia's preference for American F-111As 'undoubtedly greatly satisfies the United States and sustains their interest in this corner of the world. This is a most important by-product of the decision and one which I hope may contain some merit from your point of view': Menzies to Alec Douglas-Home, 24 Oct. 1963, DO 164/27/74.
107 Barrie Dyster and David Meredith, *Australia in the international economy in the twentieth century*, Cambridge 1990, 234. According to Dyster and Meredith, from 1961 to 1969–70 the average annual rate of real economic growth was 5.36%.
108 For the so-called mineral boom see ibid. 244. See also Geoffrey Bolton, *The Oxford history of Australia*, V: *The middle way, 1942–1995*, Melbourne 1996, 178.

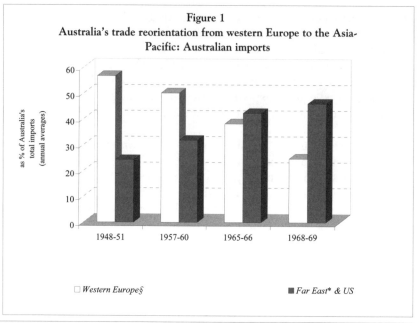

Figure 1
Australia's trade reorientation from western Europe to the Asia-Pacific: Australian imports

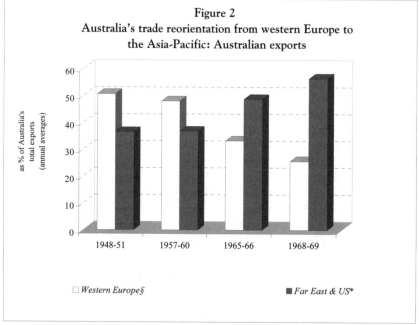

Figure 2
Australia's trade reorientation from western Europe to the Asia-Pacific: Australian exports

§ Britain, Belgium, France, Italy, Luxembourg, Netherlands, West Germany
* Brunei, Burma, Cambodia, China, Hong Kong, India, Indonesia, Laos, Macao, Malaysia, New Zealand, Pakistan, Philippines, Singapore, Sri Lanka, Taiwan, Thailand and Vietnam

Source: Dyster and Meredith, *Australia in the international economy,* 249.

132

voicing its concerns over the issue of EEC membership. In the view of Peter Lawler, Deputy Secretary to the PMD, Australia needed 'to guard against aggravating British sensitivities in a way which could be generally counter-productive for our dealings with them particularly on the fundamental defence issue'.[109] Holt agreed and made it clear that any Australian reply should take into account the question of British forces in south-east Asia. He believed that Australia was already pressing Britain strongly on the east of Suez question and that 'we might not be able to press on EEC at the same time'.[110] In this he was supported by his Treasurer, William McMahon, who also thought it 'unwise for Australia to open up a "second front"'.[111] Thus, in seeking advice from McEwen on the drafting of a possible reply, Holt suggested that Australia 'should not at this stage make any general comment on the policy issues but simply say that the extent to which Australian interests would be affected by British entry into the Community depends upon safeguards [the British] could provide to cover our interests'.[112]

McEwen concurred. In the reply to the British, which was for the most part drafted by McEwen, Holt simply pointed out that 'in general Australia's problems are much the same as in 1962. While there has been some diversification of [Australia's] trade, no substantial new markets have been found for the sensitive items in our commodity exports. In fact in absolute terms Australia has more at risk now than [in] 1962 and this is growing'. He reiterated the importance of commodity agreements as a means of overcoming some of the problems of British entry and urged the British to take a positive attitude on them within the Kennedy Round. Holt also drew attention to the possible implications of entry on sterling and on the future capital inflow from Britain. He observed that Australia had always adopted a responsible attitude with regard to sterling holdings and had consistently stood by Britain in times of adversity. He concluded: 'We trust you will keep these considerations in mind.'[113] Whether the British would do so was of course a matter for the UK-EEC negotiations to reveal. The Australian government, however, was under no illusion. As the Secretary of the DTI, Alan Westerman, explained to Harry, 'there was no point in Australia putting in a lot of work to devise safeguard arrangements unless we knew that the British would seriously attempt to negotiate them ... but we should be under no illusion that the British would do anything effective'.[114]

109 Lawler to Holt, 27 Apr. 1967, NAA, A1209/43, 1967/7117 pt 2.
110 Bunting to D. J. Munro, 23 Apr. 1967, ibid.
111 Lawler to Holt, 27 Apr. 1967, ibid.
112 Holt to McEwen, cablegram 3245, 24 Apr. 1967, ibid.
113 DEA to London, cablegram 3360, 28 Apr. 1967, ibid.
114 Notes of discussions with Westerman, 15–16 May 1967, NAA, A1838/275, 727/4/2 pt 7.

7

The 'Approach to Europe',
May–December 1967

'I just cannot understand Britain's refusal to consider any ideas we put up for future trading agreements. The door is being shut on almost all hopes of future expansion of trade between Britain and Australia, and in view of the doubts about de Gaulle ever letting you into the Common Market, this seems damn silly to us': Alan Westerman, 17 October 1967.[1]

The news that the British Cabinet had decided on 2 May 1967 to apply again to the EEC was received with remarkable restraint in Canberra; the British High Commissioner, Charles Johnston, informed the CO that 'by contrast to the vehement outburst on the part of Australian Ministers with which the British application was greeted in 1961, the reception accorded to the announcement on this occasion was relatively restrained'.[2] He attributed such self-control to the fact that Australia had long since taken Britain's willingness to join the EEC for granted.[3] There was certainly an element of truth in this. Yet other factors were more instrumental in shaping the Australian attitude. Of particular importance in the late spring of 1967 was Holt's reluctance to 'open up a second front' while his administration was exerting strong pressure on the British government to maintain a military presence in south-east Asia.

The Holt government may have restrained itself publicly, but it did not remain completely silent on the EEC issue. In private it sought to draw London's attention to the blow that the combined effect of both the withdrawal and the EEC application would inflict on Anglo-Australian relations. In mid-May Downer warned Healey that if the British persisted in their plans to withdraw, and simultaneously entered the EEC, then the effect on the Australian public would be disastrous. The Australian High Commissioner added 'that this would extend, in our lifetime, even to the Queen's position in Australia, and that in the not-so-long-run the British connection with Australia and New Zealand would be lost'.[4] A few days previously, the Australian governor-general, Richard Casey, had made the same point. He

---

[1] As quoted in the *Evening Standard*, 17 Oct. 1967.
[2] Charles Johnston to Bowden, 19 May 1967, FCO 20/50.
[3] Ibid.
[4] Downer to Holt, cablegram 6177, 18 May 1967, NAA, A2908/1, D25 pt 1.

had told Healey that 'these two things [the withdrawal and the EEC question] combined would be interpreted in Australia as definite and inescapable evidence of British indifference and isolationism so far as Australia is concerned'.[5] In his view 'it would be almost a fatal knock to the most loyal Commonwealth countries'.[6]

Policy-makers in Canberra were in the meantime assessing the effects of the British application on the Wilson government's defence policy. They were in no doubt that London's bid for EEC membership had paved the way for the decision to withdraw from the Far East. As the DEA noted in May 1967, 'it seems clear that the sudden collapse in British East of Suez policy is due to the decision to apply for membership of EEC'. DEA officials added that, while clearly 'brought on by the issue of applying for membership of EEC … the sudden reversal of the 1966 policy' was not so much the product of foreign policy considerations, but rather of economic concerns and Labour Party politics. Officials in External Affairs did not deny, for instance, that Britain's new attitude on the east of Suez question could, to some extent, be ascribed to the fact that the British were perhaps 'clearing their decks for entry [in]to the Common Market – the implication being that they were making themselves more acceptable to de Gaulle' by shedding military commitments east of Suez. Yet they thought that it was domestic factors that had played a greater role – namely, Callaghan's concerns about the heavy initial costs of joining the EEC and the widespread desire within the Labour Party to see the government reduce defence expenditure in favour of increased spending on social services. Under these circumstances, the DEA observed, 'bargains are undoubtedly necessary within the Labour Party to produce a workable pro-E.E.C. policy. Something had to be done about the divisive issue of East of Suez if the central policy [the application to the EEC] was to be secured within the Party'.[7]

Rather different was the assessment tendered to Canberra by the Senior External Affairs Representative in London. In a cable dated 15 May Critchley informed the DEA that, strictly speaking, 'Britain's bid to enter the Common Market was probably not a motivating factor in the defence planning', yet 'it is now a complication and provides arguments for the British to stick to their intentions', that is, to leave the Far East and retreat into Europe.[8] In other words, the Common Market issue reinforced rather than determined the British Cabinet's decision to withdraw. Although it is not possible

5   Diary entry, 9 May 1967, R. G. Casey papers, NLA, Canberra, MS 6150, series 4, box 31.
6   Diary entry, 15 May 1967, ibid.
7   External Affairs assessment: east of Suez, 5 May 1967, NAA, A1209/84, 1967/7334 attachment 1; Australian policy on British defence policy east of Suez, DEA working paper, 19 May 1967, NAA, A1209/84, 1967/7334 attachment 1.
8   Critchley to DEA, cablegram 5930, 15 May 1967, NAA, A1209/80, 1966/7335 pt 3. See also Critchley to DEA, cablegram 5660, 9 May 1967, A1838/346, TS691/1/1 pt 1.

from the British records to establish a clear and unambiguous correlation between Wilson's approach to Europe and his east of Suez policy, the important element here is the fact that Australian policy-makers generally took for granted that such a correlation existed. First, the timing of both decisions was seen as highly suspect. Second, statements made by some British ministers strengthened the Australian belief that a connection did indeed exist.[9] Last, and perhaps more important, political trends in Britain were perceived as working in favour of a British shift towards Europe.

The British bid runs into quicksand

Yet, 'taking Britain into Europe [was] not all plain sailing', to use a metaphor employed by the *Sydney Morning Herald* in early May.[10] Uncertainty about Britain being able to join the EEC remained strong, even within Whitehall. Saville Garner, Permanent Under-Secretary of State at the CO, told Downer that 'no-one, and I mean no-one, in the British Government machine knows what will be the result of the application and conjecture ranges from black pessimism to the rosiest optimism, but there can be no certainty'.[11] As ever, the French position remained crucial. From Paris, Ambassador Walker informed Canberra that the French remained 'opposed to British entry and in their effort to draw negotiations out they will raise precisely those questions about British entry which the Five and European opinion within France could not challenge as unreasonable'.[12]

Developments in Europe proved Walker's assessment accurate. At a press conference on 16 May, de Gaulle questioned whether Britain was really ready to join.[13] While not exercising a formal veto, de Gaulle intended to prevent the opening of negotiations. For his part, Wilson could not afford to back down after having staked his personal credibility, and that of his government, on the new bid. On 17 May he told de Gaulle that Britain would not take the General's negative remarks as a final answer and proceeded to instruct government departments to carry on with plans for negotiations.[14] As Arthur Snelling, Deputy Under-Secretary of State at the CO, put it,

> the message from the summit to senior officials in all departments in Whitehall was to ignore [the] [G]eneral's pronouncements and to press on vigorously with preparations for early negotiations with the Six. This message ...

---

[9] See chapter 6 above.

[10] *Sydney Morning Herald*, 9 May 1967.

[11] Knott to Bunting, 12 May 1967, NAA, A1209/43, 1967/7208.

[12] Ronald Walker to DEA, cablegram 1741, 3 May 1967, NAA, A1838/275, 727/4/1 pt 8.

[13] For de Gaulle's speech see Uwe Kitzinger, *The second try: Labour and the EEC*, Oxford 1968, 179–88. See also Parr, 'British policy', ch. vi.

[14] Wilson, *Labour government*, 505.

continued to reverberate throughout the corridors of power in loud, clear tones, and heaven help those who choose to take it lightly.[15]

De Gaulle, however, remained unmoved. On 29 May he told the EEC Council of Ministers in Rome that the Six should have 'profound and prolonged discussions' among themselves on the overall issue of enlarging the Community, before they could examine the merits of the British application.[16] It was evident that the General was doing his utmost to sabotage Wilson's 'approach to Europe'.

Anglo-Australian consultations, June 1967

Despite these early difficulties, London remained determined to conclude bilateral negotiations with Commonwealth governments on safeguarding their interests before the summer holidays, so that it would be able to announce to the Six that Britain was ready to enter into negotiations.[17] Whitehall was under strong pressure to dispose of the Commonwealth problem as expeditiously as possible.[18] To this end, consultations with Australia, which had been requested by the British to discuss essential Australian interests, were scheduled for early June.[19] The talks were expected to be preliminary and entirely non-committal.[20] Yet the British approached them with a degree of anxiety. They were concerned that 'Australia may cut up very rough when [it] hears that we take the view that it will be impossible for us to secure for her any special arrangements extending beyond the transitional period for our entry into the EEC'. It was felt that the Australians could 'make a big row' and, if that was the case, could 'get widespread support in the British press and Parliament … on the ground that [the British government] is letting down [its] truest friends'.[21]

In the event, when Australian and British officials met in London on 6–8 June, British concerns proved unfounded.[22] Despite being told that Britain would probably be unable to negotiate more than transitional arrangements for Australia,[23] the Australian team raised no objections, maintaining a low-

---

15 Snelling quoted in Canadian High Commission (London) to Canadian Department of External Affairs, telegram 2721, 19 May 1967, NAA, A1838/275, 727/4/2 pt 7.

16 Kitzinger, *Second try*, 52.

17 Canadian High Commission (London) to Canadian Department of External Affairs, telegram 2721, 19 May 1967, NAA, A1838/275, 727/4/2 pt 7.

18 See again Snelling quoted ibid.

19 Rooke to Bunting, 9 May 1967, NAA, A1838/275, 727/4/2 pt 7.

20 Official committee on approach to Europe: Britain and EEC, 2 June 1967, FCO 20/47.

21 Snelling to Garner, 5 June 1967, ibid.

22 Canberra to CO, telegram 823, 22 May 1967, ibid.

23 Consultations with Australian officials: first session, 6 June 1967, ibid.

key approach. Australian officials made it clear that they 'had no brief to discuss "essentiality" of items' and confined themselves to 'describing facts on commodities', and 'assessing loss in [Australia's] trade if there were no safeguards'.[24] Australian officials were, of course, following a strict brief. Canberra had advised them 'to confine this round to getting the facts across and not be led into any suggestions about safeguards or selection of some commodities as being more or less essential then others'. The team had also been warned that the British would 'no doubt seek to play it in a manner which continually puts pressure on us'.[25]

Not surprisingly, the British were irritated, finding the discussions with the Australian officials 'difficult 'and 'unproductive'. Clearly, the British had hopes that the Australians would not only avoid creating undue problems, but would also be more amenable than they actually were. They wanted the Australians to indicate what interests were regarded as essential for even 'New Zealand was limiting her request for special arrangements to three commodities (butter, cheese and lamb)'.[26] But the Australians 'could not agree to follow suit'.[27] The British team ended the three days of talks by making a unilateral distinction between those commodities which they regarded as being not 'seriously at risk' and those likely to be significantly affected by British entry. The first group included meats, cheese, apples and pears, wines, eggs, honey, lead, zinc and cereals with the exception of wheat. The second category included butter, wheat, canned and dried fruit, and manufactured goods. As for wool, a major source of foreign earnings, it was to remain unaffected by British entry.[28] In relation to sugar, Australian and British officials agreed that this item should be discussed at a conference of sugar-producing countries to be held in London in late June.[29] While seeking to categorise Australian commodities, the British team was careful, at this stage, to avoid drawing too firm a distinction between 'essential' and 'inessential' interests.[30] They were wary of making commitments or 'agreeing with [the Australians] the opening position to be adopted with the Six'.[31] Godfrey Shannon, Assistant Under-Secretary at the CO, noted in mid-May that

in 1961–63 the British government [was] handicapped by having to negotiate on two fronts, that is, with the Commonwealth as well as the EEC. [The British government] ought to try to avoid getting into the same position again

[24] London to DEA, cablegram 7262, 9 June 1967, NAA, A1838/275, 727/4/2 pt 7.
[25] DEA to Allan Fleming, cablegram 4800, 2 June 1967, ibid.
[26] CO to Canberra, telegram 1247, 9 June 1967, FCO 20/47.
[27] Short report on talks with Australian officials, undated, ibid.
[28] Ibid.
[29] CO to Canberra, telegram 1222, 6 June 1967, ibid.
[30] Consultations with Australian officials: second session, 8 June 1967, and short report on talks with Australian officials, undated, ibid.
[31] Draft brief for talks between prime minister and Holt, 8 June 1967, FCO 20/48, Euro (67)74 (Final).

... [T]he consultations with the Commonwealth should be conducted on the basis of asking them what they want to tell us, but making no commitments to them about what we shall do about their representations, and keeping our hands free to decide what we say to the Six and at what stage of our negotiations. We should, moreover, not disclose to the Commonwealth in advance what our negotiating position is to be.[32]

Australian interests in the UK-EEC negotiations

The Australian refusal to distinguish between essential and non-essential Australian interests was reiterated by Holt in his talks with Wilson in mid-June. Holt had flown to London primarily to discuss the important developments in Britain's east of Suez policy. On the Common Market issue the Australian leader confined himself to explaining briefly the Australian attitude to the EEC question.[33] He told Wilson that 'his main purpose would be to explain and put in its political context the reason why Australia could not at this stage at least identify "essential trade interests" that she would wish to see protected as opposed to the lesser or inessential interests'.[34] As he pointed out, 'he could not go home and suggest that any particular industry was regarded as expendable'.[35]

Holt's tactics, dilatory as they might have appeared to the British, were of course motivated by domestic and foreign policy concerns, as set out in a cable that McEwen had sent to him on the eve of his arrival in London. Holt had let McEwen take the lead on the Common Market issue, and in the absence of any substantive discussion in Cabinet on the matter Australian tactics were principally determined by the Trade Minister and his department. In the cable, McEwen argued that it would not be possible for the British to achieve entry without damaging Australia's interests. 'Because of the British determination to enter Europe', he admitted candidly, 'there is very little scope for us ... to influence the terms upon which Britain might enter the E.E.C.' Hence, the course of action he envisaged was 'to adopt a posture which is determined primarily by domestic political and economic considerations and which will give us the best presentational position with the Australian public and with the industries concerned, if and when market damage occurs'.[36] Accordingly, McEwen recommended that

[w]e must continue to maintain that all our trade interests are important and that we welcome Britain's undertaking to safeguard them ... We should, I

32 Shannon to Snelling, 15 May 1967, FCO 62/10.
33 Wilson and Holt, memcon, 15 June 1967, PREM 13/1323.
34 Ibid. See also London to DEA, cablegram 7766, 17 June 1967, NAA, A1838/275, 727/4/2 pt 7.
35 Wilson and Holt, memcon, 15 June 1967, PREM 13/1323.
36 McEwen to Holt, cablegram 514, 8 June 1967, NAA, A1838/275, 727/4/2 pt 7.

think, recognize that at some later stage there may be a 'crunch' which will force us to engage in a salvage operation … Decisions of this kind would involve jettisoning some industries to attempt to preserve the interests of others. You will be aware of the domestic political and economic implications of such a course. It, therefore, seems important to me that we should defer taking decisions of this kind as long as possible … For these reasons I believe we should not be shifted from our present line. This is that we recognise that decisions in respect of entry are matters for Britain and the E.E.C. We welcome Britain's assurances … We present the facts of our interests to Britain. We cannot select some of them as being more, or less, essential than others. We welcome the opportunity for consultation to ensure they understand the realities of the situation.[37]

Meanwhile, in Britain, the Ministerial Committee on the Approach to Europe met in June 1967 to discuss the length of the transitional periods which Britain would seek in negotiations with the Six. The committee included George Brown and those Cabinet ministers most directly concerned with the British application.[38] Whitehall departments had already given preliminary consideration to the terms of entry. While the FO preferred a five-year transitional period for all purposes, other departments, such as the CO, favoured different periods for different purposes, with agricultural products being generally accorded a seven-year transitional period.[39]

Douglas Jay, President of the Board of Trade and the most obdurate opponent of the 'approach to Europe' in the Cabinet, had by now come to the conclusion that Wilson and 'the pro-marketeers' were unwilling to safeguard Commonwealth interests effectively. He demanded that the government seek complete free entry for Commonwealth food products, as he thought 'all previous discussions [in Cabinet] had assumed that substantial and lasting safeguards would be essential'.[40] Wilson replied to Jay in a minute dated 27 June in which he not only disowned Jay's view as inconsistent 'with the decisions reached by the Cabinet and particularly with the terms of the statement of government policy of 2 May', but also urged Jay not to take the matter further.[41] Despite the committee's failure to make a final decision in June,[42] it was evident that Wilson's aim was to keep British requests on Commonwealth safeguards to a bare minimum. This seemed an ines-

[37] Ibid.
[38] These were Callaghan, Frederick Peart, Bowden, Jenkins, Michael Stewart and Jay. William Ross (Scotland Office) and Lord Chalfont (Minister of State for Foreign Affairs) were also included.
[39] F. G. K. Gallagher to Thomson, 28 Sept. 1967, FCO 20/38.
[40] Jay, *Change and fortune*, 405–6.
[41] Ibid., 406.
[42] According to F. G. K. Gallagher, Counsellor at the CO and Head of the Common Market Department, 'ministers took the view that, while the balance of opinion favoured seeking a seven year transitional period for agriculture, the right course would be to defer a decision until the Committee had had an opportunity of considering the transitional

Table 6
Australia's main export markets, 1959–66

	1959–60		1965–6	
	A$ (million)	% of total exports	A$ (million)	% of total exports
NZ	109	5.8	171	6.3
Japan	269	14.3	470	17.3
EEC	351	18.7	417	15.3
UK	495	26.5	473	17.4
USA	152	8.1	338	12.4

Source: Australian overseas trade, n.d., NAA, A1209/43, 1967/7117 pt 2.

capable course of action in the light of continuing French hostility. As far as Australian interests were concerned, the British view was that Australia could look after itself. Garner put it in the clearest possible terms, claiming that 'the countries which, in many ways, will be affected most [by British entry] are fortunately those about whom we need to concern ourselves least, viz. Canada and Australia – both are booming and prosperous and have considerably diversified their trade'.[43]

While the British were attempting to work out their opening negotiating position, the Australian government machinery had not remained idle. The Australian DTI had begun to assess, by means of a series of briefs and position papers, the economic effects of British entry on Australia's trade. Its approach was predictable. Despite the diversification of Australia's trade away from Britain, the DTI still held the view that British entry would be detrimental to Australian interests and regarded the ultimate loss of preference as 'a matter of considerable concern'.[44] The DTI stressed the fact that Britain was still Australia's biggest export market in terms of both value and volume (*see* table 6). Although exports to Britain had declined as a percentage of Australia's total exports, the country's dependence on the British market had actually increased in the case of some key commodities. Exports of beef, butter, fresh and canned fruit, and sugar had risen by volume between 1959–62 and 1962–5. On this point, the argument of the DTI was unconvincing, as the share taken by the UK had in fact decreased (*see* table 7). As if trying to drive home a point at any cost, the department insisted that alternative

periods for which we should need to ask in other sectors': Gallagher to Thomson, 28 Sept. 1967, FCO 20/38. See also Parr, *Britain's policy*, ch. vi.
43 Garner to Gallagher, 3 Oct. 1967, FCO 20/38.
44 UK-EEC: Australian negotiating position, PM's brief, 20 May 1967, NAA, A1838/275, 727/4/2 pt 7.

Table 7
Australia's reliance on the British market:
a comparison between 1959–62 and 1962–5

	Change in average volume	Change in share taken by the UK of key Australian commodities
Beef and veal	+ 8.9 %	30 to 20 %
Butter	+ 20.9 %	84 %
Apple and pears	+ 4.3 %	63 to 54 %
Canned fruit	+ 20.1 %	95 to 87 %
Sugar	+ 20 %	45 to 36 %

Source: British entry into EEC, conspectus of Australian position, NAA, A1838/275, 727/4/2 pt 7.

markets were difficult to find and that there were 'whole communities and industries in Australia which are geared to the British market'.[45]

This of course was true, but the problem was that the DTI over-emphasised the potential damage Britain's entry would inflict on Australia. As L. D. Thomson, Assistant Secretary at the DEA observed, the DTI (as well as Treasury) were too 'preoccupied with the injuries [Australia] may suffer'.[46] In this context it is noteworthy that, in January 1966, Ken Campbell, the EEC policy desk officer in the DTI, conceded privately that 'British entry into the Common Market would not seriously affect Australian trading interests as before ... The situation was not the same as 1963'.[47] None the less, British entry would force painful readjustments on certain sectors of the economy. The farm sector would suffer the most, as Britain would have to accept the EEC's CET and CAP (*see* tables 8, 9). Yet trade diversification and the incipient mineral boom would help soften the blow of entry overall. Notwithstanding these facts, the DTI took the line that nothing much had changed since the first application in 1961.

Traditional commodities apart, Britain's application for entry had raised a further concern: sterling. During Wilson's visit to Paris in January 1967, de Gaulle had drawn attention to the problem of sterling by pointing out that Britain's recurrent balance of payment problems could seriously undermine its position in the international financial markets. Unlike the other European currencies, sterling was a reserve currency and de Gaulle feared that, under the provisions of the Treaty of Rome, Britain would be able to

---

[45] Alan Westerman and Downer, memcon, 23 Feb. 1967, NAA, A4092/T1, 78. For a commodity-by-commodity analysis see UK-EEC consultations 1967, n.d., NAA, A4092/T1, 85.
[46] Thomson to Robert Hamilton, 25 May 1967, NAA, A1838/275, 727/4 pt 37.
[47] H. D. White to Thomson, 28 Jan. 1966, ibid. pt 36.

Table 8
Exports of Australian agricultural produce to Britain, 1965–6

	Total exports	Exports to the UK	% UK of total exports
All items	**£1090m**	**£190m**	**17.4**
Mutton and lamb	£18.2m	£2m	11.0
Butter	£20.0m	£15.5m	77.4
Cheese	£5.4m	£1.6m	29.6
Wheat	£105.5m	£13m	12.3
Apples	£10.3m	£5.1m	49.5
Pears	£3.0m	£1.3m	43.3
Tinned fruit	£15.2m	£9.9m	65.0
Sultanas and raisins	£8.5m	£3.7m	43.5
Currants	£0.8m	£0.2m	25.0
Barley	£4.6m	£0.7m	46.5
Sugar	£37.6m	£17.5m	46.5
Wool, greasy	£280.0m	£28.2m	10.0
Wool, washed and scoured	£34.0m	£3.6m	10.6
Beef and veal	£78.2m	£21.8m	27.8.

Source: Draft brief for talks between the prime minister and Holt, note by the Secretaries, 7 June 1967, FCO 20/49, Eur(S) (67)2.

seek financial assistance from the EEC should difficulties arising from the role of sterling as a reserve currency threaten its exchange rate. He did not intend to bail sterling out. In the course of 1967 the French would repeatedly refer to the sterling issue as a stumbling block on Britain's road to entry.

The sterling problem could not leave the Australian government indifferent. Despite a growing diversification towards the US dollar, Australian reserves held in sterling still accounted for approximately 70 per cent of the total in 1966. Canberra recognised that British entry would have no automatic implications for Australian sterling balances, acknowledging that it was impossible to predict the likely financial effects on Australia of British entry. Yet there was concern about four possible outcomes. First, Australia feared that it would not only lose its preferential treatment, but could also be discriminated against as Britain progressively abolished restrictions on capital movements with the EEC. In 1965–6 the capital inflow from Britain amounted to A$250 million.[48] Second, as a member of the sterling area, Australia continued to enjoy some preference in the London capital market for governmental and semi-governmental borrowings. In 1967 Australia

[48] British entry into the EEC, position paper, undated, ibid. pt 7.

Table 9
Commonwealth preferences and EEC tariffs

	Margin of preference on Commonwealth exports to the UK	EEC external tariff
Beef and veal	Nil; 3s. 4d. per 1b; 20%	Not above 20% Varies with world prices
Mutton and lamb	Nil	20%
Butter	Nil; quota arrangements	Varies with world prices
Cheese	10–15%	Variable. Cheddar type 23%
Wheat	Nil	Varies with world prices
Apples	3s; 4s. 6d. per cwt	9%–14%
Pears	3s; 4s. 6d. per cwt	9%–14%
Tinned fruit	Approx. 12% peaches and pears	17%–25%. If containing added spirit 32%
Sultanas and raisins	8s.6d. per cwt	8%
Currants	2s. per cwt	8%
Barley	10%	Variable
Sugar	Average 15%	80%
Wool greasy	Nil	Free; carded or combed 3%
Wool washed and scoured	Nil	Free; carded or combed 3%

Source: Draft brief for talks between the prime minister and Holt, note by the Secretaries, 7 June 1967, FCO 20/49, Eur(S) (67)2.

owed Britain A$750 million in government loans.[49] With Britain inside the EEC, Canberra was concerned that Australia's opportunities for government borrowing would be reduced.[50] Third, the Australian government also worried that under the Treaty of Rome Britain could find itself compelled to impose financial restrictions on the sterling area. Fourth, as a member of the EEC, Britain would be expected to treat its exchange rate policy as a matter of common interest, and this would imply close consultations with other EEC members. Canberra was concerned that, in spite of being the single largest holder of sterling balances, Australia would have less influence than EEC members on a matter of considerable importance to it.[51] Finally,

[49] Ibid.
[50] Until the mid-1960s Australia depended on the Bank of England to arrange a prompt reconversion of government loans through preferential access to the British money market. Australia was concerned that this kind of arrangement would no longer be possible once Britain entered the EEC, leaving Australia with the prospect of repaying debts out of its reserves.
[51] Trade and economic brief for the prime minister, May–June 1967, NAA, A1209/84, 1967/7334 attachment 2.

as far as the concept of the sterling area was concerned, DTI officials felt that 'British entry into the E.E.C. would certainly have a deleterious effect'. They recognised, however, that 'this may not mean much in practice. Since World War II, the sterling area has changed fundamentally ... This concept of a closely knit preferential group has now largely disappeared and the only preference which remains is in the field of capital transfers (and even here it is being progressively whittled away) and a few relatively unimportant current payments'.[52]

Anglo-Australian consultations, September–October 1967

On 18 June, the day after Holt left London, Wilson flew to Paris for talks with de Gaulle. He hoped that his visit would encourage the French president to take a less disruptive attitude. French obstruction had prevented the application from being formally acknowledged by the EEC Council of Ministers until 5 June, and then it was merely acknowledged without any meaningful discussion. Regrettably for the British, Wilson's personal diplomacy produced no breakthrough and, as a result, the application failed to gather momentum.[53] On 4 July Brown momentarily managed to circumvent French obstructionism and presented the British case for entry at the WEU Council of Ministers.[54] On 3 October the European Commission issued a Preliminary Opinion on British Membership, recommending that negotiations with Britain should be initiated.[55] But in spite of this nothing happened.

Under these circumstances, Anglo-Australian consultations on issues relating to British entry soon took on a surrealistic air. A second round of talks between Australian and British officials was scheduled for early autumn. These had been proposed by the Australians with a view to exploring 'the bases of future continuing bilateral relationship [sic] in the alternative situations of Britain gaining, or not gaining, entry to the E.E.C. on the present application'.[56] According to the Australian delegation, it was apparent from the beginning that the British 'were too damned frightened to speak about it [that is, retaining trade benefits in Australia] in case any of the discussion leaked and was capable of being used by the French as a reason for obstructing

[52] Ibid.
[53] CAB 128/42, CC(67)41st, 22 June 1967. See also Wilson, *Labour government*, 524–6, and Parr, *Britain's policy*, ch. vi.
[54] Parr, *Britain's policy*, ch. vi. In order to by-pass French obstructionism, Patrick Hermel, the Belgian foreign minister, had suggested that the foreign secretary present Britain's case at the said WEU Council.
[55] 'Opinion on the application for membership received from the United Kingdom, Ireland, Denmark and Norway for submission to the Council under articles 237 of the EEC Treaty, 205 of the Euratom Treaty, and 98 of the ECSC Treaty', quoted in Kitzinger, *Second try*, 205–99.
[56] Westerman to Richard Powell, 7 Aug. 1967, FCO 20/50.

their application for entry'. This being the case, it was not surprising that the talks ended in disappointment on 4 October, following the announcement that the Australian delegation had been recalled to Canberra. Despite further talks between Alan Westerman, the head of the Australian delegation, and his British counterpart, Richard Powell, on 16 October, differences between London and Canberra could not be reconciled. In explaining his decision to recall the Australian team to the Cabinet, McEwen argued that 'Britain is so determined to maintain a position of willingness, even anxiety to join the E.E.C. that she will take no action at this stage that might appear as the slightest contradiction of that position'.[57]

Disagreements centred on how Britain intended to safeguard Australian trade interests in negotiations with the EEC. The Australians claimed that 'even after reading the Foreign Secretary's W.E.U. statement of 4 July they were still not clear as to [Britain's] negotiating aims in so far as they related to Australia'.[58] They added that 'they could not see the relevance of the Foreign Secretary's statement to the question of safeguards for Australian essential interests'.[59] By contrast, according to British officials, the statement made by Brown on 4 July clearly implied that Britain would seek only transitional arrangements for the Commonwealth with the exception of special provisions for New Zealand and for Third World sugar-producing countries.[60]

Privately, British officials were frustrated with what they saw as a deliberate Australian attempt to avoid recognising the implications of Brown's speech.[61] They likened the Australian attitude to that of an ostrich.[62] But, however the British Foreign Secretary wanted to dress it up, Canberra was well aware of the sort of safeguards that the British had in mind. On 17 October McEwen informed the Cabinet that it was by now 'abundantly clear that the only "safeguards" Britain will seek for Australia for all products except sugar, is a transitional period during which all our existing preferences would be phased out'.[63]

The Australian government's uncooperative tactics at the October talks were not difficult to understand. They were consistent with the stance Canberra had taken since the launch of the new British bid. In London, officials now saw these tactics as an attempt either 'to delay the date on which the Australian government would have to explain the position to their own public' or 'to enable Australia later to claim that we tried to pull the wool over their eyes – a charge which could be very damaging to

---

57 Cabinet submission 504, 12 Oct. 1967, NAA, A10206, EHEC03.
58 Anglo-Australian trade talks, Rooke report, 5 Oct. 1967, FCO 20/54.
59 Christopher Audland to Snelling, 9 Oct. 1967, ibid.
60 Ibid. For Brown's statement to the WEU see Cmnd. 3345, *The United Kingdom and the European Communities*, London 1967, paras 22–42.
61 Audland to Snelling, 9 Oct. 1967, FCO 20/54.
62 Snelling to Thomson, 11 Oct. 1967, ibid.
63 Cabinet submission 504, 12 Oct. 1967, NAA, A10206, EHEC03.

H.M.G'.[64] The British were concerned that an altercation with Australia could become unavoidable, sooner or later, particularly if negotiations with the EEC were successful. However, with the future of the British application then uncertain, the risk of a public row with Australia looked remote and unlikely. Unwilling to put the situation to a test, British officials did not seek clarification on the issue of transitional arrangements. For their part, the Australians were equally reluctant to confront the British. In his talks with Powell on 17 October, Westerman said that the Australians 'were content to leave matters stand with the exchange of schedules incorporating the Kennedy Round changes'.[65]

Despite their success in obstructing progress on the question of safeguards, the Australian party did not get much joy out of the London talks as it was unable either to renegotiate the Anglo-Australian Trade Agreement, or to secure a new deal on meat.[66] Equally disappointing from an Australian perspective was the fact that a proposal put forward by Westerman on long-term arrangements between Australia and an enlarged Community was received coolly in London. Westerman had envisaged:

(a) the maintenance of British preferences in the Australian market by the establishment of preferential quotas open to all members of an enlarged EEC, but limited in total to the level of British exports in a base year; (b) the extension of British preferences to an enlarged EEC with no quota limit but with a reduced margin of preference; (c) the retention of a range of existing margins of preference but over a narrower range of goods; (d) the abolition of British preferences and the reduction of m.f.n. rates on selected goods of particular importance to the enlarged EEC. [67]

From an Australian point of view, this scheme had the merit of guaranteeing continued access for Australian exports to the British market 'in return for concessions by Australia aimed at preserving United Kingdom advantages in Australia while necessarily offering sufficient benefit to overall Community exports to Australia'.[68] For the British, however, the Australian offer, whatever its merits, was a non-starter as they had no intention of jeopardising their bid for EEC membership; nor were they in a mood to do Canberra a favour. Hence, British officials politely let the Australians know that it would not be appropriate for their government to discuss the Australian proposal with the Six, arguing that it should instead be a matter for negotiation between the enlarged Community and Australia.

---

[64] Snelling and Audland to Powell, draft report, 9 Oct. 1967, FCO 20/54. See also Snelling to Thomson, 11 Oct. 1967, ibid.
[65] Powell and Westerman, note of a meeting, 18 Oct. 1967, ibid.
[66] The Anglo-Australian Trade Agreement was allowed to continue at six months' notice. As for the Meat Agreement, it was allowed to expire without renewal.
[67] Anglo-Australian talks (September 1967), undated, ibid.
[68] Ibid.

De Gaulle says 'non'

As the Anglo-Australian talks deadlocked, the Australian High Commissioner in London drew public attention to the current state of affairs between the two countries. In a speech to the Royal Commonwealth Society in Bath on 11 October 1967, Downer complained about the negative effects of the British application on Anglo-Australian ties. He pointed out that 'the old traditional trade relationship ... is declining ... due to the desire of not only the present British government but its predecessor ... to revolutionise Britain's economy by joining the European Economic Community'. Despite making it clear that 'no Australian government ... would presume to dictate what Great Britain should do', it was depressing to see Britain and Australia drift apart. Downer did not of course attribute the weakening of Anglo-Australian ties only to the EEC problem. He was quick to explain that 'our paths ... are diverging in other aspects of the overall Commonwealth relationship', citing, as a main example, the proposed British withdrawal from east of Suez. The High Commissioner pointed out that 'if the ultimate destination of Britain is merely to become one of a group of European states ... then her diplomatic influence will be confined chiefly to Europe'. As a consequence, he added, 'this remarkable land of our ancestors ... is going to count less and less in world affairs'. As for Australia, it would 'have to re-design [its] foreign, defence and commercial policies, and proceed in some directions quite independently of what most Australians regard as the Mother Country'. In concluding his speech, he pleaded for a 'recrudescence of feeling in Westminster and Whitehall towards the Commonwealth idea', and advocated tighter bonds between Britain and the old Commonwealth.[69] This was, of course, wishful thinking. As developments in Europe since May 1967 had shown, Wilson was determined to enter the EEC and, consequently, a rapid reorientation of British foreign policy priorities was underway. Turning back the clock appeared well-nigh impossible despite the fact that in the autumn of 1967 the British bid was running into the ground.

Wilson's European aspirations received their *coup de grâce* on 27 November. It was the day de Gaulle declared at a press conference that 'for the British Isles to be really able to tie up with the continent, a very vast and very deep transformation is still needed', thus dealing a fatal blow to Wilson's hopes of joining the EEC.[70] Despite the British Cabinet's decision to 'urge the Five to insist on fixing a date in January for the opening of the negotiations, and so force the issue with the French', de Gaulle's opposition could not be overcome. On 19 December the EEC Council of Ministers concluded that the conditions did not exist for the application to proceed further.[71] The British bid was over for the second time.

---

69 Downer to Royal Commonwealth Society, 11 Oct. 1967, FCO 20/50.
70 Kitzinger, *Second try*, 311–17.
71 *Communiqué* issued by the Council of Ministers, 19 Dec. 1967, quoted ibid. 319.

In Australia, Britain's failure to open negotiations with the Six allayed local concerns about the economic aspects of the British application. Although no Australian any longer doubted Britain's resolve to join the EEC, this temporary set-back allowed the Australian farm sector more time to reduce its reliance on the British market and to find new outlets elsewhere. This seemed to remove an irritant in Anglo-Australian relations, but did not rejuvenate the relationship. Britain's failed application did not end what Downer described as 'the story of disassociation, which has become so marked in the last eighteen months'.[72] Rather, it represented one further step in that direction.

[72] Downer to Royal Commonwealth Society, 11 Oct. 1967, FCO 20/50.

PART III

THE 'TURN TO EUROPE' AND ITS AFTERMATH

8

Facing the Blow East of Suez, 1968–1971

'It is of much importance that the renewed presence of the British does not reverse or hinder the healthy adjustments of attitude and thinking that has taken place and is continuing to take place in Australia': Australian position paper, July 1970.[1]

The failure of Wilson's 'approach to Europe' in December 1967 was swiftly overshadowed by the decision taken by the British government in January 1968 to hasten the withdrawal of all its defence forces from Malaysia and Singapore. With British military disengagement now to be completed by December 1971, Australia's traditional reliance on British military power as a bulwark against regional threats was rapidly coming to an end. But then, following a narrow victory in the June 1970 general election, the new Conservative government of Edward Heath announced its intention to retain a military presence in the region, thereby seemingly reversing the policy of the previous Labour government. This decision, however, was by no means a return to the past. The Heath government soon made it clear that the British military presence would be limited in size and scope. The deployment of a token force in south-east Asia would be subject to stringent political constraints. British forces would be committed under the Five Power Defence Arrangements, which would replace the Anglo-Malaysian Defence Agreement. Contrary to the AMDA provisions, the FPDA did not entail an automatic British commitment to the defence of the Malaysian region. On the contrary, it terminated Britain's open-ended post-colonial undertaking since it contained only an obligation to consult under certain circumstances.

While welcoming the British decision to maintain a token presence in south-east Asia, the Australian government was initially rather cautious in its response. Far from accepting British proposals wholeheartedly, Canberra was careful to ensure that a continued British presence should accord with a more independent formulation of Australia's regional interests and objectives. Australia's military co-operation with the British under the FPDA would continue well into the new millennium, but the Australian approach to the announcement of a new-style British military presence in south-east Asia was an indication of how Australian thinking had evolved since the

---

[1] Discussions with Lord Carrington, DOD position paper, July 1970, NAA, A5882/2, CO988.

Wilson government's decision to withdraw from east of Suez. At the beginning of the 1970s Australian dependence on British military power was a relic of the past. This chapter therefore examines Anglo-Australian defence relations in the aftermath of the British decision to withdraw from Malaysia and Singapore, and brings to a conclusion a controversial phase in the bilateral relationship, even as negotiations over EEC membership had once again been assigned to a state of limbo.

A token military presence in south-east Asia

In January 1968 Heath, then leader of the opposition, had strongly criticised Wilson's decision to disengage from east of Suez by the end of 1971. In his view, withdrawal represented 'a flagrant breach of pledges' to Britain's allies, and a 'humiliation' for the country.[2] On 18 January he told the Commons that 'when the time comes ... we shall ignore the time phasing laid down by the Prime Minister and his Government for the Far East and the Middle East. We shall support our friends and allies and we shall restore the good name of Britain'.[3] In August 1968, during a visit to Australia, Heath declared that, if elected, his government would make a small but permanent military contribution to south-east Asia within the framework of a five-power military arrangement between the governments of Britain, Malaysia, Singapore, Australia and New Zealand.[4] In 1970 the Conservative electoral manifesto proposed a five-power defence force to help maintain peace and stability in south-east Asia.[5] Shortly after his victory in the polls, Heath despatched the Secretary of State for Defence, Lord Carrington, to Malaysia, Singapore, Australia and New Zealand for consultations with the local governments. Carrington's brief was to sound out Britain's Commonwealth partners on London's plans for the renegotiation of AMDA, and for the retention of a token military presence in Malaysia and Singapore.

On 21 July, in the lead-up to his tour, Lord Carrington explained the provisional considerations informing British thinking to Australian representatives in London. He made it clear that it was his government's intention to seek 'the abandonment of AMDA'. In so doing, Britain would terminate its open commitment to the security of Malaysia. The government's view was that 'it would be unrealistic to expect a British government to-day to be able to find the resources necessary to keep AMDA in being'.[6] However, Britain was willing to replace AMDA with five-power arrangements on the

---

2 Britain, *PD*, HC, 1966–7, dcclvi.1969.
3 Ibid. dcclvi.1971.
4 Canberra to FCO, telegram 1077, 14 Aug. 1968, FCO 24/203.
5 Extract from the Conservative Party manifesto, FCO 15/1146.
6 London to DEA, cablegram 12501, 21 July 1970, NAA, A5882/2, CO988.

basis of equal partnership and obligation.[7] In order to avoid misunderstandings, Carrington made the point that 'what was done east of Suez had to be subtracted from NATO and that this put close limitations on the British effort in Malaysia/Singapore'. In other words, he emphasised his government's primary commitment to NATO and to European defence, thereby leaving Wilson's European-centred defence policy virtually unchanged.[8] As he told the Australians, he 'had to take pains … to reassure the Germans that there was no question of Britain redeploying in the Far East the sort of forces it previously had had stationed there'.[9] The following day the British Cabinet gave Carrington his guidance for the forthcoming talks with Australia and the other three Commonwealth allies.[10] Within twenty-four hours Patrick Nairne, Deputy Under-Secretary at the Ministry of Defence, had provided the Australian High Commission with the specifics of the Cabinet's deliberations. He informed the Australians that 'Cabinet had authorised a "modest" contribution from all three services, comprising a battalion group, ships similar in character to the Australian contribution plus a contribution to afloat support, and aircraft'. Nairne also explained that, contrary to pre-election pronouncements made by the Conservative Party in relation to a 'five power joint force', the British government 'would prefer now to word this in terms of arrangements [rather] than a joint force'.[11] The new government clearly wished to avoid making too firm a commitment to the region.

The Australian response

With Carrington due to arrive in Australia at the end of July, the Gorton government took steps to work out a defined policy. In fact, the Australian Cabinet had already agreed, on 11 June 1970, to a Five Power Joint Declaration, which the British Labour government had proposed should replace AMDA from January 1972. Although this did not commit Britain and its Commonwealth partners beyond a mere pledge to consult, senior ministers in Canberra saw 'advantages for Australia' in the British proposal, judging it 'preferable to a complete cessation of British commitment'. In backing the proposal, ministers indicated that the Australian government was willing to negotiate the continuation of even a minimal regional commitment by the British.[12] Within a week, however, Wilson's unexpected electoral defeat on 18 June made Australian support superfluous, forcing the Gorton govern-

---

7 London to DEA, cablegram 12646, 23 July 1970, ibid.
8 Michael Dockrill, *British defence policy since 1945*, Oxford 1988, 103.
9 London to DEA, cablegram 12501, 21 July 1970, NAA, A5882/2, CO988.
10 CAB 128/47, CM(70)8th, 23 July 1970.
11 London to DEA, cablegram 12646, 23 July 1970, NAA, A5882/2, CO988.
12 Cabinet decision 430, 11 June 1970, NAA 5869/1, 316. The British proposal was made by Defence Secretary Healey in April 1970: Chin, *Defence*, 171.

ment to rethink its broad interests and objectives with regard to British policy in south-east Asia. These were eventually elaborated in a position paper prepared by the Department of Defence in July 1970.

DOD officials acknowledged without reservation that 'the new British presence will be severely limited in numbers of men and other resources and hence ultimately in political commitment'. Within these constraints they hoped that a British presence would be 'large enough to contribute to confidence and stability' in the region, and 'sufficiently substantial to weigh with the Americans and with our SEATO allies'. At the same time, it was argued, the British presence should 'be no larger than can be endured by the British (present and possibly succeeding Governments) rather than one so large as to stimulate fresh domestic pressures for withdrawal, and add to doubts in the region as to its permanence'. This presence, however, should 'be backed up, and through appropriate exercises, to be seen to be backed up, by a substantial reinforcement capability'.[13] These considerations were broadly in line with past Australian views. Following the Wilson Cabinet's decision in mid-1967 to withdraw, Canberra had come to expect a much reduced, yet continuing, British presence in south-east Asia through the rundown phase, and the maintenance of a general capability after the mid-1970s. To the Australian government's great disappointment, the decision in January 1968 to accelerate the withdrawal had led to the discarding of these options. While there was no intention of reintroducing a large British military contingent, Heath's plans for a continuing British presence in Malaysia and Singapore appeared, in a sense, to turn the clock back to late 1967, reversing the policy of the previous Labour administration. So it was not surprising that Australian officials regarded the reintroduction of a small British presence as a positive development.

What was surprising – and this was an indication of how Australian thinking had changed since late 1967 – was that the Gorton government was prepared to welcome the deployment of a token British force provided certain Australian requirements were met. As DOD officials put it, 'it is of much importance that the renewed presence of the British does not reverse or hinder the healthy adjustment of attitude and thinking that has taken place and is continuing to take place in Australia'. What is remarkable here is the change of tone when compared to Australian defence calculations as little as five years earlier. Far from articulating the traditional anxiety that British defence forces be maintained in the region at all costs, the Australian Department of Defence raised the possibility that a continued British military presence might actually hinder Australia's adjustment to the new post-imperial realities. As DOD officials explained:

[13] Discussions with Carrington, DOD position paper, July 1970, NAA, A5882/2, CO988.

[Australia does not] want the renewal of the British presence to introduce influences that could obstruct the independently Australian purposes we had in mind when deciding to leave our own forces in the region (on the contrary, we should be looking to harness the renewed British presence to those purposes); to antagonise Indonesia, complicate the development of our defence relations with that country or other countries in the region, or tend to restore the previous high level of militarization across the Southeast Asian Archipelago; to focus our presence (and our thinking) too narrowly for too long on Malaysia/Singapore.

British defence co-operation, it seemed, was both an asset and a liability. Having faced up to the logic of Wilson's withdrawal of British forces from the region, the Australian government had now to consider whether Britain's influence might draw Australia into commitments that were not only inimical to Australian interests, but possibly also antipathetic to Australia's nearest neighbours, particularly Indonesia. It was therefore deemed essential that the British presence 'be directed towards enhancing defence co-operation between the local countries, and to assist the rational development of those forces', while at the same time discouraging Malaysia and Singapore 'from economically unwise decisions in defence'. Above all, the Australian government would have to remain 'cautious lest the renewal of the British presence lead to notions of a self-contained "Commonwealth" military community and induce inward-looking attitudes among our people in the region'. The DOD view was that the Australian government

> needs to keep in mind that we had already made decisions as to the forces we would retain, and the commitments we would accept, after the British left the region. We don't want what may still prove to be merely a temporary renewal of the British presence to leave us saddled later with undertakings (either forces in the region, or political commitment) any larger or more enduring than we would have made if the British had stuck to Labour's timetable for departing from Malaysia and Singapore.

While the DOD was anxious 'to make things as easy as we can for the British', it was equally clear that there was more at stake than simply 'renewing our defence connection with the U.K.'. On the contrary, this was an entirely new situation, which might well 'introduce risks'.[14] There could be no clearer indication of the shift in the Australian outlook than this. Although Australian governments had long sought to harness British power and influence to Australian interests, this had rarely been so self-consciously calculated. Nor had Australia been so wary of what the possible cost might be.

[14] Ibid.

Anglo-Australian defence relations on a new footing

Lord Carrington held talks with the Gorton government in Canberra on 31 July and 1 August 1970. He repeated the views that he had already expressed to Australian representatives in London. Essentially, he reiterated his government's intention to terminate AMDA, and to have it replaced by a much looser agreement 'with the five powers being equal partners and the three overseas nations having the same political commitment'.[15] In this context Carrington made it clear that the British government did not intend to make any undertaking which would go further than a simple obligation to consult 'in the event of external aggression or the threat of external aggression'. He also re-emphasised the limited size and scope of the planned British military contribution to future five-power arrangements in view of Britain's limited resources, and its primary commitment to European security.[16] He emphasised that the British contribution should not be too onerous financially and went on to tell Gorton and his ministers that 'if the British commitment East of Suez were not too costly it could possibly become in Britain a bipartisan policy'. Carrington was also able to give the Australian government a provisional outline of the planned British force. Its naval capability in the area would amount to five frigates or destroyers (one located in Hong Kong) and a share in afloat support. Visits by RN vessels for training and exercises were also contemplated. The ground contribution would include one battalion group to be stationed in Singapore, and some supporting elements. Britain's aerial capacity would consist of four Nimrods and a flight of Whirlwind helicopters. The British government envisaged a rotation of aircraft in and out of the area (at the rate of about 600–700 movements a year).[17]

Lord Carrington is said to have been taken aback by the change in Australia's position, and is cited by one Australian minister as having complained: 'One would almost think that Australia did not want us back in the area.'[18] This, however, is not supported by archival evidence, or indeed the recollection of the people involved, including Carrington himself; on the whole it seems that the Australian government received the British proposal warmly.[19] While expressing 'regret at the British intention to

---

[15] Under AMDA Britain was responsible for the defence of Malaya/Malaysia against external aggression. This did not apply to Australia and New Zealand as they were not signatories to AMDA. Only in 1959 did they associate themselves with it. In 1963, when the Federation of Malaysia was established, Australia and New Zealand extended their association with AMDA.

[16] It is noteworthy that by 1970 internal security problems in Northern Ireland had already begun to place British military resources under strain. See Carver, *Tightrope walking*, 100–1.

[17] Cabinet decision 575 (ad hoc), 31 July 1970, NAA, A5882/2, CO988.

[18] Howson, *Diaries*, 648.

[19] In a letter to the author (15 Oct. 2002) Lord Carrington wrote that 'I can't think why Peter Howson would have written anything so unlikely. There is and there was no

terminate AMDA', Gorton claimed that 'the Australian Government was pleased at the decision to have a continuing British presence in the area'. In keeping with the DOD's concerns, however, Gorton introduced a note of caution into the proceedings as 'it was not yet clear precisely what the five power arrangement would mean'.[20] The Australian government was unsure as to 'what political commitment each Government would accept, what force contribution each would make, whether joint approval by all partners would be necessary … and if there would be distinction between East and West Malaysia'.[21] The last point was of particular concern to Australia. First, as Gorton himself had declared on 25 February 1969, Australian troops would only be used 'against externally promoted and inspired infiltration and subversion … [on] … the Peninsula (including Singapore)'.[22] Australia had no intention of making troops available for use in Eastern Malaysia (Sabah and Sarawak). By contrast, the British saw no problem in the five-power arrangement covering Eastern Malaysia.[23] Second, Australia 'intended to include externally-promoted subversion and insurgency amongst the causes that would activate the commitment to consult'.[24] As McMahon, now Minister for External Affairs pointed out, 'if insurgency were not covered in the commitment to consult, the commitment would be virtually useless in military terms since insurgency was the only real threat'. The Australians, therefore, were clearly attracted by a more inclusive formula. As the Minister of Defence, Malcolm Fraser, put it, the formula should indicate that the five powers would 'consult in the event of any form of armed attack organised or supported from outside, or the threat of such attack'.[25]

---

reason to suspect that "Australia did not want us back in the area". The reverse was true.' Carrington's interpretation is also supported by Malcolm Fraser, then Australian Minister of Defence, in a letter to the author of 18 Nov. 2002.

[20] Cabinet decision 575 (ad hoc), 31 July 1970, NAA, A5882/2, CO988. It is interesting to note that, according to Fraser, 'there was some tension between Gorton himself and defence officials because Gorton did not believe in forward defence and did not believe in the stationing of Australian forces in Malaysia and Singapore': personal communication with Malcolm Fraser, 18 Nov. 2002. Gorton was in fact known for his scepticism towards a continuing Australian military presence in south-east Asia: Edwards, *Nation at war*, 199–201; Alan Reid, *The Gorton experiment: the fall of John Grey Gorton*, Sydney 1971, 143.

[21] Cabinet decision 575 (ad hoc), 31 July 1970, NAA, A5882/2, CO988.

[22] Gorton quoted in McDougall, 'Australia and the British withdrawal', 191.

[23] The Gorton government was concerned that Australia could become involved in an awkward diplomatic dispute between Malaysia and the Philippines over the Malaysian state of Sabah. In 1968 the Marcos government had revived the claims of the Philippines over Sabah: Chin, *Defence*, 149–62.

[24] McMahon, Malcolm Fraser and Carrington, memcon (Saturday morning), 1 Aug. 1970, NAA, A5882/2, CO988.

[25] McMahon, Fraser and Carrington, memcon (Friday afternoon), 31 July 1970, ibid.

The Five-Power Defence Arrangements

These problems were ironed out in the immediate aftermath of Carrington's visit. In September 1970 and January 1971 officials of the five countries met in Singapore to agree on the military aspects of future five-power arrangements, including the establishment of an air defence council for the supervision of an integrated air defence system (IADS).[26] On 15 February 1971, at the end of the Commonwealth Prime Ministers' Conference in Singapore, Heath met the four prime ministers for an informal five-power meeting. On 16 February Fraser announced that British, Australian and New Zealand forces would be organised as a single ANZUK force (*see* table 10) under an Australian 'two-star' commander.[27] On 15 and 16 April 1971 ministers representing the five countries gathered in London to conclude the five-power defence arrangements.[28] The understanding included an obligation that 'in the event of any form of armed attack externally organised or supported or the threat of such attack against Malaysia and Singapore, their Governments would immediately consult together for the purpose of deciding what measures should be taken jointly or separately in relation to such attack or threat'.[29] A Joint Consultative Council was established to serve as a forum for regular consultations at senior official level.[30] In November 1971 Australia, Britain and New Zealand formally terminated AMDA with Letters of Exchange to the governments of Malaysia and Singapore, thus bringing to an end the final vestiges of imperial defence co-operation.

In the end, the Heath government's deployment of a token military force in south-east Asia within the FDPA framework was only a marginal reversal of policy and did not amount to a return to the past. By 1970 the ambit of British defence policy was largely confined to Europe. The Australian government understood this and accepted the British decision. For Australia, a continued, albeit limited, British presence would in fact make a contribution to regional confidence and stability. It would also 'help give pause to radical nationalistic elements that might in the future attempt to upset the status quo in the region'.[31] At first, however, Australian policy-makers responded rather cautiously to the British initiative. Before agreeing to British proposals,

---

[26] Five-power officials talks on defence, agreed conclusions, 8 Jan. 1971, FCO 24/975; five-power official talks, Singapore, 7–8 January 1971, FCO 24/976. See also Chin, *Defence*, 175.

[27] David Hawkins, *The defence of Malaysia and Singapore: from AMDA to ANZUK*, London 1972, 42.

[28] For the legal basis of this loose consultative framework see Kin Wah Chin, *The five power defence arrangements and AMDA: some observations on the nature of an evolving partnership* (Institute of Southeast Asian Studies occasional paper xxiii, 1974), 17–18.

[29] Idem, *Defence*, 176.

[30] Idem, *Five power*, 1–2.

[31] Discussions with Carrington, DOD position paper, July 1970, NAA, A5882/2, CO988.

Table 10
ANZUK forces

Australia	Britain	New Zealand
2 squadrons of Mirage fighter aircraft	1 battalion group up to 6 frigates	1 battalion
		1 frigate
1 battalion group	up to 4 Nimrod aircraft	
		transport aircraft
1 destroyer or frigate	1 squadron of Whirlwind helicopters	
		other air units if needed
1 submarine in rotation with Britain		
	1 submarine in rotation with Australia	
	combat units, ships and aircraft on visit	
total troops 3,300	total troops 2,550	total troops 1,150

Source: Chin, *Five-power*, 3–4.

Canberra sought to ensure that a continued British presence would accord with a more independent formulation of Australia's regional interests and objectives. Less than three years after Wilson's announcement in January 1968 of an accelerated withdrawal, 'Australian dependence on the projection of British power in Southeast Asia was now a thing of the past.'[32]

Although the Five-Power Defence Arrangements are still in place today and FPDA military exercises are conducted at regular intervals with all five nations usually contributing forces to each exercise, the military complexion of the Australian, British and New Zealand commitment has changed since the mid-1970s. In 1973 the Australian Labor government, led by Gough Whitlam, decided to withdraw the Australian infantry battalion from the ANZUK force based in Singapore. Britain pulled out its ground contribution in 1974.[33] The New Zealand battalion was brought home in 1989. The Australian Mirage squadrons were withdrawn from Butterworth (Malaysia) in 1988. Australia left behind some P3C reconnaissance aircraft and an infantry company.[34]

The Whitlam government's decision to withdraw the Australian ground contribution to FPDA (with the exception of 150 men, consisting of tech-

[32] Grey, *Military history of Australia*, 246.
[33] Cabinet decision 392 (FAD), 29 Mar. 1973, and Cabinet decisions 821, 823 (FAD), 2 July 1973, NAA, A5915.
[34] Post-1971 FPDA is discussed in Kin Wah Chin, 'The five power defence arrangements: twenty years after', *Pacific Review* iv (1991), 196.

nical aid, training and exercise personnel, and their support) was disappointing news for the British. As Lord Carrington told his Australian counterpart, Lance Barnard, on 18 June 1973, 'the British Government did not like or welcome [the Australian decision] or even think it a good idea'.[35] Having decided to maintain a military presence in south-east Asia, the Heath government had expected a strong and continued commitment to FPDA on the part of Australia. To its frustration, Australia did not oblige. Despite British attempts to urge the Australians to reconsider their plans for withdrawal – in April 1973 Carrington went so far as to make a veiled threat to the visiting Australian prime minister, warning him that Britain 'might find it impossible' to remain in Malaysia and Singapore if Australia failed to retain its ground contribution – Whitlam did not give in.[36] In the end, his sole 'concession' was a pledge to abstain from carrying out further withdrawals – that is, 'to take no decision at this stage on the actual time of withdrawal of [Australian] Mirages from Butterworth'.[37] Coming only a few years after calls made by the Holt and Gorton governments on Wilson to maintain a military presence in south-east Asia, the Australian decision to withdraw its ground forces from Singapore was a rather ironic, if not totally unexpected, twist to the tale. While the decision had been taken primarily to appease the left-wing section of the Australian Labor Party, which had forcefully demanded the withdrawal of Australian forces from south-east Asia, there was little doubt that the Whitlam government was also inclined to call into question that erstwhile bedrock of Australia's foreign and defence policies, the assumption that British troops in Australia's neighbourhood were vital to Australian interests.[38]

[35] Lance Barnard and Carrington, memcon (Australian minute), 18 Apr. 1973, FCO 24/1559; Gough Whitlam, Douglas-Home and Carrington, memcon (Australian draft minute), 24 Apr. 1973, FCO 24/1614.
[36] Ibid.
[37] Whitlam did however agree to review the matter before March 1975: Cabinet decision 823, 6 July 1973, NAA, A5915.
[38] Sydney Morning Herald, 6 July 1973; Age, 6 July 1973.

9

Coming to Terms with Europe, 1970–1972

'The British move into the Common Market had brought home to Australia that it was now a completely independent country': William McMahon, 6 November 1971.[1]

Britain's final and successful diplomatic push to join the EEC in 1970–2 marked the end of an era in Anglo-Australian relations. Although by the end of the 1960s the bilateral relationship had been significantly transformed as a result of Britain's shift to Europe, it was only with British entry in January 1973 that the change was fully realised. In no way did Britain's final attempt to enter the Community arouse the kind of widespread public and official uproar that the original Macmillan application in 1961 had occasioned.[2] Yet, while far from having the same impact as the first application and, to a lesser extent, the second, the 1970–2 attempt had important symbolic and practical implications. At a practical level British entry spelled the end of the imperial preference system, which had governed trade between Australia and Britain for forty years. At a more symbolic level, entry sealed Britain's European destiny and, in Australian eyes, represented a formal departure from the close ties of empire. Consequently, following the British signing of the Treaty of Accession in January 1972, the Australian government introduced a number of symbolic reforms which formalised the changed reality of Anglo-Australian relations. This chapter argues that, despite its demands for transitional arrangements to protect its trade interests, the Australian government had little faith in Britain's capacity to safeguard these interests adequately. Hence, while urging the British to seek long transitional arrangements for Australia's farm exports, policy-makers in Canberra considered moves to strengthen Australia's political and economic ties with Japan, Asia's emerging economic power. A closer relationship with Tokyo was seen in Canberra as the first step towards a much closer political and economic engagement with Asia. As Britain set about joining the EEC, Australia increasingly reoriented its external and economic policies towards Asia.

---

[1] As quoted in New York to PMC and Treasury, cablegram 998, 6 Nov. 1971, NAA, A1838/2, 727/4/2 pt 19.
[2] Ward, *British embrace*, 253.

Britain tries again

The French veto of 27 November 1967 brought the Wilson bid to join the EEC to an end. However, the veto did not sap the Wilson government's resolve to seek entry.[3] On 20 December George Brown informed the House of Commons that the British application remained on the agenda of the EEC Council of Ministers, and that the government did not intend to withdraw it.[4] There was a widespread feeling in Britain that, as long as de Gaulle remained in office, the country's prospects for entry would be gloomy, and British chances of joining were certainly not enhanced by the Gaullists' victory in the 1968 French elections or by the 'Soames Affair' in February 1969.[5] Throughout this period no significant progress was made. Nevertheless the Labour government 'maintained its determination to join the Community and declined to endorse any objective falling short of that'.[6] Events, however, were to take a sudden turn when de Gaulle resigned on 28 April 1969. As Con O'Neill, Deputy Permanent Under-Secretary in the Department of European Integration at the Foreign and Commonwealth Office, recalled in a report on Britain's 1970–2 negotiations for entry, 'the Labour Government immediately recognised that our prospects for membership of the Community had changed from nil to good'.[7] In early December 1969 the Six agreed at a summit in The Hague to open negotiations with Britain and the other candidate countries.[8] Wilson seized the opportunity and lobbied for talks to start as soon as possible. A date of 30 June 1970 was finally fixed.

In the meantime, Britain went to the polls and, surprisingly, the Labour government was defeated. On 18 June 1970 the Conservative Party was returned to power, led by the well-known Europeanist Edward Heath. Under Macmillan he had been the Cabinet minister in charge of the British delegation during the ill-fated negotiations with the Six in 1961–3. Subsequently, in his capacity as leader of the opposition between 1965 and 1970, Heath had steered the Conservative Party along a markedly pro-European course.

---

[3] Melissa Pine, 'Application on the table: the second British application to the European Communities, 1967–70', unpubl. PhD diss. Oxford 2003.

[4] Brown quoted in David Hannay (ed.), *Britain's entry into the European Community: report by Sir Con O'Neill on the negotiations of 1970–1972*, London 2000, 11.

[5] In a conversation with Sir Christopher Soames on 4 February 1969, de Gaulle told the British ambassador in Paris that he wanted to see the EEC change into a loose free trade area. He suggested that this new grouping, which would include the existing members of the Community as well as the EFTA countries, be directed by Britain, France, Germany and Italy. To explore this possibility, the French president proposed secret Anglo-French talks. However, anxious not to offend France's EEC partners, Wilson leaked de Gaulle's proposals to them, thereby provoking a bitter Anglo-French row. For the 'Soames Affair' see John Dickie, *Inside the Foreign Office*, London 1992, 165–71.

[6] Britain's entry into the EEC, report by O'Neill, 1972, FCO 75/1.

[7] Ibid. 13–14.

[8] Ireland, Denmark and Norway.

His commitment to EEC entry was unequivocal. According to John Young, 'there was never any doubt that Edward Heath would press for EEC membership with greater vigour than Wilson'. Heath was firmly convinced that EEC entry would not only help regenerate Britain's economy, but would also lead his country to regain its political influence in world affairs. Young also pointed out that 'unlike Wilson, Heath did not have such a divided party with which to contend ... The new Cabinet was carefully chosen to support EEC membership'.[9] Within a few days the new administration endorsed all the previous commitments made by the Labour government, agreeing to attend the formal opening meeting in Luxembourg on 30 June, and the first ministerial meeting scheduled for 21 July.[10] On 20 June Anthony Barber was appointed Chancellor of the Duchy of Lancaster with the task of leading the British team in the negotiations with the EEC. Britain was again knocking on the EEC's door.

Developments in Britain did not catch the Gorton government by surprise. Despatches from London had noted Wilson's determination to reopen the European chapter as soon as circumstances permitted.[11] Sensing after the EC summit in The Hague that negotiations between Britain and the Six would take place soon, Australian ministers met in late May to discuss a Cabinet submission put forward by the Minister for Trade, John McEwen. As with the previous bids, the Australian approach to Britain's 1970–2 attempt to join the EEC was mainly the responsibility of McEwen and his department, the DTI. Although his political career was about to come to an end – he would in fact step down in early 1971 – McEwen was still a powerful political figure in Canberra in 1970. He ensured that the formulation of Australia's EEC policy remained firmly in his own hands.

In his submission, McEwen noted that the British government was unlikely to seek any special safeguards for Australian trade interests. Aware that all British political parties were publicly committed to EEC membership, McEwen argued that 'no amount of representations, personal or otherwise, are going to achieve a special position for Australia such as New Zealand has'. McEwen pointed out that, as a consequence of this, there were not too many options which Australia could pursue to protect its own interests. Of those which could be considered he referred to a multilateral effort urging the EEC to modify its agricultural system, the negotiation of international commodity agreements and some form of association with the EEC. While the prospects of achieving worthwhile results from any of the three options were minimal, the Australian government could not afford to 'be seen to be doing nothing to try to safeguard [Australia's interests], particularly as New Zealand has been very active in seeking to have accepted that it has a

9 Young, *Britain and European unity*, 107.
10 CAB 148/47, CM(70), 1st and 2nd, 23, 25 June 1970.
11 See London to DEA, cablegram 12218, 19 July 1968, NAA, A1838/2, 727/4/1/3 pt 3; London to DEA, cablegram 967, 15 Jan. 1970, A1838/2, 727/4 pt 38.

special position'. According to McEwen, therefore, it was 'imperative that our public position, particularly as seen by the producers of those commodities likely to be most affected, be that ... we are doing everything possible to influence the enlargement of the Community in such a way as to cause the least damage to Australia'. He acknowledged that British entry into the EEC would be less disruptive to Australian trade now than it would have been in the early 1960s, but the effect on particular industries such as sugar, dairy and fruit would create very serious problems in the current economic position.[12]

Cabinet endorsed McEwen's recommendations. In particular, ministers agreed first, 'to confirm Australia's former attitude that it is for Britain to decide whether or not it joins the E.E.C. but that important Australian trade interests stand to be seriously damaged'; second, 'to make it clear that the enlargement of the Community should be done on the basis consistent with G.A.T.T.'; third, 'to make it publicly clear that we are doing what we can to influence the U.K. and the Community in such a way as to cause the least damage to Australia'; and, finally, 'to explain Australia's position clearly in Brussels and London'.[13]

With this brief in hand, McEwen flew to Europe in July 1970. His expectations were low. Yet on his arrival in London on 6 July he declared that he expected the British to 'press quite hard for our interests, recognising that the relationship between Britain and Australia hasn't been by any means one-sided. I can remember a couple of wars'.[14] A consummate politician, McEwen was clearly speaking to his domestic audience and, in particular, to farming communities scattered around Australia. Privately, however, McEwen 'was resigned rather than demanding', as the British remarked.[15] In talks with the Chancellor of the Duchy of Lancaster, McEwen reminded Barber of the damage that Australian farm interests would suffer if Britain entered the EEC, and complained about the EEC's protectionist farm policies. He urged his British counterpart to seek as long a transitional period as possible for Australian farm exports.[16] In response, Barber recognised that entry would have a considerable effect on Australia's traditional exports to Britain and pledged that 'the United Kingdom team would be seeking to achieve the longest transitional stage possible'.[17] However, he reminded

---

[12] Cabinet submission 258, 8 May 1970, NAA, A5619/1, C743 pt 2.
[13] Ibid.
[14] McEwen press conference, 7 July 1970, NAA, A10206/1, EHEC06.
[15] Britain's entry into the EEC, report by O'Neill, 1972, FCO 75/1.
[16] McEwen and Anthony Barber, memcon, 8 July 1970, NAA, A10206/1, EHEC06.
[17] Ibid. Britain's brief as circulated to ministers on 30 June 1970 stated that 'the previous administration decided in 1967 that we should not aim at securing more for New Zealand (apart from the field of dairy products), Canada and Australia than the gradual application of tariffs and levies over whatever transitional periods are negotiated': Britain's entry into the EEC, report by O'Neill, 1972, FCO 75/1.

McEwen of the fact that the British government 'had to bear in mind the possible views of the E.E.C. Member States'.[18]

This was indeed a crucial point. While sympathetic to British entry, France's new president, Georges Pompidou, was likely to demand something in return for letting Britain in.[19] From a French viewpoint, British entry had to be accomplished without damaging French interests. This attitude was also shared by the other EEC members. Despite having been traditionally supportive of British entry, the so-called 'friendly Five' were also determined to make sure that British membership would not occur at their expense. The Heath government knew only too well that 'the Community would inevitably set the limits of negotiation with any aspirant for membership at a rather narrow span'. 'Over the years', Con O'Neill wrote in his report, 'we had to make a judgment of what was possible and what was not ... The experience of many years, including those of the negotiations, taught us, if it needed teaching, that the power of any country outside the Community to influence its decisions and actions is extremely limited'. It was for this reason that, in the opening statement on 30 June, Barber expressed the wish that the negotiations be kept 'short' and 'confined to the essentials', indicating that Britain's 'main problems ... concern matters of agricultural policy; [its] contribution to Community budgetary expenditure; Commonwealth sugar exports; New Zealand's special problems; and certain other Commonwealth questions'.[20]

The omission of any reference to Australia and its interests was not an oversight. It was yet another indication that London did not envisage special safeguards for Australia.[21] As Barber had told McEwen in July, all Britain could hope to do was to seek the longest possible transitional arrangements for Australia's agricultural produce. This assurance was reiterated by Barber's successor, Geoffrey Rippon, in the late summer of 1970.[22] It is important to note these pledges, as they sparked a fierce public row between London and Canberra in the summer of 1971. On 14 October 1970, however, the British negotiating team in Brussels adhered to its undertakings and proposed a six-year period for agriculture. This proposal was rejected by the Six. Conse-

---

[18] McEwen and Barber, memcon, 8 July 1970, NAA, A10206/1, EHEC06.
[19] In February 1970 President Georges Pompidou told his American counterpart, Richard Nixon, that France wanted Britain to join the EEC. According to Henry Kissinger, then Nixon's national security adviser, 'it was fear of a resurgent Germany, Pompidou averred, that had caused him to reverse de Gaulle's opposition to Britain's entry into Europe': *The White House years*, London 1979, 422.
[20] Britain's entry into the EEC, report by O'Neill, 1972, FCO 75/1.
[21] CAB 134/2596, AE(70)2nd, 6 July 1970, and AE(70)7, Negotiating aims for the Commonwealth, 30 July. 1970.
[22] DFA to London, cablegram 7926, 16 June 1971, NAA, A1838/2, 727/4/2 pt 12; Geoffrey Rippon and McEwen, memcon, 15 Sept. 1970, A10206/1, EHEC06. On 25 July 1970 Barber had been moved to the Treasury to replace Ian Macleod as Chancellor of the Exchequer.

Table 11
Major Australian exports to Britain, 1968–9

	Australian exports to the UK		Estimated loss	
	Value A$ million	% of total exports	Value A$ million	% of total exports
Beef or veal	2.2	6.2%	1.1	31%
Butter	27.6	70%	27.6	70%
Apples	9.7	49%	3.6	18%
Apricots	1.0	58%	0.4	23%
Peaches	7.7	53%	3.8	26%
Pears	9.3	82%	4.6	41%
Fruit salad	2.5	47%	1.2	23%
Cheese	2.0	14%	2.0	14%
Eggs in liquid form	1.5	35%	1.5	35%
Wheat, unmilled	42.3	16%	9.1	4%
Pears, fresh	1.2	29%	0.4	10%
Sultanas	5.4	32%	2.7	16%
Cane sugar	39.2	34%	8.0	7%
Wine	1.2	35%	0.8	23%

Source: Cabinet submission 258, May 1970, NAA, A5619, C743 pt 2.

quently, on 8 December, Rippon scaled down British demands, proposing a five-year period for agriculture.[23]

Australian trade interests at stake

British entry was expected primarily to affect Australia's farm exports. Wool and some minerals would continue to enter the EEC market freely, as no quota or tariff restrictions were levied on these commodities.[24] Manufactured goods, while subject to the CET, would in general benefit from the Community's liberal regime on manufacturing trade.[25] As far as the farm sector was concerned, Australia's problems centred upon dairy products, fruit, sugar and meat (see table 11).[26]

[23] CAB 128/47, CM(70)28th, 13 Oct. 1970; CAB 134/2596, AE(70)8th, 7 Dec. 1970.
[24] Other minerals would be subject to the CET.
[25] In this category, gluten, leather and coils would be particularly affected: Cabinet submission 258, May 1970, NAA, A5619, C743 pt 2.
[26] Another source of concern for Canberra was the economic future of Papua New Guinea (PNG). In the early 1970s PNG was still a non-self-governing trust territory under Australian administration and, because of its constitutional position, could not

While the dependence of these commodities on the British market had lessened somewhat since the mid-1960s, diversification had been far from satisfactory. For some of these commodities (dairy products, dried and canned fruit, meat and sugar) there was limited scope for alternative markets. A further problem was that certain regions around Australia had, over the years, specialised in producing specific commodities for the British market and would be hit hard by British entry into the Community.[27] Overall, however, estimated trade losses were in 1970 less than in 1967. According to DTI figures, total losses would be in the region of A$86 million a year – that is, 2.7 per cent of Australia's total exports in 1968–9.[28] In 1967 initial losses had been put at around A$125 million a year.[29] Figure 3 clearly shows the significant decline since the early 1960s in the dependence on British markets of much Australian produce.

Australia's declining trade with Britain made the Australian economy less vulnerable to British entry, as McEwen himself acknowledged in his submission to Cabinet. This was an important factor that made the 1970–2 negotiations different from those of 1961–3, but it was not the only one. The declining relevance of the Commonwealth connection in Australian eyes constituted another significant factor. In 1961 the Australian government had been seriously concerned about the harmful effects of British entry on the cohesion of the Commonwealth as a political entity. This was no longer the case. In a November 1970 policy planning paper, the Department of Foreign Affairs claimed that 'Australia's interests are not vitally bound up with the Commonwealth' and argued that 'little advantage accrues to Australia from its Commonwealth link'.[30] On the one hand, Australia's

become associated with the enlarged EEC. This meant that, like Australia itself, PNG would face the imposition of the CET on some of its tropical exports over whatever transitional period was negotiated. Under the UK-Australia trade agreement (1956), PNG had in fact enjoyed tariff preferences in the British market. In 1969 Britain absorbed almost 29% of PNG total exports. Coconut oil, copra, coffee, cocoa and tea, which constituted the backbone of the territory's economy, all depended on the British market. See M. A. Pakenham to M. J. Robinson, 1 Oct. 1970, FCO 30/611. Hence, British entry was expected to inflict serious economic damage on PNG. Canberra was concerned that, unless provisions were made to accommodate PNG trade, British entry could hamstring the territory's development effort and complicate Australian plans to grant PNG independence as an economically viable country.

27 For instance, the loss of the British market for dairy products would particularly hit Tasmania and Victoria. The disappearance of British outlets for dried fruit would have serious repercussions in the Murray region.

28 Cabinet submission 258, 8 May 1970, NAA, A5916, C743 pt 2.

29 Britain and the EEC, 15 Nov. 1967, NAA, A10206, EHEC03. Initial losses were expected to rise to nearly A$200 million after 1974, when the Commonwealth Sugar Agreement expired and when the Community was likely to reach self-sufficiency over a large spectrum of farm commodities.

30 Commonwealth: its prospects for survival, DFA policy planning paper, 11 Nov. 1970, NAA, A1838/367, 899/1/2. In early November 1970 the DEA was renamed Department of Foreign Affairs (DFA).

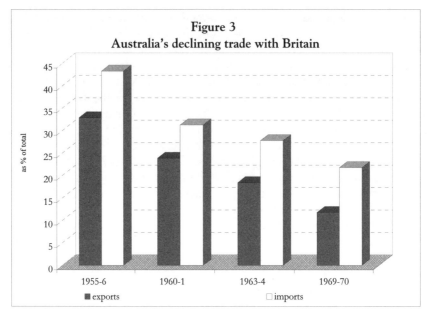

Figure 3
Australia's declining trade with Britain

Source: NAA, A1838/2, 727/4/1 pt 13.

ties with major Commonwealth countries such as Britain, New Zealand and Canada were no longer dependent on the Commonwealth link. On the other, Australia's relations with less important Commonwealth members were seen in Canberra as of little value since these countries felt 'able, by virtue of their Commonwealth status, to make political and economic demands on Australia which are not infrequently an embarrassment and a burden'. Furthermore, according to the DFA, 'very little value will be left of Commonwealth trade preferences after Britain's entry into the E.E.C.'. In short, the paper concluded, 'Australia could manage quite well without the Commonwealth'.[31]

Australia and the EEC negotiations

Australia's approach to the 1970–2 negotiations was clearly dictated by stringent political realities. After two failed attempts it was evident that London was determined to join the EEC and that no Commonwealth interest would be allowed to stand in the way. Moreover, it was felt in Canberra that there

[31] Ibid. However, as the paper also noted, 'we [the Australian government] should bear in mind that some of our particular friends in the Commonwealth ... see value in association; and that an organization which provides channels for formal and informal consultation with a wide range of countries on a wide range of issues should not be lightly dismissed'.

was, on the British side, an 'evident lack of sympathy' towards the Australian case.[32] Lack of sympathy was also manifest in continental Europe, as McEwen discovered during his talks with the European Commission in July 1970.[33] Within the Community it was generally held that Australia was a wealthy country that could withstand the impact of British entry. Hence, despite its various attempts between 1970 and 1972 to undertake 'simultaneous representations to a number of the numerous points of power or influence in the Communities', the Australian government failed to be heard within the EEC.[34]

Not everyone in Canberra was prepared to lay all the blame on the Six. The DFA was particularly critical of 'Trade's aggressive attitude to the Community', claiming that it was 'no wonder there is little sympathy for us … It's time we looked at [the] results of McEwen's approach'.[35] The DFA felt that Australia's interests could 'best be guarded in the long-term by making every endeavour, in association with the U.S., Canada, New Zealand and possibly Japan and South Africa, to discourage the enlarged Communities from becoming inward-looking'. According to the department, there were a number of ways of achieving this objective. For instance, Australia should try 'to influence the British, the Netherlands and Germany, to take care in their policies'. Second, the Australian government should 'continue pressures in the GATT for the upholding of its basic purposes and principles related to reducing trade barriers'. Third, were Australia to become a member, it should also use the Organisation for Economic Co-operation and Development 'as a forum'.[36] In truth, the DTI was not opposed to this approach. In the May 1970 submission to Cabinet, McEwen had in fact referred to the need for a multilateral effort designed to urge the EEC to overhaul its agricultural system. However, he also recognised that the conditions for such an ambitious exercise barely existed. In particular, the Nixon administration was not yet ready to challenge the EEC head-on, despite growing pressure from its economic departments (Treasury, Commerce and Agriculture) to do so.[37] McEwen and his department were neither able nor willing to wait. With the Gorton administration increasingly unpopular domestically, they were under pressure to show that the government was doing its best to safeguard Australia's interests and to push the EEC to reform its protectionist farm regime.

---

[32] L. Corkery to McMahon, 13 Aug. 1970, NAA, A1838/2, 727/4/1 pt 11.
[33] Britain's entry into the EEC, report by O'Neill, 1972, FCO 75/1.
[34] Corkery to minister, 13 Aug. 1970, NAA, A1838/2, 727/4/1 pt 11.
[35] Annotated comment to cablegram 401 (DFA to Paris), 27 Jan. 1971, ibid.
[36] Corkery to minister, 13 Aug. 1970, ibid. Australia joined the OECD in 1971.
[37] Kissinger, *White House*, 425–9. In February 1970 President Nixon declared in his Foreign Policy Report that American 'support for the strengthening and broadening of the European Community has not diminished'. Yet, as Kissinger recalled, 'the economic agencies insisted that we use the forthcoming negotiations for British entry into the Community to conduct the battle' against the protectionist farm policies of the EEC.

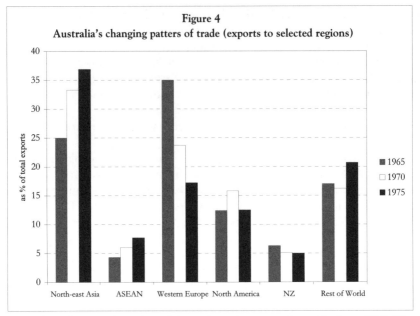

Figure 4
Australia's changing patters of trade (exports to selected regions)

Source: Ross Garnaut, *Australia and the northeast Asian ascendancy,* Canberra 1989, 72.

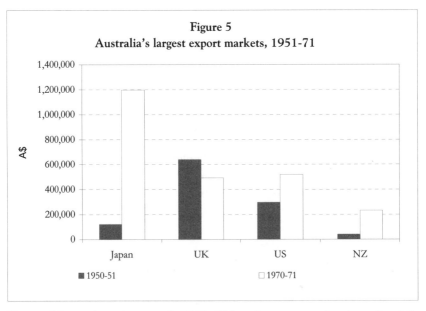

Figure 5
Australia's largest export markets, 1951-71

Historical data in Australian pounds (1901–65) have been converted to Australian dollars at the rate of one pound to two dollars.

Source: Department of Foreign Affairs and Trade, *Directions of trade time series: one hundred years of trade,* Canberra 2002, 6.

The way in which it handled the EEC was not the only criticism levelled at the DTI. In May 1970 McEwen had sought Cabinet approval for 'the development of a new dynamic relationship with Japan particularly [but by no means exclusively] in the trade and economic field'. This initiative was not accidental, but linked to the imminent opening of negotiations between Britain and the Six. As Britain turned to Europe, Australia had to look elsewhere for new markets and export opportunities. Reorientation of Australia's trade was no doubt an important factor in McEwen's initiative, but it was not the only one. McEwen was also concerned that, as a result of Britain's entry, Australia would face the prospect of becoming more isolated in a world trade system increasingly polarised around three major blocs (the EEC, the North/Latin Americas and the Communist countries). Australia therefore needed 'a bold new formula for future co-operation fashioned to meet not only today's needs, but more importantly a framework capable of dynamic development'. As Japan was 'apprehensive of the prospects she faces of being similarly excluded from the major trading blocs', Australia should explore the possibility of a closer relationship with Tokyo. McEwen's submission pointed out that 'Japan and the surrounding countries offer the best prospects for increasing Australian exports in the world, and are the only area where, by developing closer relations, we can hope that the doors are opening to us'.[38] Between 1965 and 1970, Australian exports to north-east Asia had grown significantly and, by 1970, the region had already replaced western Europe as Australia's major export destination (*see* figure 4). And Japan had already established itself as Australia's largest exporting market (*see* figure 5). A new relationship with Japan, as envisaged by McEwen, represented a major change in Australian foreign and trade policies. Foreign Minister McMahon noted that 'the submission contained concepts which if pursued would bring about significant changes in Australian attitudes' and he advocated caution.[39] The PMD went further and expressed the view that 'to go out and woo the Japanese' was not the sole option open to Australia, as McEwen arguably contended.[40] The problem was not that Australian policy-makers were reluctant to reorient Australia's external and trade polices. Rather, the problem was that strong sensitivities still remained – particularly within the Australian public – towards Japan. In the end, Cabinet accepted McEwen's proposal despite some reservations.[41] Thus, one of the outcomes for Australia of Britain's 1970–2 bid was in play even before London began negotiations with the EEC. The Gorton government was already considering strengthening Australia's political and economic ties with Japan, accepting McEwen's view that a closer relationship with Tokyo would be the first step towards a much closer political and economic engagement with other

---

38 Cabinet submission 257, May 1970, NAA, A5619/1, C742.
39 McMahon to John Gorton, 13 May 1970, ibid.
40 Notes on Cabinet submission 257, 11 May 1970, ibid.
41 Cabinet decision 387, 18 May 1970, ibid.

countries in the region. Australia had been striving to diversify its trade by finding new markets ever since Britain's first application in 1961.[42] This time Australia seemed even more determined to expand its politico-economic ties with its Asian neighbours. This represented a further step away from the traditional links with Britain. It is noteworthy that, in commending his policy initiative to the Cabinet, McEwen drew attention to the fact that British entry 'would mean the dismantling of the British Preferential System'. He advised the Cabinet to act without delay and revoke British preferences. This would allow the government to accord Japan greater trade advantages in the Australian market, in exchange for preferential treatment for Australian goods in Japan. McEwen argued that an early move 'would in itself make Australia a much more attractive market partner to Japan but our ability to capitalise on that will decrease progressively as the U.K. moves closer to taking its final decision on movement into Europe'.[43] It was indeed the end of an era.

Australia protests

Rarely does the end of an era occur without recriminations, however, and Anglo-Australian relations proved no exception. Australia strongly criticised Britain's handling of the negotiations with the Six, accusing London of completely disregarding Australian interests. The rift became public in the summer of 1971, but did not last long. Despite its disappointment, Australia had to live with the fact that, in the words of Con O'Neill, 'what mattered [to Britain] was to get into the Community, and thereby restore [its] position at the centre of European affairs ... The negotiations were concerned only with the means of achieving this objective at an acceptable price'.[44] The trouble was, of course, that what was acceptable to Britain was hardly palatable to Australia.

During the first half of 1971 Britain and the Six gradually moved towards a settlement of those agricultural issues that most concerned Australia: agricultural transition and sugar.[45] The Gorton government had asked for the longest transitional periods possible and the British had reassured Australia on

---

[42] John Singleton, 'After the veto: Australasian commercial policy in the mid sixties', *AEHR* xli (2001), 287–307.
[43] Cabinet submission 257, May 1970, NAA, A5619/1, C742.
[44] Britain's entry into the EEC, report by O'Neill, 1972, FCO 75/1.
[45] During the 1970–2 negotiations, Britain and the EEC treated the question of sugar – a complex and politically sensitive matter – separately. All Commonwealth sugar producers, with the exception of Australia, were developing countries. In general, they were heavily dependent on their sugar exports. Under the CSA Britain was contractually bound to buy fixed quotas of sugar from CSA producers. Without proper safeguards, the economies of CSA countries would be badly affected by British entry. For a brief account of the sugar issue see ibid.

this. Yet in December 1970 EEC opposition to long transitional arrangements led London to settle for a proposed five-year transition period. In February 1971 Britain and the Community agreed provisionally to a programme of tariff transition: Britain would phase in the CET in five stages between 1973 and 1977. Then, in early March, the EEC Council of Ministers decided that, as far as agricultural prices were concerned, the transitional period should be restricted to four years.[46] More important, under pressure from the French, the Council also decided that Britain and the other candidate countries should accept Community Preference in full from the beginning. This meant not only that these countries would have to accept the Common Agricultural Policy without derogations from the date of entry, but also that Australia's traditional exports of butter, sugar, meat, cheese, eggs, wheat and flour would be practically shut out of the British market upon entry, due to protectionist CAP barriers.[47] Britain rejected this decision and as late as 21 April was still insisting on the need for the full five years of transition in relation to agricultural prices. Yet, unbeknownst to the Australians, British negotiators were discreetly signalling to the EEC that their government's 'position on Community Preference was no longer absolute'.[48] The British clearly realised that the EEC position on this point was firm and felt that a partial breakthrough was needed if the Heath-Pompidou summit, which was scheduled for late May, were to help break the back of the negotiations.[49] Hence the British Cabinet decided on 6 May to accept the Community Preference in return for concessions by the Community on agricultural prices.[50] Consequently, at the UK-EEC ministerial meeting in Brussels on 11–13 May, Rippon informed the Six that Britain accepted the Community Preference in full from the start. In return, the Six agreed to a provision for dealing with sudden agricultural problems.[51] This, which became widely known as the 'safeguard clause', specified that should significant volumes of trade risk serious disruption during the transitional period, then the enlarged Community would seek remedial action.[52] The Six also accepted Britain's request for a full five-year period for agricultural prices. A final settlement on agricultural tariffs was also agreed upon: tariffs would be dismantled in

---

[46] Ibid. According to the EEC Council of Ministers agricultural prices would be phased in in five steps between 1973 and July 1977.

[47] Other important Australian farm commodities including lamb, canned and dried fruit were instead subject to the CET.

[48] Ibid.

[49] Ibid. Given the crucial role of France in the negotiations, Heath set great store on an Anglo-French summit as a means of paving the way to a successful application. It was clearly in Britain's best interest that the summit did not take place at a time when the Brussels negotiations were still deadlocked.

[50] CAB 129/48, CM(71)24th, 6 May 1971.

[51] Britain's entry into the EEC, report by O'Neill, 1972, FCO 75/1.

[52] Brussels to DFA, cablegram 135, 4 Mar. 1971, NAA, A1838/2, 727/4/1 pt 12.

five equal steps of 20 per cent beginning from January 1974.[53] Last but not least, Britain and the EEC reached a broad understanding on sugar which, contrary to previous British assurances to the Australian government, did not include any transitional period for Australian sugar.[54]

Britain's climb-down on the Community Preference was badly received in Canberra. The new Australian government, led by William McMahon, strongly criticised the British for failing to keep their word and protect Australia's interests.[55] It drew particular attention to the deal struck by the UK and EEC negotiators on 11–13 May, and protested that this was in stark contrast with the assurances given by both Barber and Rippon. In a message to Heath on 15 June, McMahon complained that Australia

> had been led to believe that the problems which would be caused to [its] industries would be very much in the minds of the British negotiators and that those problems would be raised in the negotiations with a view to mini-mising the disturbance to [Australian] trade and ensuring that there would be a reasonable transitional period.

The Australian leader reminded his British counterpart that 'during his visit to Australia Mr Rippon has placed special emphasis on this concept of a transitional period and has said it was what he would be seeking in order to safeguard the Australian position'. McMahon pointed out that the UK-EEC deal on agriculture 'would not comply with the understanding the Australian Government was given of the type of transition period the British Govern-ment would be seeking'.[56] While couched in careful diplomatic language, the import of McMahon's words could not be mistaken: they clearly suggested that the British had reneged on their previous assurances.

The tensions in the Anglo-Australian relationship increased further when McEwen's successor, Douglas Anthony, arrived in London in mid-June 1971.[57] According to High Commissioner Downer, Anthony 'expressed himself with restraint' during press and television interviews on arrival at Heathrow, but

---

[53] Britain's entry into the EEC, report by O'Neill, 1972, FCO 75/1.

[54] In 1970 Britain had informed Australia that the CSA would run until 31 December 1974. After that, Australia's arrangements under the CSA would be phased out during the remainder of the transitional period for agriculture. However, under the terms of the understanding reached in Brussels, no transitional period for Australian sugar was granted. The general assurance, whereby the enlarged Community would 'have as its firm purpose' the safeguarding of the interests of all Commonwealth sugar-producing countries, did not apply to Australia: W. Weemaes to Philip Flood, 4 June 1971, NAA, A1838/2, 727/4/2 pt 12. See also Britain's entry into the EEC, report by O'Neill, 1972, FCO 75/1.

[55] McMahon had replaced Gorton in March 1971.

[56] Bunting to Downer, cablegram 7856, 15 June 1971, NAA, A1838/2, 727/4/2 pt 14.

[57] London to DFA, cablegram 12150, 25 June 1971, ibid. pt 17. Upon McEwen's retire-ment from parliament on 5 February 1971, Anthony inherited the leadership of the Country Party and replaced him as Minister of Trade and Industry.

'his mood soon changed'.[58] In recalling his visit to London more than thirty years later, Anthony described his meeting with Rippon as

> one of the most disorderly, rude and vulgar meetings I have ever attended. And that's saying a lot having dealt with discontented farmers and trade unionists during my political career. After an introduction by Geoffrey Rippon and a few indiscreet comments the whole meeting exploded and each officer virtually took on his counterpart across the table. It was bedlam and the language was pretty raw. I finished up leaving the meeting in disgust.[59]

Anthony complained to Rippon that in their desire to enter the EEC, the British had 'jettisoned the safeguards and transitional arrangements that they had earlier promised to Australia'.[60] In reply, Rippon took the line that even if the British government had, during the spring of 1971, changed its policy on transitional agricultural arrangements, Australian officials had been informed of this change. He suggested that if the Australians had any complaint they should have raised it at that time, thereby ruling out the possibility of taking any further action with the EEC on Australia's behalf. He claimed that what Australia was seeking was not negotiable. In any case, Rippon argued, a generalised safeguard clause represented a better result for Australia.[61]

Rippon's claims were only partially true. He was certainly right to point out that, in the light of EEC intransigence on Community Preference, Australian requests were not negotiable. But, as far as the safeguard clause was concerned, it was doubtful that Britain really believed that it represented a better result. Until the 11–13 May ministerial meeting the British had in fact insisted on 'firmer' and 'more specific' guarantees than a safeguard clause.[62] To the Australians this was irrelevant in any case: they did not believe that it was a better result. More important, Rippon's claim that Canberra had been informed in advance of Britain's change of mind on Community Preference was simply not true.[63] Despatches from the Australian High Commission in London or the Australian Embassy in Brussels relayed no such news. This is not surprising. In the spring of 1971 the British were gradually coming to the conclusion that, for the sake of a breakthrough in the negotiations, they would have to scale down their requests on Community Preference. Fearing complications with their Commonwealth partners, they kept their cards close to their chests and played the deception game. On 22 April, at

---

58 Alexander Downer, *Six prime ministers*, Melbourne 1982, 273.
59 Personal communication with author, 21 Aug. 2003.
60 Ibid.
61 London to DFA, cablegram 12150, 25 June 1971, NAA, A1838/2, 727/4/2 pt 17.
62 Brussels to DFA, cablegram 215, 22 Apr. 1971, NAA, A1838/2, 727/4/1 pt 13.
63 See, for example, O. L. Davies to Waller, 8 July 1971, NAA, A1838/2, 727/4/2 pt 15; Brussels to DFA, cablegram 141, 10 Mar. 1971, and Brussels to DFA, cablegram 215, 22 Apr. 1971, A1838/2, 727/4/1 pt 13.

a briefing with Commonwealth representatives in Brussels, British officials still maintained that 'there would be serious political problems if the British market for products for which there were no other outlets were "brutally and abruptly" ended for the traditional suppliers'.[64] But the British Cabinet agreed to accept the EEC's demands on Community Preference on 6 May. In strict confidentiality, the British informed the Six of their decision in advance to ensure that 'an approach on these lines would be acceptable to the [EEC] member countries and the Commission, and could lead to an agreement'.[65] Australians were of course left in the dark, and Rippon's claims that the McMahon government had been kept informed were groundless. As O'Neill pointed out in an internal minute,

> [o]n the whole, it is difficult to refute the Australian case ... We had hoped to get clearer and more precise arrangements for running down third country supplies over the transitional period. We told Commonwealth representatives this, eg 22 April. We did not give them much if any notice of the switch we felt obliged to make at the Ministerial meeting on 11 to 13 when we had to accept the principle of Community preference from the start.[66]

Unappeased and dissatisfied, Anthony left London resentful at the British sleight of hand. Before departing, he made a bitter statement, which, according to Downer, 'angered British Ministers and upset many people sympathetic to the Australian cause'.[67]

Unsurprisingly, the Heath government found the Australian reaction unpleasant. At a press conference Heath said that he 'regretted' Anthony's comments.[68] According to Con O'Neill, 'from May to July 1971 [Australia's] complaints and accusations rose to an embarrassing public crescendo'.[69] Even before Anthony's arrival in London, the British had already voiced their annoyance with Australia. In early June, at a meeting with the foreign diplomatic corps, Rippon lashed out at Downer about Australia's accusations. According to the Australian High Commissioner, Rippon

> embarked on a bitter tirade against Australia. We were a selfish country ... We cared nothing for Britain. 'It would matter nothing to you if this country sank under the North Sea', he shouted. We thought of our own interests and nothing else. Australia was a rich country – richer than Britain ... 'You cannot', he proceeded, 'continue to live on England's back'.[70]

---

64 Brussels to DFA, cablegram 215, 22 Apr. 1971, NAA, ibid.
65 Britain's entry into the EEC, report by O'Neill, 1972, FCO 75/1.
66 O'Neill to C. Tickell and N. Statham, 16 July 71, FCO 24/1055.
67 Downer, *Prime ministers*, 273.
68 London to DFA, cablegram 13643, 20 July 1971, NAA, A1838/2, 727/4/2 pt 15.
69 Britain's entry into the EEC, report by O'Neill, 1972, NAA, A1838/2, 727/4/2 pt 15.
70 Downer, *Prime ministers*, 271–2.

Inevitably, the controversy became public. On 30 June the *Financial Times* condemned the McMahon government's attempts 'to blame the British hardheartdness' for its own domestic political gains. The newspaper observed that 'a strong Government could handle these undoubted difficulties with more finesse and dignity. Mr Macmahon's [*sic*] position is not strong. Yet, the very facts which he adduces to defend his policies to his own electorate strengthen the European case that Australia taken as a whole has no need for special consideration'.[71] That the controversy left some ill feeling between Canberra and London was clear from the fact that in October the *Economist* still commented that 'bad feeling between countries often starts when politicians talk to their home constituencies through the medium of international negotiations'.[72] In January 1972 the Melbourne newspaper, *The Age*, still referred to Anthony's 'tardy and tactless efforts in London' as one of the main reasons for Australia's failure to soften the blow inflicted by British entry.[73]

Such a verdict was unfair for two reasons. First, the vociferous attitude of the McMahon government in the summer of 1971 was not the cause of Britain's decision to accept Community Preference. Rather, it was its consequence. Second, Australian reactions had not been 'tardy'. London had only informed Commonwealth countries of its new position on Community Preference on 13 May. Geoffrey Bolton has argued that McMahon and Anthony perhaps 'relied too much on the hope that Britain would hold out for concessions on behalf of Australia'.[74] But there was little such hope in Canberra. Moreover, from a diplomatic point of view, Australia had no other option than to rely on British assurances – any alternative would have amounted to holding the British responsible for negotiating in bad faith.[75] Here was a predicament experienced by Australian policy-makers during the previous decade. As Britain felt it necessary to alter its own policies, Australia was left out in the cold, having not only to face a *fait accompli* but also to contemplate a series of worthless assurances.

Criticism of Australian tactics, however, was not confined to the press or to Whitehall. The DFA in Canberra had followed the unfolding of Anthony's mission to Britain closely and had found Anthony's protests objectionable. It had endorsed McMahon's message of 15 June to Heath. While regarding the message as a 'futile exercise', the DFA 'conceded that it was a game that had to be played' and 'the British would no doubt see it in that light'.[76] However, the DFA objected to the confrontational line taken by

71 *Financial Times*, 30 June 1971.
72 *Economist*, 3 Oct. 1971.
73 *Age* quoted in Geoffrey Bolton, 'The United Kingdom', in W. J. Hudson (ed.), *Australia in world affairs, 1971–75*, Sydney 1980, 213.
74 Ibid.
75 UK-EEC, DFA departmental note, n.d., NAA, A1838/2, 727/4/2 pt 17.
76 James Cumes to Flood, 15 June 1971, ibid. pt 14.

Anthony. According to James Cumes, First Assistant Secretary to the DFA's International Organisations Division, 'rather than complain about being let down on transitional arrangements, [Australia] should now seek to make the most of what we have got and, inter alia, to try hard to breathe life into the disruption provision'. Despite his criticism, Cumes did not disregard the fact that 'in respect of meaningful consultations, the British had again behaved abominably'. 'This', he added, 'had been part of the pattern established over the past ten years in the current and the earlier negotiations. However, we had to realise that the British wanted the negotiations to succeed and when they struck trouble – especially in matters affecting Australia – they were loath to allow this trouble to develop into a threat to the negotiations.' 'For the future', Cumes advised, 'it would be better to eschew recriminations.'[77]

On his return to Australia, Anthony tried to put a positive gloss on the Anglo-Australian row. Giving the House of Representatives his account of the controversy, he declared that 'this must all be accepted as history' and added that Australia 'must now look to the future'. He told the House that 'if the United Kingdom joins the EEC then Australia will be on its own'. Yet, Anthony was quick to add, in his view, Australia could 'stand on its own feet'.[78] He assured the House that the Australian government would take all possible steps to ensure that the safeguard clause would be given meaningful application.[79] He also stressed the need to place increasing reliance on ties with Japan and to ensure that 'this relationship is developed as much as possible'.[80]

In the end Australian discontent faded away. Despite its disappointment, Canberra had no option but to accept the minimal terms negotiated by Britain to safeguard Australian interests. The British retreat on the Community Preference had enabled McMahon to blame them for the unsatisfactory terms which Australia had obtained, and in so doing was able to justify his government's actions to the Australian public. In purely political terms, McMahon had at least succeeded in defusing a potentially damaging domestic issue. Hence, in mid-November 1971, during his talks with British ministers in London, McMahon set Australian complaints to one side. Not only did he thank Rippon 'for his efforts on Australia's behalf', but he also expressed his wish that 'the Anglo-Australian relationship could be effectively maintained'. The British attitude appeared equally positive. The Foreign and Commonwealth Secretary, Alec Douglas-Home, told McMahon that Britain intended 'to keep the most intimate relationship it could with Australia'. In claiming that British intentions were 'good ... and the machinery to give effect to those intentions is in a good order', Douglas-Home, emphasised that

---

77 Cumes to Flood, 5 July 1971, ibid.
78 Australia, HR, PD, lxxiii, 1971, 354–6.
79 The final text of the safeguard clause as incorporated in the Treaty of Accession can be found in London to DFA, cablegram 900, 19 Jan. 1972, NAA, A1838/2, 727/4/2 pt 20.
80 Australia, HR, PD, lxxiii, 1971, 357.

Britain would do its 'absolute damnest [*sic*] to help', and represent Australia's interests within the EEC.[81] In fact, as Australia's future awkward dealings with the Community were to prove, there was actually nothing much Britain could do to represent Australian interests in Brussels.[82]

In the ensuing months the Heath government worked hard to smooth Britain's path into the Community and, following Heath's successful summit with Pompidou, the road was clear for a positive result. Although settlements were still pending on a number of important issues, namely fisheries, political agreement at the highest level between the governments of France and Britain ensured that EEC-UK negotiations could now be brought to a successful conclusion. This duly happened on 22 January 1972 when Heath signed the Treaty of Accession in Brussels. Britain finally joined the EEC in January 1973.

In September 1972, recognising that British entry spelled the end of the imperial preference system, the McMahon government announced two important measures: the abolition of preferences granted to British imports and the termination of the UK-Australia Trade Agreement (UKATA) as from 1 February 1973.[83] With the adoption of these measures, the Australian government was not simply responding to Whitehall's inability to retain imperial preferences after entry, it was taking the first steps towards dismantling the preferential arrangements hitherto accorded to Britain.[84] As a result, Australia's trade with Britain shrank even further. Between 1970–1 and 1974–5 Britain's share of the Australian export market tumbled from 11.26 per cent to 5.47 per cent while its share of Australian imports fell from 21.36 per cent to 15.03 per cent.[85] In response to the end of its guaranteed access to the British market, Canberra was compelled to pursue diversification of its overseas trade more aggressively. Alternative export outlets for grains, sugar and beef were found in Asia and North America, but not every sector was successful in recovering from the loss of the British market: the dairy and canned fruit industries suffered serious contraction.[86]

The 'EEC saga', which had marred the Anglo-Australian relationship for

[81] London to DFA and PMC, cablegram 20753, 13 Nov. 1971, NAA, A1838/2, 727/1/3 pt 3.
[82] For an examination of Australia's difficult relations with the EEC following British entry see Andrea Benvenuti, 'Australian-European negotiations on agriculture: a study in economic diplomacy, 1983–93', unpubl. MA diss. Monash 1997, and 'Australia's battle against the Common Agricultural Policy: the Fraser government's trade diplomacy and the European Community', *AJPH* xlv (1999), 181–96.
[83] Bolton, 'United Kingdom', 215.
[84] Further adjustments were made between the mid-1970s and early 1980s. Remaining preferences were removed in 1981: Richard Snape, Lisa Gropp and Tal Luttrell, *Australian trade policy, 1965–1997: a documentary history*, Sydney 1998, 452.
[85] Bolton, 'United Kingdom', 215.
[86] Bureau of Agricultural Economics, *Agricultural policies in the European Community: their origins, nature and effects on production and trade*, Canberra 1985, 334.

a decade, had finally come to a close, and with it an era of intimate attachment. In early December 1972 a new Australian government, led by Labour leader Edward Gough Whitlam, came to power. Whitlam had no particular fondness for the British connection, and even though he would later claim that he knew of no one else in Australian public life 'who has a greater love for Britain than I have', he wasted no time in assuming a less pro-British stance in international affairs.[87] In his first hundred days in office Whitlam took a number of steps that irritated the British, first warning the British High Commissioner, Morrice James, that in the process of achieving 'a truly independent image for Australia ... there would be occasions when he would have to say and do things which would appear anti-British'. To illustrate this point, Whitlam said that he was very doubtful whether his government would allow the British Broadcasting Corporation to relocate its Far East relay station from Tebrau in Malaysia to the Australian territory of Christmas Island since he did not want to give the impression that 'Australia was still acting as a biddable client of Britain'.[88] He then instructed the Australian delegation at the United Nations to support an Afro-Asian resolution in the General Assembly condemning London's refusal to take effective measures to bring down the Smith government in Rhodesia.[89] In January 1973, unlike past Australian leaders who had always made a point of visiting London early in their premierships, he informed the British authorities that a tour of the major Asian capitals was a higher priority than a state visit to Britain.[90] Finally, but more important, in early February 1973 Whitlam informed the British Defence Secretary, Lord Carrington, that his government would stand by his electoral pledge to withdraw the Australian infantry battalion from the ANZUK force based in Singapore.[91]

In his desire to downplay the British connection and to distance himself from his predecessors, Whitlam went even further, openly supporting British participation in the process of European integration. During a visit to Brus-

[87] Whitlam, quoted in James Curran, *The power of speech: Australian prime ministers defining the national image*, Melbourne 2004, 77.

[88] Morrice James to FCO, telegram 1808, 21 Dec. 1972, FCO 24/1610. The BBC Far East relay station had been located at Tebrau since the 1950s. When the lease expired in the early 1970s, the Malaysian government asked the BBC to vacate Tebrau by April 1975, thus forcing the British authorities to look for an alternative site. Their choice fell upon Christmas Island, which combined security of tenure with technical suitability. Whitlam's refusal to give the go-ahead persuaded the Heath government to settle for a new site in Singapore, from which the BBC began to transmit in 1979. See Whitlam's visit to London: brief for Secretary of State, 16 Apr. 1973, PREM 15/1299.

[89] M. A. McConville to D. A. Campbell, 6 Dec. 1972, FCO, 24/1335; Whitlam's visit to London: brief for Secretary of State, 16 Apr. 1973, PREM 15/1299.

[90] James to Eric Norris, telegram 158, 30 Jan. 1973, and James to FCO, telegram 191, 3 Feb. 1973, FCO 24/1600.

[91] Canberra to FCO, telegram 731, 31 May 1972, FCO 24/1294; Secretary of State's meeting with Whitlam, 29 June 1972, FCO 24/1294; Canberra to FCO, telegram 192, 3 Feb. 1973, FCO 24/1553.

sels in December 1974 he criticised the new Wilson government's attempts to renegotiate Britain's terms of entry into the EEC, arguing that London needed to stop 'shilly-shallying' about whether to stay in the EEC or withdraw from it. He made it clear that Australia saw no advantage in Britain leaving the Community and added that 'the days when Australia wanted a special relationship are past'.[92] Furthermore, convinced that certain aspects of the Anglo-Australian relationship 'urgently needed up-dating', Whitlam set out to implement a number of constitutional and legal changes.[93] Between 1973 and 1975 he introduced the Royal Styles and Title Act, which changed the queen's title to 'Queen of Australia', abolished British royal honours and substituted 'Advance Australia Fair' for 'God Save the Queen' as the country's national anthem.[94] The 'British subject' caption also disappeared from Australian passports. While symbolic, these changes emphasised the impact that Britain's reorientation towards Europe had had on Anglo-Australian relations. Although cultural ties between Australia and Britain remained fairly strong, and relations between the two governments cordial, Britain's relevance to Australia's political life as well as to its economic and strategic policy-making had greatly diminished. Whitlam's reforms, therefore, served to bring largely outdated constitutional symbolism into line with the changed realities of Anglo-Australian relations.

[92] Whitlam quoted in J. D. B. Miller, *The EEC and Australia*, Melbourne 1976, 99–100, and Bolton, 'United Kingdom', 227. For the Wilson government's renegotiation of Britain's terms of entry see John Pinder, 'Renegotiation: Britain's costly lesson', *IA* li (1975), 153–65.

[93] Whitlam quoted in James to FCO, telegram 1808, 21 Dec. 1972, FCO 24/1610.

[94] He would also try to eliminate legal appeals to the Judicial Committee of the Privy Council in London, but would run into constitutional difficulties: Millar, *Australia in peace and war*, 331.

Conclusion

'Australia is still (with New Zealand) Britain's best friend in the world. The bond of attachment runs deep'. So British High Commission officials in Canberra wrote in a steering brief dated March 1962. Yet, as they were ready to acknowledge, Anglo-Australian relations had begun to change fundamentally during the previous two years and were bound to change further over the next decade. The bonds of empire were becoming 'increasingly a matter for the historian'. Change had been accelerated by significant developments within the Commonwealth that included its transformation into a multi-racial body with an increasing Afro-Asian membership and new restrictions under Britain's immigration laws. Yet, the factor identified as most likely to undermine Anglo-Australian relations was Britain's bid to join the EEC, first launched in July 1961. Officials claimed that there was widespread concern in Australia about the consequences of Britain's entry. Apart from the economic damage, Australians felt that Britain's role as a European power would increasingly affect its policies outside Europe and that these would not necessarily accord with Australian interests. Unsettling as it was, the British bid was not the only disturbing aspect of Britain's closer engagement with Europe. There were also politico-strategic factors which fuelled Australian apprehension. 'As we withdraw into Europe', the brief continued, 'British power, interests and influence in South-East Asia are seen as waning rapidly.' Understandably, the contraction of Britain's politico-military presence in that region was viewed in Canberra with anxiety at a time of growing instability in south-east Asia.[1]

These observations provide an interesting insight into the changing nature of the Anglo-Australian relationship in the early 1960s. They also foreshadow the emergence of a major conflict of interest between Australia and Britain as policy-makers in London increasingly came to see Europe as the future locus of Britain's power and influence in the world. Through its extensive examination of newly-released material from the Australian and British archives, this book has shown that Britain's turn to Europe did indeed provoke serious dissension between what had once been the closest of allies. The radical redefinition of Britain's post-imperial role, together with its reorientation towards Europe, did not accord, nor could it accord, with Australian political, economic and strategic interests in south-east Asia. Australia and Britain had faced tough challenges before the 1960s: important disagreements over defence, trade and financial issues were, for instance, recorded

---

[1] Steering brief: Anglo-Australian relations, Mar. 1962, DO 169/2.

between London and Canberra in the 1940s and 1950s. This time, however, the scale of the conflict was quite different. Anglo-Australian tensions could not now be reconciled in reaffirmations of Commonwealth unity or imperial kinship. As a result, the intimate relationship, which had hitherto existed between Australia and Britain, could not withstand the strains imposed by this fundamental clash of interests.

In seeking to explain how Australia reacted to the challenges posed by Britain's reorientation towards Europe, this book makes two important contributions to post-war Australian and Commonwealth diplomatic history. First, it offers a detailed analysis of the impact of Britain's turn to Europe on Anglo-Australian relations, taking into account the political, strategic and economic consequences of Britain's reorientation for the Australian government as it struggled to accept the inevitability of the British decision. The Anglo-Australian relationship did not weaken as a consequence of one specific crisis. Rather, it declined rapidly as a result of the cumulative effect of four perceived crises centred upon the three British attempts to join the EEC (1961–3, 1967, 1970–2) and the proposed military withdrawal from east of Suez (1967–8). Impact on the Australian sense of vulnerability was compounded by the fact that Britain's actions not only occurred one after another, indeed overlapping in the case of Britain's 1967 application and the military withdrawal, but also took place within a relatively short period of time. As Stuart Ward has argued, Australia's attachment to the idea of Britishness was profoundly shaken as a result of Britain's first application to join the EEC. But this was by no means 'the end of the affair', for it was the close succession and cumulative impact of the four crises that brought an era in Anglo-Australian relations to a close.[2]

Second, this book integrates the politico-strategic and the politico-economic dimensions of the Anglo-Australian relationship. Australian scholars have emphasised either the first or the second, which has resulted in noticeably different explanations for the unravelling of bilateral ties. On the one hand, politico-strategic analyses have stressed the significance of strategic questions in shaping post-war Australian perceptions and policies towards Britain, and by extension, in weakening relations. In this context, the fall of Singapore in 1942 has been commonly regarded as a defining moment. The surrender of Britain's largest, and supposedly unassailable, military base in the Far East shattered Canberra's complete trust in London's ability to defend the most distant outposts of the empire, thus forcing Australia to look to the United States for its own security. According to this view, Anglo-Australian relations never recovered from the implications of the fall of Singapore and were further weakened by the steady decline of British power in the years following the end of the Second World War.[3]

---

[2] Ward, *British embrace*, passim.
[3] See, for instance, Day, *Great betrayal*, passim; Bell, *Dependent ally*, 18; Macintyre; *Oxford history of Australia*, 335; Bolton, 'United Kingdom', 210; Farrell, *Defence and fall*, 392; and Millar, *Australia in peace and war*, 122.

Politico-economic analyses, on the other hand, have stressed the significance of economic and financial issues. Here, the most disparate factors have been advanced to explain the fraying of Anglo-Australian ties. Paul Robertson and John Singleton, for instance, argue that the erosion of both the Commonwealth preference system and the sterling area in the 1950s acted as a catalyst for change in post-war relations.[4] Sandra Tweedie identifies the renegotiations of the Anglo-Australian trade agreement in 1956 as a major turning point, while Ward and Gelber emphasise the crucial role of Britain's 1961–3 application to join the EEC.[5] Yet none of these factors individually caused lasting damage: Australia's political, economic and strategic links with Britain remained remarkably close until the early 1960s and only then began to unravel under the combined impact of London's applications to the EEC and its military retrenchment from east of Suez.

By examining both the politico-strategic and politico-economic dimensions of Britain's turn to Europe, a new and comprehensive explanation for the erosion of the Anglo-Australian partnership is provided. This is more than just another attempt to date the crucial turning point in Australia's political and diplomatic relations with Britain and it is not without important implications for the study of post-war Commonwealth diplomatic history. It suggests that Britain's shift towards Europe had more far-reaching implications for some of London's closest Commonwealth allies than has previously been assumed. Studies of British history in the twilight of empire have tended to focus on the impact of the British quest for EEC membership on London's 'old dominions'. Such studies have generally seen London's diplomatic push to enter the community as the key factor in transforming Britain's ties with these nations. While recognising the importance of London's European quest in redefining Commonwealth relations, this work argues that for some of Britain's Commonwealth allies the strategic aspect of the British shift towards Europe was also extremely important.

Macmillan's decision to seek EEC membership in 1961 no doubt dealt the first blow. British plans to join the Community came as a shock to Australian policy-makers given that, during the 1950s, they had accepted in good faith British assurances that Australian and Commonwealth interests would not be sacrificed on the altar of the EEC. Understandably, Macmillan's change of heart was a source of great anxiety: Australian authorities felt that Britain's apparent resolve to join a close-knit group of European nations presented the government with a number of seemingly intractable problems. Not only was EEC membership thought likely to undermine Britain's political ties with Australia and the Commonwealth, but it was also expected to have serious implications for Australian trade, threatening Australian exports to the British market. Furthermore, British entry was viewed as having a potentially

---

4 Robertson and Singleton, 'Commonwealth', 241–66.
5 Tweedie, *Trading partners*, 97; Ward, *British embrace*, 254, 260; Gelber, *Australia, Britain*, 258.

harmful impact on Australia's strategic interests in Asia: Australian policy-makers were concerned that closer engagement with the Six would weaken London's determination to maintain a politico-military role in south-east Asia where Australia's main strategic interests lay.

It is important to underline the strategic implications of Britain's reorientation towards Europe as they introduced a further element of concern, and likely friction, in the already tense political climate created by Macmillan's decision to bid for EEC membership. Under these circumstances it was inevitable that the Australian response to the 'Common Market' crisis was initially vociferous and rigid. The Menzies government demanded that all Australian trade interests be protected and, in urging the British to safeguard Australian interests, it sought to play the 'sentiment card'. In addition, as Menzies himself reminded the British repeatedly, London should carefully consider the potential damage that entry would inflict on the unity of the Commonwealth. The Australians also sought to enlist the diplomatic support of the United States in their efforts to persuade Britain to rethink. However, as negotiations in Brussels between the British delegation and the representatives of the six member states of the EEC dragged on, it became evident that Australian and British interests were too far apart to be reconciled. Resigned to the fact that London would allow no Commonwealth interest to stand in the way of British entry, the Menzies government modified its approach. Although, in the event, de Gaulle's veto meant that the application was unsuccessful, the fifteen months of negotiations between Britain and the Six left an indelible mark on Anglo-Australian relations. They dramatically brought to a head the extent to which London's European concerns took precedence over its Commonwealth interests, thereby destroying Australia's strongly-held belief that differences between 'British nations' could be reconciled in the name of strong Commonwealth loyalty.

Although de Gaulle's rebuff left Macmillan's policy on closer engagement with Europe in tatters, the clock could not be turned back as far as Anglo-Australian relations were concerned. Australian policy-makers remained convinced that Britain would be increasingly drawn into a European orbit at the expense of its traditional ties with the Commonwealth. Their views appeared to be vindicated when London's tentative steps towards the EEC overlapped with its attempts to reassess Britain's global and imperial role. This became particularly evident in the painful process of military retrenchment undertaken by the Wilson government in the second half of the 1960s. In attempting to disengage from burdensome politico-military commitments in Asia, Britain set itself on a collision course with Australia. Military withdrawal from south-east Asia thus introduced a further element of discord only a few years after the acrimony of 1961–3, and in doing so inflicted another significant blow upon the Anglo-Australian relationship.

While a number of historians have drawn attention to Australian concerns about the strength of Britain's commitment to post-war Asian security, they have made scant mention of how these fears played out in the two decades following the end of the Second World War.[6] In filling this gap, this book places the erosion of Anglo-Australian defence ties into a wider international context while exploring Britain's 'end of empire' as a factor that impinged on the western alliance's strategic aims in Cold War Asia. Notwithstanding the post-war decline in British power in the Far East, Britain's politico-military presence in south-east Asia continued to play an important role in Australia's foreign and defence policy-making in the 1950s and the early 1960s. Throughout this period, the Australian government remained seriously concerned about Britain's long-term willingness and ability to remain in south-east Asia – concerns that were heightened by Britain's plans to join the EEC in the early 1960s. As the British resolve to remain engaged east of Suez dwindled during 1965, and the Wilson government contemplated plans for a much reduced military presence, London was careful to present its plans not only as part of a broad settlement to end *Konfrontasi*, but also as an exercise in contingency planning in the event that the British were forced to quit their bases in Malaysia and Singapore. The Australian government, however, discerned an appreciable change of emphasis in British thinking and, as a result, became increasingly anxious about British intentions. Canberra was concerned that Britain, despite its claims to the contrary, was seeking a way out of south-east Asia at a time when Australia was increasing its involvement in regional crises. In early 1965 the Australian government had agreed to deploy troops in Vietnam and Borneo. Canberra was not just worried that British disengagement would undermine Australia's forward defence strategy, but also that it would leave a political and military vacuum in an unstable region that could in turn prompt an American withdrawal from Indochina. Under intense lobbying from Australia, the United States and New Zealand, London was temporarily compelled to shelve its plans.

Throughout 1966 Australia and its ANZUS allies repeatedly attempted to strengthen Britain's resolve to remain engaged in south-east Asia and, for a time, it appeared that this pressure might have had some success. In the end, however, it failed either to gain an unequivocal British commitment to the defence of south-east Asia, or to secure British support for a common strategic concept for the area. The gap between Australian and British politico-strategic interests had widened. Inevitably, Australian policy towards Britain hardened. As its suspicions that Britain planned to withdraw from the region increased, Canberra became less forthcoming, fearing that a co-operative attitude towards Britain would in the end facilitate, rather than prevent, British disengagement. Throughout these difficult negotiations the re-emergence of 'the EEC question' in British policy-making only served to confirm Australian suspicions about Britain's intentions.

Australian efforts to gain a British commitment to the security of the region did not succeed because London's objective remained a gradual disen-

6   Edwards with Pemberton, *Crises and commitments*, 206.

gagement from south-east Asia. Partly, but not exclusively, in response to the growing uncertainty surrounding Britain's long-term plans, the Holt government sought closer alignment with the United States. The news that the British government was considering withdrawal from south-east Asia by the mid-1970s reached Australia in late April, just days before the British decision to seek EEC entry on 2 May 1967. Both the withdrawal and the EEC application were serious blows to Australia and were seen in Canberra as linked.

In dealing with these two major crises, the Holt government gave priority to the most urgent question: Britain's planned withdrawal from the region. As part of its tactics, Australia sought to secure the diplomatic support of the United States and other Commonwealth allies. In his talks with Wilson in mid-June, Holt emphasised the importance to Britain of a continued presence in south-east Asia. In British eyes, however, south-east Asia was a growing burden and Holt found little agreement with his arguments from his counterpart. Australian and British interests and aims were clearly at variance. In the end, in July 1967, the British Cabinet confirmed its decision to withdraw by the mid-1970s. In January 1968 the date of withdrawal was brought forward to the end of 1971. After constant assurances that Britain would remain in south-east Asia, the setting of a date for withdrawal caused consternation. Yet the Australian government's reactions were muted in the hope of gaining British co-operation through the rundown phase to ease Australia's task of maintaining its own military presence in Malaysia and Singapore. In the final analysis, the British withdrawal forced the Australian government to rethink its defence role in south-east Asia. In so doing, it laid the foundations for Australia's closer engagement with its neighbours and hence for a more prominent and independent role in the region.

While the consequence of the second application were not as far-reaching as those of the 1961–3 bid, further strain to Anglo-Australian relations was undoubtedly added. Apart from the inevitable economic damage to Australia, the application was now also regarded as being likely to weaken further Britain's resolve to maintain its politico-military role in south-east Asia. Australian policy-makers became persuaded in mid-1967 that Wilson's 'approach to Europe' had paved the way for the almost concomitant decision to withdraw from east of Suez. The withdrawal, combined with the decision to seek EEC entry, was perceived in Australian official circles as irrefutable evidence that London was reorienting its external policies towards Europe. The 1967 application sent a clear and powerful message that, in pursuing Britain's European objectives, London regarded Australian interests as expendable. While Macmillan had to some extent tried to reconcile the divergent interests of Britain and Australia at the time of the 1961–3 bid, such consideration was of little interest to Wilson. Yet the response of the Holt government was low-key and non-committal. J. D. B Miller, a keen observer of Anglo-Australian relations in the 1960s, has attributed this to the fact that Australia's fast-expanding economy and its discovery of alternative trading outlets had made Canberra less apprehensive about the economic consequences of British entry than a few years earlier.[7] Stuart Ward, however, has explained Holt's restrained reaction by claiming that Canberra now regarded efforts to resist Britain's EEC ambitions as pointless.[8]

While such views go some way towards explaining the situation, this book has argued that other factors were more instrumental in determining the Australian attitude. These included continuing French opposition to British entry throughout the 1966–7 period, which made the outcome of the Wilson bid doubtful; Australia's concern not to expose itself to British pressure for trade compensation should any Australian action be seen as an attempt to thwart Britain's entry into the EEC; Canberra's desire in 1967 to defer informing the Australian public of the grim outlook for Australian farm exports should Britain join the EEC; and Australian concerns that Wilson's approach to Europe would undermine Britain's willingness to remain east of Suez. Given that this bid for entry coincided with the British defence review, the Holt government even canvassed the possibility of giving Britain some trade benefits if these could help strengthen its resolve to remain in south-east Asia. Australia was also careful to avoid confrontation on the EEC question in its other dealings with the British government, fearing that this could drive a wedge between Australia and Britain at a time when British goodwill was still needed. In the event, while the Wilson bid collapsed, its impact was none the less lasting. In contrast to 1963, Britain's application remained on the table and would be revived by Heath's Conservative government in 1970. The lessons of the 1967 bid left Canberra in no doubt that Britain was committed to joining the EEC and under no illusion that the British would not jeopardise their chances of success in order to protect Australian interests. The Australian government accepted the realities of the situation and made no attempt to sabotage the British bid, recognising that such a course of action would only prove counterproductive and ultimately futile.

Consequently, by the late 1960s, Anglo-Australian relations had changed profoundly. At an economic level, despite the fact that the imperial preference system was still in place, Australian dependence on the British market had diminished as Australia diversified its external trade, notably towards the Asia-Pacific region. At the strategic level, the days of Australia's reliance on the British security blanket were now numbered with the British decision to withdraw from south-east Asia by 1971. At the political level, relations between Canberra and London had lost most of the 'instinctive intimacy, warmth, generosity and genuine appreciation of each other's position' which had characterised Anglo-Australian relations through to the 1950s.[9] However, despite these far-reaching changes, Britain's shift to Europe

[7] Miller, *Commonwealth affairs*, 336, and *The EEC and Australia*, 93–4.
[8] Ward, *British embrace*, 252.
[9] Ibid.

had still to be fully accomplished since London had not as yet been accepted in the EEC. It was only with entry in January 1973 that the change in Anglo-Australian relations was realised.

Before turning to Britain's 1970–2 bid for EEC membership and its implications for Australia, this book dealt with the decision of the Heath government in 1971 to deploy a token military force in south-east Asia under the aegis of the FPDA. Far from being a complete reversal of previous Labour policy, the successful negotiation of the FPDA in 1971 terminated the open-ended commitment to the defence of the Malaysian region that Britain had made under AMDA. The Conservative government's decision to deploy a small presence in south-east Asia did not reverse Wilson's reorientated, more European-centred, defence policy. The Australian government was initially rather cautious in its response to the British deployment. Far from endorsing British proposals unconditionally, Canberra looked to ensure that a continuing British military presence accorded with a more independent formulation of Australia's own regional interests. This attitude was an indication of the extent to which Australian thinking had evolved since Wilson's initial decision to pull out of Malaysia and Singapore. By the beginning of the 1970s, Australian dependence on British military power was very much a thing of the past.

This was also the period of Britain's final bid for EEC membership under Heath's premiership. While an apparent sense of inevitability pervaded Commonwealth responses to it, London's final bid none the less had important symbolic and practical implications for Australia. At a practical level, British entry ended the imperial preference system that had regulated trade between Australia and Britain for four decades. Although this was expected to be less disruptive to Australian trade in the early 1970s than it would have been a decade earlier, a number of Australian commodities still stood to be damaged. At a more symbolic level, entry finally sealed Britain's European destiny and, in Australian eyes, signalled a formal departure from the close ties of empire. With little hope of seeing its trade interests properly safeguarded by Britain, the Australian government centred its policy on demands for protective transitional arrangements. At the same time Canberra considered steps to strenghten its political and economic ties with Japan. A closer relationship with Asia's emerging economic power was seen in Canberra as the first step towards a much closer political and economic engagement with other countries in the region. Thus, as Britain was poised to join the EEC, Australia was positioning itself to reorient its own external and economic policies towards the Asian region.

British entry into the Community in January 1973 marked the end of an era in Anglo-Australian relations. The bonds of empire had indeed become a matter for the historian. Gone were the imperial preferences that had underpinned commercial relations between Australia and Britain; and after the British entry into the EEC, Australia's trade with Britain further declined in relative terms.[10] Despite Heath's decision to deploy a token military force in Malaysia and Singapore under FPDA, Anglo-Australian defence relations changed beyond recognition. Gone was Australia's dependence on British military power. Despite continuing friendship, gone also was the intimacy that had been the hallmark of political relations between the two governments before the first bid.

More widely, the importance of the Commonwealth network was also much diminished. It ceased to be the valuable forum in which members sought to co-ordinate policies of mutual interest. The transformation of the Commonwealth into a composite and multi-racial organisation certainly played a role in bringing about these changes, but so too did Britain's turn to Europe. Throughout all the negotiations, the signals were unmistakable – if forced to choose between the Commonwealth and Europe, London would downgrade its ties with the Commonwealth rather than imperil those with Europe. Last but not least, while the monarchy remained a link between Australia and Britain, between 1973 and 1975 the Whitlam government made many symbolic changes, such as adopting a new national anthem, which emphasised the fact that Britain's importance in Australian political life, as well as in its economic and strategic policy-making, had declined significantly. The close ties of empire that had bound Australia and Britain since Australian federation had been severed.

[10] In the period 1978–82 exports to Britain represented 4% of total Australian exports while imports from Britain amounted to 9% of Australia's total imports: Goldsworthy, *Facing north*, 427.

Bibliography

Unpublished primary sources

Canberra, National Archives of Australia (NAA)

Australian Embassy, Washington
A3093 Correspondence files, 1954–7
A3092 Correspondence files, 1958
A5462 Secret/top secret correspondence files, 1954–7

Australian High Commission, London
A2908 Correspondence files, 1920–68
A3211 Correspondence files, 1960–95

Department of Defence
A816   Correspondence files, 1928–58
A1945 Correspondence files, 1957–74
A2031 Defence Committee minutes, 1926–
A5799 Defence Committee agenda, 1932

Department of External Affairs/Department of Foreign Affairs
A1838 Correspondence files, 1948–

Department of Trade/Department of Trade and Industry
A1310   Correspondence files, 1948–62
A2051   Correspondence files, 1954–
A3917   UK-EEC negotiations, 1961–3
A4092   UK-Europe, briefs and papers, 1932–73
A10206   UK-EEC, papers, 1956–70
AA1974/35 UK-Europe, correspondence, Cabinet submissions and papers,
      1957–72

Department of Treasury
A571 Correspondence files, 1901–78

Prime Minister's Department and Cabinet Office
A463   Correspondence files, 1956–
A1209 Correspondence files, 1957–
A4926 Cabinet submissions, 1956–8
A4940 Cabinet files, 1949–67
A5619 Cabinet files, 1949–72
A5821 Cabinet decisions, 1958–63
A5839 Cabinet and Cabinet committees decisions, 1966

A5840 Cabinet and Cabinet committees decisions, 1966–7
A5842 Cabinet submissions, 1966–7
A5867 Cabinet submissions, 1968
A5868 Cabinet submissions, 1968–9
A5869 Cabinet submissions, 1969–71
A5871 Cabinet and Cabinet committees decisions, 1968
A5872 Cabinet and Cabinet committees decisions, 1968–9
A5882 Cabinet files, 1968–72
A5915 Cabinet submissions, 1972–5
A6706 Prime minister's correspondence, 1950–66
M2576 Menzies papers, 1945–67

Canberra, National Library of Australia (NLA)

MS 4654 J. McEwen papers
MS 4936 R. G. Menzies papers
MS 5274 P. Hasluck papers
MS 6150 R. G. Casey papers

London, National Archives (TNA)

Cabinet Office
CAB 128 Cabinet minutes, 1945–74
CAB 129 Cabinet memoranda, 1945–71
CAB 130 Cabinet committees, 1945–70
CAB 133 Commonwealth and international conferences, 1944–71
CAB 134 Cabinet committees, 1945–74
CAB 148 Defence and Overseas policy committees, 1944–74

Commonwealth Office
FCO 20 Common Market Department files, 1967–8
FCO 22 Economic General Department and Commonwealth Trade Department
    files, 1967–8
FCO 62 Western Economic Department files, 1967–8

Commonwealth Office and Foreign and Commonwealth Office
FCO 24 Far East and Pacific Department and South West Pacific Department
    files, 1967–71

Commonwealth Relations Office
DO 164 Defence files, 1957–67
DO 169 Far East and Pacific Department files, 1960–7
DO 207 Rhodesia Department files, 1965–6

Commonwealth Relations Office and Commonwealth Office
DO 215 Economic General Department files, 1964–7

Foreign Office
FO 371 Correspondence files, 1906–66
FO 953 Information Policy Department and Regional Information Department
    files, 1947–66

Foreign and Commonwealth Office
FCO 15 South East Asian Department files, 1967–71
FCO 21 Far Eastern Department files, 1967–71
FCO 30 European Economic Organisations Department files, 1967–77
FCO 75 Internal histories, 1972

Foreign Office and Foreign and Commonwealth Office
FCO 41 Western Organisations Department files, 1967–72

Ministry of Defence
DEFE 11 Chiefs of Staff Committee files, 1946–75

Prime Minister's Office
PREM 11 Prime Minister's correspondence and papers, 1951–64
PREM 13 Prime Minister's correspondence and papers, 1964–70
PREM 15 Prime Minister's correspondence and papers, 1970–4

Treasury
T 225 Defence Policy and Material Divisions files

Official documents and publications

Ashton, Stephen and William Roger Louis (eds), *British documents on the end of empire: east of Suez and the Commonwealth, 1964–71*, London 2004
Australia, *Hansard parliamentary debates* (House of Representatives), Canberra 1961–73
Australia, *Hansard parliamentary debates* (Senate), Canberra 1961–73
Britain, *Hansard parliamentary debates* (House of Commons), London 1961–73
Central Statistical Office, *Annual abstract of statistics, no. 96*, London 1960
—— *Annual abstract of statistics, no. 97*, London 1960
Cmnd. 91, *Trade agreement between the government of the United Kingdom and Northern Ireland and the government of the Commonwealth of Australia*, London 1957
Cmnd. 2592, *Statement on defence estimates, 1965*, London 1965
Cmnd. 3203, *Statement on defence estimates, 1967*, London 1967
Cmnd. 3264, *Membership of the European Communities*, London 1967
Cmnd. 3345, *The United Kingdom and the European Communities*, London 1967
Cmnd. 3357, *Supplementary statement on defence policy 1967*, London 1967
Department of Foreign Affairs and Trade, *Directions of trade time series: one hundred years of trade*, Canberra 2002
—— 'The Australian national anthem' at http://www.dfat.gov.au/facts/pdfs_2004/aust_national_anthem.pdf
Foreign Relations of the United States, 1961–63, XIII: *West Europe and Canada*, Washington 1994
—— *1964–68*, XII: *Western Europe*, Washington 2001
—— *1964–68*, XIII: *Western European region*, Washington 1995

—— *1964–68, XXVII: Mainland Southeast Asia: regional affairs*, Washington 2000

Goldsworthy, David (ed.), *The Conservative government and the end of empire, 1951–57*, London 1994

Hyam, Ronald and William Roger Louis (eds), *The Conservative government and the end of empire, 1957–1964*, London 2000

Newspapers and periodicals

Age (Melbourne)
The Australian
Economist
Evening Standard
Financial Times
Sydney Morning Herald
Times

Published primary sources

Ball, George, *The past has another pattern*, New York 1982

Brown, George, *In my way: the political memoirs of Lord George-Brown*, London 1971

Callaghan, James, *Time and chance*, London 1987

Carrington, Peter, *Reflect on things past: the memoirs of Lord Carrington*, London 1988

Crossman, Richard, *The diaries of a cabinet minister*, I: *Minister of Housing, 1964–66*, London 1975

—— *The diaries of a cabinet minister*, II: *Lord President of the Council and Leader of the House of Commons, 1966–68*, London 1976

Denman, Roy, *Missed chances: Britain and Europe in the twentieth century*, London 1996

Hasluck, Paul, *The chance of politics*, Melbourne 1997

Healey, Denis, *The time of my life*, London 1990

Heath, Edward, *The course of my life: my autobiography*, London 1998

Howson, Peter, *The Howson diaries: the life of politics*, Ringwood 1984

Jay, Douglas, *Change and fortune: a political record*, London 1980

Jenkins, Roy, *A life at the centre*, London 1991

Judt, Tony, *Postwar: a history of Europe since 1945*, London 2005

Kissinger, Henry, *The White House years*, London 1979

Macmillan, Harold, *At the end of the day, 1961–63*, London 1973

Stewart, Michael, *Life and Labour: an autobiography*, London 1980

Wilson, Harold, *The Labour government, 1964–70: a personal record*, Harmondsworth 1971

Secondary sources

Adamthwaite, Anthony, 'Overstretched and overstrung: Eden, the Foreign Office and the making of policy, 1951–5', *IA* lxiv (1998), 241–59

Alexander, Philip, 'From imperial power to regional powers: Commonwealth crises and the second application', in Daddow, *Harold Wilson*, 187–210

Andrews, E. M., *A history of Australian foreign policy*, Melbourne 1988

—— *The Department of Defence: the Australian centenary history of defence*, v, Melbourne 2001

Arnold, John, Peter Spearritt and David Walker (eds), *Out of empire: the British dominion of Australia*, Melbourne 1993

Arnold, Lorna, *A very special relationship: British atomic weapons trials in Australia*, London 1987

Audland, Christopher and Roy Denman, *Negotiating Britain's membership of the European Communities: 1961–3 and 1971–2* (University of Manchester working paper xliii, 2000)

Bell, Coral, *Dependent ally: a study in Australian foreign policy*, Sydney 1988

Benvenuti, Andrea, 'Australia's battle against the Common Agricultural Policy: the Fraser government's trade diplomacy and the European Community', *AJPH* xlv (1999), 181–96

—— and Stuart Ward, 'Britain, Europe and the "other quiet revolution" in Canada', in Phil Buckner (ed.), *Canada and the end of empire*, Vancouver 2005, 165–82

Beresford, M. and P. Kerr, 'A turning point for Australian capitalism: 1942–1952', in Edward Wheelwright and Kenneth Buckley (eds), *Essays in the political economy of Australian capitalism*, iv, Sydney 1980, 148–71

Bolton, Geoffrey, 'The United Kingdom', in W. J. Hudson (ed.), *Australia in world affairs, 1971–75*, Sydney 1980, 209–30

—— *The Oxford history of Australia*, V: *The middle way, 1942–1995*, Melbourne 1996

Boyd, Martin, 'Their link with Britain', in Arnold, Spearritt and Walker, *Out of empire*, 199–210

Bridge, Carl (ed.), *Munich to Vietnam: Australia's relations with Britain and the United States since the 1930s*, Melbourne 1991

Brivati, Brian and Harriet Jones (eds), *From reconstruction to integration: Britain and Europe since 1945*, London 1993

Bureau of Agricultural Economics, *Agricultural policies in the European Community: their origins, nature and effects on production and trade*, Canberra 1985

Cain, Frank (ed.), *Menzies in war and peace*, Sydney 1997

Camps, Miriam, *Britain and the European Community, 1955–63*, London 1964

Carver, Michael, *Tightrope walking: British defence policy since 1945*, London 1992

Chin, Kin Wah, *The five power defence arrangements and AMDA: some observations on the nature of an evolving partnership* (Institute of Southeast Asian Studies occasional paper xxiii, 1974)

—— *The defence of Malaysia and Singapore: the transformation of a security system, 1957–71*, Cambridge 1983

—— 'The five power defence arrangements: twenty years after', *Pacific Review* iv (1991), 190–203

Coleman, Jonathan, 'The London ambassadorship of David K. E. Bruce during the Wilson-Johnson years, 1964–68', *Diplomacy and Statecraft* xv (2004), 327–52

Curran, James, *The power of speech: Australian prime ministers defining the national image*, Melbourne 2004

Daddow, Oliver (ed.), *Harold Wilson and European integration: Britain's second application to join the EEC*, London 2002

Darby, Phillip, *British defence policy east of Suez, 1947–1968*, London 1973

Darwin, John, 'Britain's withdrawal from east of Suez', in Bridge, *Munich to Vietnam*, 140–58

—— *Britain and decolonisation: the retreat from empire in the post-war world*, Basingstoke 1992

Day, David, *The great betrayal: Britain, Australia, and the onset of the Pacific war, 1939–42*, Melbourne 1992

—— *Reluctant nation: Australia and the allied defeat of Japan, 1942–45*, Melbourne 1992

Deighton, Anne, 'The Labour Party, public opinion and the "second try" in 1967', in Daddow, *Harold Wilson*, 39–55

—— and Piers Ludlow, ' "A conditional application": British management of the first attempt to seek membership of the EEC, 1961–63', in Anne Deighton (ed.), *Building postwar Europe: national decision-makers and European institutions, 1948–63*, London 1995, 106–27

Dennis, Peter and Jeffrey Grey, *Emergency and confrontation: Australian military operations in Malaya and Borneo, 1950–1966*, Sydney 1996

Dickie, John, *Inside the Foreign Office*, London 1992

Dockrill, Michael, *British defence policy since 1945*, Oxford 1988

Dockrill, Saki, 'Britain's power and influence: dealing with three roles and the Wilson government's defence debate at Chequers in November 1964', *Diplomacy and Statecraft* xi (2000), 211–40

—— *Britain's retreat from east of Suez: the choice between Europe and the world?*, Basingstoke 2002

Downer, Alexander, *Six prime ministers*, Melbourne 1982

Dumbrell, John and Sylvia Ellis, 'British involvement in Vietnam peace initiatives, 1966–67: Marigolds, Sunflower and "Kosygin week"', *Diplomatic History* xxvii (2003), 113–49

Dyster, Barrie and David Meredith, *Australia in the international economy in the twentieth century*, Cambridge 1990

Edwards, Peter with Gregory Pemberton, *Crises and commitments: the politics and diplomacy of Australia's involvement in Southeast Asian conflicts, 1948–1965*, Sydney 1992

Edwards, P. G., *A nation at war: Australian politics, society and diplomacy during the Vietnam war, 1965–75*, Sydney 1996

—— 'Singapore and Malaysia, 1965', in Lowe, *Australia and the end of empires*, 187–98

Ellison, James, 'Dealing with de Gaulle: Anglo-American relations, NATO and the second application', in Daddow, *Harold Wilson*, 172–87

Farrell, Brian, *The defence and fall of Singapore, 1940–1942*, Stroud 2005

Fielding, Jeremy, 'Coping with decline: US policy toward the British defence reviews of 1966', *Diplomatic History* xxiii (1999), 633–56

Garnaut, Ross, *Australia and the northeast Asian ascendancy*, Canberra 1989

Garner, Joe, *The Commonwealth Office, 1925–1968*, London 1968

Gelber, H. G., *Australia, Britain and the EEC, 1961 to 1963*, Melbourne 1966

George, Stephen, *Britain and European integration since 1945*, Oxford 1991

—— *An awkward partner: Britain in the European Community*, London 1994

Golding, Peter, *Black Jack McEwen: political gladiator*, Melbourne 1996

Goldsworthy, David (ed.), *Facing north: a century of Australian engagement with Asia, I: 1901 to the 1970s*, Melbourne 2001

—— *Losing the blanket: Australia and the end of Britain's empire*, Melbourne 2002

—— 'Australian external policy and the end of Britain's empire', *AJPH* li (2005), 17–29

Greenwood, Sean, *Britain and European co-operation since 1945*, Oxford 1992

Grey, Jeffrey, *A military history of Australia*, Cambridge 1999

Hack, Karl, *Defence and decolonisation in Southeast Asia, 1941–1968*, London 2001

Hannay, Sir David (ed.), *Britain's entry into the European Community: report by Sir Con O'Neill on the negotiations of 1970–72*, London 2000

Hawkins, David, *The defence of Malaysia and Singapore: from AMDA to ANZUK*, London 1972

Heinlein, Frank, *British government policy and decolonization, 1945–1963: scrutinising the official mind*, London 2002

Hennessy, Peter, *The prime minister: the office and its holders since 1945*, London 2000

Holland, Robert, *The pursuit of greatness: Britain and the world role, 1900–1970*, London 1991

Horne, Donald, *The lucky country*, Melbourne 1964

Horner, David, *Defence supremo: Sir Frederick Shedden and the making of Australian defence policy*, Sydney 2000

Jackson, William, *Withdrawal from empire: a military view*, New York 1986

—— *Britain's defence dilemma: an inside view*, London 1990

Jones, Matthew, *Conflict and confrontation in South East Asia, 1961–1965*, Cambridge 2002

—— 'A decision delayed: Britain's withdrawal from South East Asia reconsidered, 1961–68', *English Historical Review* cxvii (2002), 569–95

Kaiser, Wolfram, *Using Europe, abusing the Europeans: Britain and European integration, 1945–63*, London 1996

—— and Gillian Staerck (eds), *Contracting options: British foreign policy, 1955–64*, London 2000, 33–60

Kandiah, David and Gillian Staerck, 'Commonwealth international financial arrangements and Britain's first application to join the EEC', in May, *Britain, the Commonwealth and Europe*, 111–31

Kaufman, Victor, *Confronting Communism: US and British policies toward China*, Columbia, MI 2001

Kitzinger, Uwe, *The second try: Labour and the EEC*, Oxford 1968

Kristensen, Jeppe, '"In essence a British country": Britain's withdrawal from east of Suez', *AJPH* li (2005), 40–52

Kunz, Diane (ed.), *The diplomacy of the crucial decade: American foreign relations during the 1960s*, New York 1994

—— '"Somewhat mixed up together": Anglo-American defence and financial policy during the 1960s', in Robert King and Robin Kilson (eds), *The statecraft of British imperialism*, London 1999, 213–32

Lee, David, *Australia turns to the United States, 1955–57* (Menzies Centre for Australian Studies working paper lxxxiv, 1992–3)

—— *Search for security: the political economy of Australia's postwar foreign and defence policy*, Sydney 1995

—— and Moreen Dee, 'Southeast Asian conflicts', in Goldsworthy, *Facing north*, 262–309

Lee, Donna, *Middle powers and commercial diplomacy: British influence at the Kennedy trade round*, Basingstoke 1999

Leifer, Michael (ed.), *Constraints and adjustments in British foreign policy*, London 1972

Logevall, Frederik, *Choosing war: the lost chance for peace and the escalation of war in Vietnam*, Berkeley 1999

Lowe, David, *Commonwealth and communism: Australian policies towards South East Asia in the Cold War, 1949–54* (Menzies Centre for Australian Studies working paper li, 1989)

—— *Menzies and the 'great world struggle': Australia's Cold War, 1948–1954*, Sydney 1999

—— (ed.), *Australia and the end of empires: the impact of decolonisation in Australia's near north, 1945–65*, Geelong 1996

Lowe, Peter (ed.), *The Vietnam war*, Basingstoke 1998

Ludlow, Piers, *Dealing with Britain: the Six and the first UK application to the EEC*, Cambridge 1997

—— 'Too far away, too rich and too stable: the EEC and trade with Australia during the 1960s', *AEHR* xli (2001), 267–86

McDougall, Derek, 'Australia and the British military withdrawal from east of Suez', *AJIA* li (1997), 183–94

Macintyre, Stuart, *The Oxford history of Australia*, II: *The succeeding age, 1901–1942*, Melbourne 1993

McLean, David, 'ANZUS origin: a reassessment', *AHS* xxiv (1990), 64–82

Martin, A.W., *Robert Menzies: a life*, II: *1944–1978*, Melbourne 1999

May, Alex (ed.), *Britain, the Commonwealth and Europe: the Commonwealth and Britain's application to join the European Communities*, Basingstoke 2001

—— '"Commonwealth or Europe?": Macmillan's dilemma, 1961–63', in May, *Britain, the Commonwealth and Europe*, 82–110

Mayhew, Christopher, *Britain's role tomorrow*, London 1967

Millar, T. B., *Australia in peace and war: external relations since 1788*, Canberra 1991

Miller, J. D. B., *Britain and the old dominions*, London 1966

—— *Survey of Commonwealth affairs: problems of expansion and attrition, 1953–69*, London 1974

—— *The EEC and Australia*, Melbourne 1976

Milward, Alan, *The rise and fall of a national strategy*, London 2002

Morgan, Kenneth, *The people's peace: British history, 1945–89*, London 1990

—— *Callaghan: a life*, Oxford 1997

O'Brien, John, 'The British Commonwealth and the European Economic Community, 1960–63: the Australian and Canadian experiences', *Round Table* lxxxv (1996), 479–91

O'Neill, Robert, *Australia in the Korean war, 1950–53*, I: *Strategy and diplomacy*, Canberra 1982

Ovendale, Ritchie, *British defence policy since 1945*, Manchester 1994

Parr, Helen, 'Going native: the Foreign Office and Harold Wilson's policy towards the EEC, 1964–67', in Daddow, *Harold Wilson*, 75–94

—— 'A question of leadership: July 1966 and Harold Wilson's European decision', *Contemporary British History* xix (2005), 437–58

—— *Britain's policy towards the European Community: Harold Wilson and Britain's world role, 1964–1967*, Oxford 2006

Pemberton, Gregory, *All the way: Australia's road to Vietnam*, Sydney 1987

Pickering, Jeffrey, *Britain's withdrawal from east of Suez: the politics of retrenchment*, Basingstoke 1998

—— 'Politics and "black Tuesday": shifting power in the Cabinet and the decision to withdraw from east of Suez, November 1967–January 1968', *TCBH* xiii (2002), 144–70

Pimlott, Ben, *Harold Wilson*, London 1992

Pinder, John, 'Renegotiation: Britain's costly lesson', *IA* li (1975), 153–65

Ponting, Clive, *A breach of promise: Labour in power, 1964–1970*, London 1989

Prasser, Scott, J. R. Nethercote and John Warhurst (eds), *The Menzies era: a reappraisal of government, politics and policy*, Haryborough 1995

Rees, G. Wyn, 'British strategic thinking and Europe, 1964–1970', *Journal of European Integration History* v (1999), 57–71

Reid, Alan, *The Gorton experiment: the fall of John Grey Gorton*, Sydney 1971

Reynolds, David, 'A "special relationship"? American, Britain and the international order since the Second World War', *IA* lxii (1985/86), 1–20

—— *Britannia overruled: British policy and world power in the 20th century*, London 1991

Reynolds, Wayne, *Australia's bid for the atomic bomb*, Melbourne 2000

Rickard, John, 'Loyalties', in Arnold, Spearritt and Walker, *Out of empire*, 35–55

Robertson, Paul, 'The decline of economic complementarity? Australia and Britain, 1945–1952', *AEHR* xxxvii (1997), 91–117

—— and John Singleton, 'The Commonwealth as an economic network', *AEHR* xli (2001), 241–66

Rooth, Tim, 'Imperial self-sufficiency rediscovered: Britain and the Australia, 1945–51', *AEHR* xxxix (1999), 29–51

—— 'Economic tensions and conflict in the Commonwealth, 1945–c.1951', *TCBH* xiii (2002), 121–43

Sanders, David, *Losing an empire, finding a role: British foreign policy since 1945*, London 1990

Schenk, Catherine, 'The UK, the sterling area, and the EEC, 1957–63', in Anne Deighton and Alan Milward (eds), *Widening, deepening and acceleration: the European Economic Community, 1957–1963*, Baden-Baden 1999, 123–37

Schwartz, Thomas Alan, *Lyndon Johnson and Europe: in the shadow of Vietnam*, Cambridge, MA 2003

Singleton, John, 'After the veto: Australasian commercial policy in the mid sixties', *AEHR* xli (2001), 287–307

—— and Paul Robertson, *Economic relations between Britain and Australasia, 1945–1970*, Basingstoke 2002

Snape, Richard, Lisa Gropp and Tal Luttrell, *Australian trade policy, 1965–1997: a documentary history*, Sydney 1998

Stockwell, A. J., 'Malaysia: The making of a neo–colony?', *JICH* xxvi (1998), 138–56

—— 'Imperialism and nationalism in south-east Asia', in Judith Brown and William Roger Louis (eds), *The Oxford history of the British empire: the twentieth century*, Oxford 1999, 465–89

Subritzky, John, 'Macmillan and east of Suez: the case of Malaysia', in Richard Aldous and Sabine Lee (eds), *Harold Macmillan: aspects of a political life*, Basingstoke 1999, 177–94

—— 'Britain, *Konfrontasi*, and the end of empire in Southeast Asia, 1961–65', *JICH* xxvii (2000), 209–27

—— *Confronting Sukarno: British, American, Australian and New Zealand diplomacy in the Malaysian-Indonesian Confrontation, 1961–5*, Basingstoke 2000

Tarling, Nicholas (ed.), *The Cambridge history of Southeast Asia*, II: *The nineteenth and twentieth centuries*, Cambridge 1992

Tomlinson, Jim, 'The decline of the Empire and the economic "decline" of Britain', *TCBH* xiv (2003), 201–21

Tratt, Jaqueline, *The Macmillan government and Europe: a study in the process of development*, Bansingstoke 1996

Tsokhas, Kosmas, 'Dedominionisation: the Anglo-Australian experience, 1935–45', *Historical Journal* xxxvii (1994), 861–83

Tweedie, Sandra, *Trading partners: Australia and Asia, 1790–1993*, Sydney 1994

Urwin, Derek, *The community of Europe: a history of European integration since 1945*, London 1995

Ward, Stuart, *Australia and the British embrace: the demise of the imperial ideal*, Melbourne 2001

—— 'A matter of preference: the EEC and the erosion of the old Commonwealth relationship', in May, *Britain, the Commonwealth and Europe*, 156–80

—— 'Sentiment and self-interest: the imperial ideal in Anglo-Australian commercial culture', *AHS* xxxii (2001), 91–108

Waters, Chris, *The empire fractures: Anglo-Australian conflict in the 1940s*, Melbourne 1995

Watt, Alan, *The evolution of Australian foreign policy, 1938–1965*, Cambridge 1968

Wheare, K.C., *The statute of Westminster and dominion status*, London 1953

Winand, Pascaline, *Eisenhower, Kennedy and the United States of Europe*, Basingstoke 1993

Woodard, Garry, 'Best practice in Australia's foreign policy: "Konfrontasi" (1963–66)', *Australian Journal of Political Science* xxxiii (1998), 85–99

—— and Joan Beaumont, 'Paul Hasluck as Minister for External Affairs: towards a reappraisal', *AJIA* lii (1998), 63–75

Wrigley, Chris, 'Now you see, now you don't: Harold Wilson and Labour foreign policy 1964–70', in R. Coopey, S. Fielding and N. Tiratsoo (eds), *The Wilson government, 1964–70*, London 1993, 123–35

Young, Hugo, *The blessed plot: Britain and Europe from Churchill to Blair*, London 1998

Young, John, *Britain and European unity, 1945–1992*, London 1993

—— 'The Heath government and British entry into the European Economic Community', in Stuart Ball and Anthony Seldon (eds), *The Heath government, 1970–74*, London 1996, 259–84

—— 'Britain's and "LBJ" war, 1964–68', *Cold War History* ii (2002), 63–92

—— *The Labour governments, 1964–70*, II: *International policy*, Manchester, 2003

Zappalà, Gianni, 'The decline of economic complementarity: Australia and the sterling area', *AEHR* xxxiv (1994), 5–21

Ziegler, P., *Wilson: the authorised life*, London 1993

Unpublished theses and papers

Alexander, Philip, 'The Commonwealth and European integration: competing commitments for Britain, 1956–1967', PhD diss. Cambridge 2002

Benvenuti, Andrea, 'Australian–European negotiations on agriculture: a study in economic diplomacy, 1983–93', MA diss. Monash 1997

—— 'The end of the affair: Britain's turn to Europe as a problem in Anglo-Australian relations, 1961–72', DPhil. diss. Oxford 2004

Dee, Moreen, 'In Australia's own interests: Australian foreign policy during Confrontation, 1963–1966', PhD diss. New England, NSW, 2000

Easter, David, 'British defence policy in South East Asia and the Confrontation, 1960–66, PhD diss. London 1998

Elijah, Annmarie, 'Better the devil you know? Australia and the British bids for European Community membership', PhD diss. Melbourne 2003

Goldsworthy, David, 'Point of departure: the British military withdrawal from south-east Asia as a problem in Anglo-Australian relations', conference paper, Australian Historical Association, Hobart, October 1999

—— 'Australian external policy and the end of Britain's empire', conference paper, London, July 2002

House, Daniel, 'Rethinking the region: Australia and Britain's withdrawal from southeast Asia, 1965–71', PhD diss. Deakin (Geelong) 2004

Kristensen, Jeppe, 'Community of interest: Australia and Britain's "east of Suez"', 1966–68', MA diss. Southern Denmark (Odense) 2000

Parr, Helen, 'Harold Wilson, Whitehall and British policy towards the European Community, 1964–1967', PhD diss. London 2002

Pham, Phuong, 'The end to "east of Suez": the British decision to withdraw from Malaysia and Singapore, 1964 to 1968', DPhil. diss. Oxford 2001

Pine, Melissa, 'Application on the table: the second British application to the European Communities, 1967–70', DPhil. diss. Oxford 2003

Tepper, Jonathan, 'The dollar, the pound and British policy "east of Suez", 1964–67: deals and understandings between Wilson and Johnson', MLitt diss. Oxford 2004

Ward, Stuart, 'Discordant communities: Australia, Britain and the EEC, 1956–1963', PhD diss. Sydney 1998

Index

Abdul Rahman Putra, Tunku, 39, 53
Aden, 66, 67
Africa, 125
Age, 179
agricultural commodities, Australian: beef and veal, 138, 141, 142, 143, 144; butter, 138, 141, 142, 143, 144, 168, 175; cheese, 138, 143, 144, 168, 175; eggs, 138, 168, 175; fruit, 166, 168, dried 138, 169, 169 n. 27, 175 n. 47, canned, 141, 142, 143, 144, 169, 175 n. 47, 181; mutton and lamb, 19, 138, 143, 145, 175 n. 47; sugar, 31, 144, 166, 168, 169, 174, 174 n. 45, 175, 181, exports to Britain, 141, 142, 143, safeguards for, 130, 138, 146, 176, 176 n. 54; wheat and other cereals, 19, 20, 31, 114, 130, 138, 143, 144, 168, 175; wine, 168; wool, 19, 138, 143, 144, 168
agriculture, 129, 140, n. 42, 167, 168, 171, 176, 176 n. 54
aircraft: Avon Sabres, 46 n. 4; AVRO 748, 74; BAC 111, 74; Canberras, 46 n. 4, 130 n. 6; F-111A, 131 n. 106; HS86I, 62; Mirage, 105, 161, 162; Nimrod, 158; P1154 Hunter, 62; TSR2, 131 n. 106; Whirlwind helicopters, 158, 161
AMDA, *see* Anglo-Malayan (later Malaysian) Defence Agreement
America, *see* United States
Anglo-American relations, 10, 27, 63, 66, 71–2, 86, 98, 108. *See also* United States
Anglo-Australian relations: constitutional links, 17–18; cultural and social links, 23–4; erosion and decline in, 2, 10, 11, 12, 186, 188; impact of Britain's applications to EEC, 12, 14, 134, 148, 183, 187; impact of Britain's withdrawal east of Suez, 45, 94, 134, 183, 185; impact of fall of Singapore, 9, 10, 185
Anglo-Australian Trade Agreement (1956), 11, 147 n. 66, 169 n. 26, 181, 186

Anglo-French summit, 175 and n. 49, 181
Anglo-French talks, 164 n. 5
Anglo-Malayan (later Malaysian) Defence Agreement (AMDA), 69, 99, 153, 154, 155, 158, 158 n. 15, 159, 160, 191
Anthony, Douglas, 176–7, 178, 179, 180
ANZAM, 23, 51,
ANZUK forces, 160, 161, 182
ANZUS: ANZUS powers, 65, 66, 69, 75, 85, 89, 93, 98, 104; doubts about Britain's resolve to stay in south-east Asia; 86; opposition to British withdrawal, 73, 76; pressures on Britain to stay in south-east Asia, 59, 101, 188
ANZUS treaty, 3, 9, 11, 47, 104, 105 n. 104
Asia, 4, 83, 84, 85, 94, 91, 97, 124, 125, 174; allied strategic cooperation in, 80, 81, 82; Australia's relations with, 5, 12, 14, 24, 47, 109, 163, 181, 187, 191; Australia's reliance on American power in, 57; British colonial order in, 48; Cold War tensions, 79, 111; Communist penetration, 46, 72; decline of British influence, 55; security, 108, 187; western strategic interests/objectives,12, 47, 68, 72, 111, 188. *See also* Communism, Communist powers, Communist threat, Far East, south-east Asia
Asia-Pacific region, 4, 5, 131, 132, 190. *See also* Asia
Atlantic Alliance, 38
Australia: general: British bases, 69, 70, 74 n. 82, 80, 82 83,103, Australian agreement to consider, 74, 81, Australian financial contribution, 97, and Britain's peripheral strategy, 64, 65, Menzies's approach, 75, 77–8, 79, 67; de-dominionisation, 10; exports to Asia-Pacific, 132, 173; exports to Britain, 28, 29, 126, 133, 143, 147, 163, 170, decline, 18, 141, 192 n. 10, preferential entry into British market, 19; exports to Commonwealth, 36;